The Desert Flowers - Lily

Judith Keim

BOOKS BY JUDITH KEIM

THE HARTWELL WOMEN SERIES:

The Talking Tree – 1
Sweet Talk – 2
Straight Talk – 3
Baby Talk – 4
The Hartwell Women – Boxed Set

THE BEACH HOUSE HOTEL SERIES:

Breakfast at The Beach House Hotel – 1
Lunch at The Beach House Hotel – 2
Dinner at The Beach House Hotel – 3
Christmas at The Beach House Hotel – 4
Margaritas at The Beach House Hotel – 5
Dessert at The Beach House Hotel – 6
Coffee at The Beach House Hotel – 7
High Tea at The Beach House Hotel – 8 (2024)

THE FAT FRIDAYS GROUP:

Fat Fridays – 1
Sassy Saturdays – 2
Secret Sundays – 3

THE SALTY KEY INN SERIES:

Finding Me – 1
Finding My Way – 2
Finding Love – 3
Finding Family – 4
The Salty Key Inn Series – Boxed Set

THE CHANDLER HILL INN SERIES:

Going Home – 1
Coming Home – 2
Home at Last – 3
The Chandler Hill Inn Series – Boxed Set

SEASHELL COTTAGE BOOKS:

A Christmas Star
Change of Heart
A Summer of Surprises
A Road Trip to Remember
The Beach Babes

THE DESERT SAGE INN SERIES:

The Desert Flowers – Rose – 1
The Desert Flowers – Lily – 2
The Desert Flowers – Willow – 3
The Desert Flowers – Mistletoe & Holly – 4

SOUL SISTERS AT CEDAR MOUNTAIN LODGE:

Christmas Sisters – Anthology
Christmas Kisses
Christmas Castles
Christmas Stories – Soul Sisters Anthology
Christmas Joy

THE SANDERLING COVE INN SERIES:

Waves of Hope
Sandy Wishes – (2023)
Salty Kisses – (2023)

OTHER BOOKS:

The ABC's of Living With a Dachshund
Once Upon a Friendship – Anthology
Winning BIG – a little love story for all ages
Holiday Hopes
The Winning Tickets – (2023)

For more information: **www.judithkeim.com**

PRAISE FOR JUDITH KEIM'S NOVELS

THE BEACH HOUSE HOTEL SERIES

"Love the characters in this series. This series was my first introduction to Judith Keim. She is now one of my favorites. Looking forward to reading more of her books."

BREAKFAST AT THE BEACH HOUSE HOTEL is an easy, delightful read that offers romance, family relationships, and strong women learning to be stronger. Real life situations filter through the pages. Enjoy!"

LUNCH AT THE BEACH HOUSE HOTEL – "This series is such a joy to read. You feel you are actually living with them. Can't wait to read the latest one."

DINNER AT THE BEACH HOUSE HOTEL – "A Terrific Read! As usual, Judith Keim did it again. Enjoyed immensely. Continue writing such pleasantly reading books for all of us readers."

CHRISTMAS AT THE BEACH HOUSE HOTEL – "Not Just Another Christmas Novel. This is book number four in the series and my introduction to Judith Keim's writing. I wasn't disappointed. The characters are dimensional and engaging. The plot is well crafted and advances at a pleasing pace. The Florida location is interesting and warming. It was a delight to read a romance novel with mature female protagonists. Ann and Rhoda have life experiences that enrich the story. It's a clever book about friends and extended family. Buy copies for your book group pals and enjoy this seasonal read."

MARGARITAS AT THE BEACH HOUSE HOTEL – "What a wonderful series. I absolutely loved this book and can't wait for the next book to come out. There was even suspense in it. Thanks Judith for the great stories."

"Overall, Margaritas at the Beach House Hotel is another wonderful addition to the series. Judith Keim takes the reader on a journey told through the voices of these amazing characters we have all come to love through the years! I truly cannot stress enough how good this book is, and I hope you enjoy it as much as I have!"

THE HARTWELL WOMEN SERIES:

"This was an EXCELLENT series. When I discovered Judith Keim, I read all of her books back to back. I thoroughly enjoyed the women Keim has written about. They are believable and you want to just jump into their lives and be their friends! I can't wait for any upcoming books!"

"I fell into Judith Keim's Hartwell Women series and have read & enjoyed all of her books in every series. Each centers around a strong & interesting woman character and their family interaction. Good reads that leave you wanting more."

THE FAT FRIDAYS GROUP :

"Excellent story line for each character, and an insightful representation of situations which deal with some of the contemporary issues women are faced with today."

"I love this author's books. Her characters and their lives are realistic. The power of women's friendships is a common and beautiful theme that is threaded throughout this story."

THE SALTY KEY INN SERIES

<u>FINDING ME</u> – "I thoroughly enjoyed the first book in this series and cannot wait for the others! The characters are endearing with the same struggles we all encounter. The setting makes me feel like I am a guest at The Salty Key Inn...relaxed, happy & light-hearted! The men are yummy

and the women strong. You can't get better than that! Happy Reading!"

FINDING MY WAY- "Loved the family dynamics as well as uncertain emotions of dating and falling in love. Appreciated the morals and strength of parenting throughout. Just couldn't put this book down."

FINDING LOVE – "I waited for this book because the first two was such good reads. This one didn't disappoint.... Judith Keim always puts substance into her books. This book was no different, I learned about PTSD, accepting oneself, there is always going to be problems but stick it out and make it work. Just the way life is. In some ways a lot like my life. Judith is right, it needs another book and I will definitely be reading it. Hope you choose to read this series, you will get so much out of it."

FINDING FAMILY – "Completing this series is like eating the last chip. Love Judith's writing, and her female characters are always smart, strong, vulnerable to life and love experiences."

"This was a refreshing book. Bringing the heart and soul of the family to us."

THE CHANDLER HILL INN SERIES

GOING HOME – "I absolutely could not put this book down. Started at night and read late into the middle of the night. As a child of the '60s, the Vietnam war was front and center so this resonated with me. All the characters in the book were so well developed that the reader felt like they were friends of the family."

COMING HOME – "Coming Home is a winner. The characters are well-developed, nuanced and likable. Enjoyed the vineyard setting, learning about wine growing and seeing the challenges Cami faces in running and growing a business. I look forward to the next book in this series!"

"Coming Home was such a wonderful story. The author has a gift for getting the reader right to the heart of things."

<u>*HOME AT LAST*</u> – *"In this wonderful conclusion, to a heartfelt and emotional trilogy set in Oregon's stunning wine country, Judith Keim has tied up the Chandler Hill series with the perfect bow."*

"Overall, this is truly a wonderful addition to the Chandler Hill Inn series. Judith Keim definitely knows how to perfectly weave together a beautiful and heartfelt story."

"The storyline has some beautiful scenes along with family drama. Judith Keim has created characters with interactions that are believable and some of the subjects the story deals with are poignant."

SEASHELL COTTAGE BOOKS

<u>*A CHRISTMAS STAR*</u> – *"Love, laughter, sadness, great food, and hope for the future, all in one book. It doesn't get any better than this stunning read."*

"A Christmas Star is a heartwarming Christmas story featuring endearing characters. So many Christmas books are set in snowbound places...it was a nice change to read a Christmas story that takes place on a warm sandy beach!" Susan Peterson

<u>*CHANGE OF HEART*</u> – *"CHANGE OF HEART is the summer read we've all been waiting for. Judith Keim is a master at creating fascinating characters that are simply irresistible. Her stories leave you with a big smile on your face and a heart bursting with love."*

Kellie Coates Gilbert, author of the popular Sun Valley Series

A SUMMER OF SURPRISES – "The story is filled with a roller coaster of emotions and self-discovery. Finding love again and rebuilding family relationships."

"Ms. Keim uses this book as an amazing platform to show that with hard emotional work, belief in yourself and love, the scars of abuse can be conquered. It in no way preaches, it's a lovely story with a happy ending."

"The character development was excellent. I felt I knew these people my whole life. The story development was very well thought out I was drawn [in] from the beginning."

THE DESERT SAGE INN SERIES:

THE DESERT FLOWERS – ROSE – "The Desert Flowers - Rose, is the first book in the new series by Judith Keim. I always look forward to new books by Judith Keim, and this one is definitely a wonderful way to begin The Desert Sage Inn Series!"

"In this first of a series, we see each woman come into her own and view new beginnings even as they must take this tearful journey as they slowly lose a dear friend. This is a very well written book with well-developed and likable main characters. It was interesting and enlightening as the first portion of this saga unfolded. I very much enjoyed this book and I do recommend it"

"Judith Keim is one of those authors that you can always depend on to give you a great story with fantastic characters. I'm excited to know that she is writing a new series and after reading book 1 in the series, I can't wait to read the rest of the books."!

THE DESERT FLOWERS – LILY – "The second book in the Desert Flowers series is just as wonderful as the first. Judith Keim is a brilliant storyteller. Her characters are truly lovely and people that you want to be friends with as soon as you start reading. Judith Keim is not afraid to weave real life conflict and loss into her stories. I loved reading Lily's story and can't wait for Willow's!

"The Desert Flowers Lily is the second book in The Desert Sage Inn Series by author Judith Keim. When I read the first book in the series, The Desert Flowers-Rose, I knew this series would exceed all of my expectations and then some. Judith Keim is an amazing author, and this series is a testament to her writing skills and her ability to completely draw a reader into the world of her characters."

<u>THE DESERT FLOWERS – WILLOW –</u> "The feelings of love, joy, happiness, friendship, family and the pain of loss are deeply felt by Willow Sanchez and her two cohorts Rose and Lily. The Desert Flowers met because of their deep feelings for Alec Thurston, a man who touched their lives in different ways.

Once again, Judith Keim has written the story of a strong, competent, confident and independent woman. Willow, like Rose and Lily can handle tough situations. All the characters are written so that the reader gets to know them but not all the characters will give the reader warm and fuzzy feelings.

The story is well written and from the start you will be pulled in. There is enough backstory that a reader can start here but I assure you, you'll want to learn more. There is an ocean of emotions that will make you smile, cringe, tear up or outright cry. I loved this book as I loved books one and two. I am thrilled that the Desert Flowers story will continue. I highly recommend this book to anyone who enjoys books with strong women."

The Desert Flowers - Lily

The Desert Sage Inn Series
Book - 2

Judith Keim

Wild Quail Publishing

wildquail.pub@gmail.com
www.judithkeim.com

Wild Quail Publishing
PO Box 171332
Boise, ID 83717-1332

ISBN 978-1-962452-25-0

Dedication

For my friends everywhere!
During this crazy time of the Covid pandemic,
I've thought of friends near and far and am so grateful
for each of you!

CHAPTER ONE

LILY

In the early morning light on this March day in Palm Desert, California, Lily Weaver jogged in nice, easy steps on the path beside the Desert Sage Inn golf course. Her life, which had seemed so settled, had recently gone through a dramatic shift. Alec Thurston, her former employer and lover, was dying and had asked her to leave her job in New York and come to his home in California to help with the sale of the inn and its transition to the buyers, The Blaise Hotel Group. Here, she'd formed friendships with Rose Macklin and Willow Sanchez, two other women he'd asked to help him as well. Alec called them The Desert Flowers. They had separate jobs to help Alec, a man they each dearly loved.

Rose was working with a consultant for the Blaise Group to ensure that all social media and other PR going forward did nothing to destroy the panache of the upscale inn Alec had worked so hard to create.

Willow was working opposite the two young men in the hotel company's ownership family who were vying for the position of managing the inn after the sale went through.

She herself, as someone who had once been Alec's assistant, was on hand to take careful notes of meetings and to oversee and control the paperwork involved while the hotel company did property inspections, market research, and other due diligence activities. She worked alongside Brian Walden, another consultant hired by the Blaise Group to head their transition team.

As she followed the path by the golf course, she admired both the greens and the desert landscape. Some thought the bland colors of the desert were boring. She loved seeing sandy, rocky areas accented by green cacti and a variety of desert flowers. It made each color seem special. Hummingbirds were in abundance, their tiny bodies airborne by the constant fluttering of their wings, allowing them to hover about the bright flowers among the growth. In the distance, snow-capped mountains glistened in the sun, adding color to the purple-gray hue of their textured surfaces.

Hearing footsteps behind her, she turned to see Brian approaching. They sometimes met in the morning as they were jogging. At one time she'd entertained hopes of his being more than a co-worker. On their one so-called date, they'd ended up meeting a whole group working at the Desert Sage Inn, and he'd made it clear that this gathering was all business. Since then, she'd kept her distance. But despite telling herself not to dream foolishly, those secret hopes still lingered.

As he moved toward her, she observed his thick brown hair, handsome, athletic body and the ease at which he handled his prosthetic lower left leg. Brian was the sort of man she hoped to marry someday —kind, thoughtful, and smart.

"Morning!" Brian said, coming to a stop beside her. "How's it going? I haven't seen you in a while. Keeping busy with Alec?"

"Actually, I've been waiting for you to call a meeting. As lovely as it is to be here, I like to feel as if I'm doing my job."

"Ah, well, things have been put on hold while details are being worked on for the conversion of Desert Sage Inn to be the lead property in the new Corona Collection. I've missed those meetings myself."

He smiled at her. Her heart rate kicked up. That smile was

lethal. Telling herself to be professional, she said, "I'm thinking of taking up Bennett Williams' offer for me to apply for a job in his law office. Part-time, of course, until the sale of the inn takes place. I'd still help with that and any other projects Alec might have for me."

"So, you've really decided to move here?" Brian said, his hazel eyes drilling into her.

"Yes," she said. "I've already put my condo in New York State up for sale. I still have to convince my sister to move here, but the rest is underway."

"I'm scouting around for places to live here on at least a part-time basis. At the moment, Austin is still home."

She gazed up at him thinking Texas suited a big guy like him. She could even imagine him in a Stetson.

"I'd better go," Brian said. "Don't worry, I'll let you know when the next big meeting takes place. And if you need any help getting that job with Bennett Williams, call me. He owes me."

"Thanks." She lifted her hand to say goodbye as he jogged away. His steel blade made a distinctive sound as it hit the pavement in syncopation with his other foot. She sighed. The man was dreamy.

Lily watched him for a moment and then headed back to Alec's house where she and the other Flowers were living. Life here was so pleasant. Her childhood had been tough with an absentee father and an alcoholic mother who was distant, even cruel, a lot of the time. She'd been forced to be strong and self-sufficient even when she had the care of her sister, ten years younger and the daughter of a different father. A teacher had given her some guidance, but pride had kept her from asking for more help, which is why as an adult she'd sometimes found it difficult to maintain relationships. Now, at forty-two, she was hoping to find the love she'd missed so much in her life. Alec had been the one to introduce her to a calm, secure, loving lifestyle. She longed to have that again.

She sighed and picked up speed. Enough of fairy tales about finding a prince. It was time to get real.

Back at the house, Lily freshened up and then went to talk to Alec. At one time, she'd hoped he'd ask her to marry him. But Alec had been honest when they started dating, telling her marriage was not part of it. She should've known he'd stay true to his word. He was that kind of man. But their relationship was a gift. He'd taught her to open her heart to love, to find respite from the chaos that had always surrounded her. Prior to that, she'd been cautious about letting a man into her life. God knew, she didn't have the example of a wise woman to follow. She'd never known her own father, and the men her mother had hung out with were unreliable creeps she'd never accept.

As she walked toward Alec's wing of the house, sadness filled her at the thought of him dying. She considered it a real honor that he'd trusted her, along with Rose and Willow, to help him get his hotel safely sold before he died. The Desert Flowers act was like that television show with the man and his three angels, *Charley's Angels,* on a mission to save the inn. Lily loved being part of it.

At the entrance to his private space, Lily knocked gently at the door and cracked it open.

"Alec?"

"Here," came a voice weakened by the cancer that was slowly stealing his life. Lily stepped into the living area to find him reclining on a lounge chair and smiling up at her. "Lily, my dear. How are you?"

Normally a large, rangy man with thick gray hair and startling blue eyes, a Sam Elliott look-alike, Alec's thin body and weakened state tore at Lily's insides.

She pulled a chair up next to his and took hold of his hand. "I've been wanting to talk to you. I'm left doing almost nothing while meetings have been put aside. Rose and Willow are very busy, but not me. I'm used to doing my share of work and am thinking of taking Bennett Williams' offer for me to come work for him on a part-time basis. With my upcoming move here, it might be wise to have work outside of the project for you. How would you feel about that?

Alec's blue-eyed gazed rested on her. "I think if it suits you, it's something you should do. Believe me, Bennett wouldn't ask you to work for him if he wasn't serious about it. He told me he was very impressed with you. And you couldn't find a nicer guy to work with. Not only is he my lawyer, he's a friend. He now has a young partner working with him. Another great guy."

"The transition period you hired us for is three months. But you know I'd be happy to stay for as long as you wish and do anything I can to help you."

"Yes, I know. Three months seemed like such a long time. Now, I'm trying to make it through these last two months before the sale goes through," said Alec. "Any day beyond that is an unexpected gift."

Tears filled Lily's eyes. "I wish this hadn't happened to you."

His lips curved into a crooked smile. "So, do I. But after I get through all this, I'll be with Conchita and the baby. At least, I hope I will."

Lily nodded. It was a well-known story that Alec's wife and baby had died in a house fire for which he'd always blamed himself. That's one reason he had vowed never to marry again. Some people thought it was twisted thinking, but Lily understood his devotion to them. He'd shown her what love could mean, and though she'd asked for and wanted much more from him, she knew deep down it wasn't ever going to happen. After he ended their relationship, he found her a job with a business associate in Phoenix and helped her move on with her life. But he could never erase the love and gratitude she felt for him.

Juanita appeared. "Hi, Lily. Time for your medicine, Alec."

Lily got to her feet and kissed Alec on the cheek. "Have a nice day. I hope to see you tonight." She moved the chair back into place. "See you later. 'Bye, Juanita."

Juanita gave her a smile and turned back to Alec. Juanita Sanchez was a cousin of Alec's wife, Conchita. She and her husband, Pedro, were Willow's parents and had worked for Alec for years. They were lovely people. Juanita and Pedro were exactly the kind of people Lily wished she'd had as parents.

Back in her room, Lily looked at her reflection in the mirror. She was of medium height with curves in all the right places—curves she'd once done her best to hide. Her shoulder-length, blonde hair was highlighted by both her hairdresser and the desert sun. Freckles, few enough to be of interest, were sprinkled across her nose. She'd always thought she was drab. But Willow and Rose had helped her change—not only with her wardrobe but in believing in her self-worth.

Taking a deep breath, Lily called Bennett Williams' office and asked to speak to him. Her fingers were cold with nerves, and she almost dropped her phone. She was uncomfortable putting herself out there.

"Well, hello," said Bennett after her call went through. "I'm glad to hear from you. I hope you're calling about a job because I've just learned that one of the women in the office is going on maternity leave."

Lily's breath left her in a puff of surprise. Things didn't

usually come that easily to her. "As a matter of fact, that's what I wanted to talk to you about. I've decided to stay in Palm Desert following my work for Alec and will need a job. May I make an appointment to meet with you?"

"Absolutely. Send me your resumé, and I'll have my assistant schedule a time for you to come into the office." He paused. "I'm glad you called Lily. As I mentioned to you earlier, I'm impressed with your work."

"Thank you." Lily ended the call and sat down on her bed, struggling to accept what had just happened. The arrangements had fallen into place so quickly it almost seemed as if it had been preordained. That, or maybe her luck had changed. Either way, she was going to update her resumé and send it along as soon as possible.

Two days later, Lily dressed carefully for her interview with Bennett and his staff. In New York, the law firm for whom she worked had insisted on conservative clothes. Here in the desert, Lily agreed with Rose and Willow that brighter colors were acceptable.

Her black skirt, white-on-white print blouse, and hibiscus-colored soft jacket looked both professional and light-hearted. Studying herself in the mirror, Lily smiled at the changes living here had made to her appearance. The tan on her skin and the lack of stress lines on her face made her appear younger than her age and healthier than she'd ever been.

When Lily walked out to the kitchen to face the inspection Willow and Rose were sure to give her, she felt confident.

"Wow! Look at you!" said Willow, smiling at her.

"You look terrific," Rose immediately agreed. "Good luck with the interview."

Lily smiled. "Thanks. For once, I'm not a nervous wreck. Bennett made it seem as if it were a mere formality. I'm hoping so, anyway."

"He'd be lucky to have you on his staff. How many texts and calls have you received from your old job in New York?" said Rose.

Lily laughed and shook her head. "Too many. They keep promising to raise my salary if I come back. They increase the amount each time they call, but I finally told them I'm staying here no matter what they offer me."

"I'm so glad you are," said Willow. "Sarah is too."

Lily filled with pleasure. While Rose was spending time with Hank Bowers, the consultant the Blaise Group had hired and who was now her fiancé, she, Willow, and Sarah Jensen spent time in the evening together whenever they were all free. Sarah, a part-time assistant manager at the inn, was living at home with her parents and two-year-old son while her husband was serving in the military in Afghanistan. They'd quickly become friends. With this kind of support, Lily felt comfortable about her decision to move here. She hadn't yet chosen a place to live because she needed to sell her condo first. Her sister, Monica, who lived nearby her had promised to make sure the condo was ready for showings. So far, no luck, but Lily felt uncharacteristically optimistic.

Driving through the town, Lily bypassed the usual tourist places on Route 111, turned onto Cook Street and easily found the law office of Williams and Kincaid. She parked the car and entered the modern building trying to stem the nervousness that threatened to break through her shell of calmness.

She took the elevator to the third floor and exited into an attractive reception area. A young man smiled at her from behind a long desk.

"Good morning. May I help you?" he asked.

"I'm here to see Bennett Williams," she answered politely.

"Lily Weaver."

He smiled. "Of course. I'll let Mr. Williams know you're here. May I get you something to drink? Water? Coffee?"

"Water would be nice," said Lily. "The weather has turned hot."

"It's going to stay that way for a few days," said the receptionist whose nameplate said *Jonathan Waite.* He left and returned with a small, chilled bottle of water, which he handed to her.

Right then, Bennett appeared in the reception area, filling the room with his presence and his booming, jovial voice. "Ah, Lily. I'm so glad to see you. Come on back to my office. We'll talk there."

Lily followed him down a hallway to a corner office whose windows looked out at a landscaped garden below. The fronds of nearby palm trees danced in the playful breeze. But it was the beautiful fountain sitting in a small pond that caught her attention. The free-form shape, like high desert boulders that had tumbled together, was the kind of thing she'd been researching for the Blaise Group's two hotels in Arizona—the hotels they hoped to bring into the Corona Collection of Fine Hotels.

"Something peaceful about water flowing, especially in a desert setting," said Bennett standing beside her.

"Yes. Very refreshing."

"Have a seat," said Bennett. "I'll chat with you, then I'll ask my partner to join us. Okay with you?"

"Sure," Lily said. Bennett, with his easy-going manner and lack of airs made her feel comfortable. She knew enough from being in a couple of meetings with him, though, to understand he was a stickler for detail, much like her old boss.

"As you probably are already aware, our firm deals with trusts and estates, probate, and civil litigation. We've been in business here for close to forty years. Our company is hands-on, which is why we maintain a small staff of ten. It's a close-knit group."

"I like the sound of that," said Lily. "Some law firms get so big you lose some of that close feeling."

Bennett looked over her resumé. "You've got an impressive background. I took the liberty of going ahead and getting a reference from the law firm you worked with in New York." He smiled. "They'd do anything to get you back."

"I know," said Lily. "But I've decided to stay here. I've put my condo in New York up for sale."

"Great." Bennett discussed what he was looking for, how he saw someone like her fitting into the office, quizzed her on strengths and weaknesses, and asked the normal new-hire questions.

Finally, he leaned back. "I'm more than satisfied. Let me call my partner and have him come meet you. His name is Craig Kincaid."

Lily nodded politely and waited while Bennett called him on the intercom.

A low voice said, "Be right there, Ben."

Lily waited quietly for him to appear, imagining him as much of a cowboy as Bennett, whose brown cowboy boots were worn with age and activity. They and the turquoise and silver bolo tie around Bennett's neck against his crisp white shirt gave him an undeniable Southwestern flair.

A knock at the door signaled Craig's arrival. Lily turned to see a young, broad-shouldered man with caramel colored-hair studying her with a green-eyed gaze that made her catch her breath. Struggling to maintain her composure, Lily thought he was one of the most handsome young men she'd ever seen.

He came right over to her and shook her hand. "Pleased to meet you, Lily. I've heard a lot about you and have already reviewed your resumé."

The three of them sat together and talked for a while. Craig asked some of the same questions Bennett had, but she cheerfully answered them.

Finally, Craig rose and turned to her. "I'm satisfied by everything I've heard. I think you're going to make a nice addition to our staff, Lily."

She shook herself mentally. He looked like one of the heroes on the cover of an historical novel, one that showed a man in a kilt. That thought brought a flush of heat to her cheeks.

"Thank you," she finally managed to say. "I'm looking forward to it."

"You may occasionally be asked to help me out, but I have an assistant who's quite capable of taking care of me."

Bennett chuckled. "Loretta Morales is the boss of not only Craig, but the entire office. In fact, I thought you and Loretta should have a chance to talk. Do you mind?"

"Not at all," said Lily.

"Why don't I show you the way? Her office is next to mine." Craig stood and waited while Lily got to her feet.

"Thanks," said Bennett. "After you're through with Loretta, you and I will go to lunch and make final arrangements."

"That sounds nice," said Lily, hoping Bennett hadn't noticed her reaction to Craig.

Leaving the office, she walked beside Craig down a hallway, studying his easy gait from the corner of her eye.

With her short, comfy body and gray hair pulled back into a bun at the back of her head, Loretta was the image of an old-fashioned grandmother. Her dark eyes sparkled as she got to her feet. Names were exchanged, and Loretta greeted Lily with a quick, firm handshake.

"This woman is the one I can't live without," said Craig,

with a teasing smile. "I'd ask her to marry me, but she's already taken."

Loretta's laugh rose from her belly. "No woman would ever put up with your shenanigans. Not me, for sure." Still smiling, she turned to Lily. "This young man has to learn to make up his mind. Every woman in the area is after him, but he still hasn't settled down."

Craig's fair-skinned cheeks turned pink, but he gamely nodded. "I'll know when the right one comes along." He winked at Lily. "Loretta treats me like a son."

Loretta's expression turned serious. "Craig's mother and I were best friends. She died way too young. But I'm here to take over for her."

His face softened with affection. "Yeah, Mom would be pleased. I'll leave you two alone to talk. Then Ben is going to take Lily to lunch."

"Okay," said Loretta. "Sounds like a plan."

As Craig walked into his office, Loretta waved Lily to a chair in front of her desk. "Have a seat, and let's get to know one another a bit. Bennett already had me look over your resumé, but I like to meet people face-to-face, see what they're all about."

"I agree," said Lily. "So far, I like what I see here. How long have you been working in the office?"

"For over twenty years. Ben, Alec Thurston, my husband, Ricardo, and Craig's dad, Ken, play golf together. They became friends back when Bennett was growing his business and my husband was a professional golfer. When Ben knew I was looking for work, he suggested I give his office a try. I've been here ever since. The time's coming, though, when I'll want to retire." She leaned forward. "Tell me a bit about yourself. I hear you're helping Alec out. How's that going?"

"It's a sad time for me. Alec is a friend. I hate the thought of him dying. We dated for a couple of years. I moved to Arizona and then to New York to help out my sister who has a precious three-year-old daughter whom I adore."

"Ah, so you like children?" Loretta said, smiling.

"Very much. I'd still like to try for a child of my own," Lily said, then wondered why on earth she'd say something like this on a job interview. It was just that Loretta made her feel so comfortable.

"I've got three boys, all decent men," said Loretta with obvious pride. "I count Craig as one of them. Ben tells me you've decided to relocate here. May I ask why?"

Lily hesitated, not knowing if this was some sort of trick question. "In the time I've been here, I've been happier than I've been in years. I've learned to enjoy being outdoors, have already made great friends, and I want a better lifestyle." She cleared her throat and recalled the words she'd rehearsed with Rose. "I'm very good at my job and can work anywhere. I choose to do it here."

Loretta nodded. "Smart answer." She got to her feet. "I'm sure we're going to get along just fine. I mostly work for Craig, and you'll be on Ben's team, but it's important for all of us to be able to work together. Welcome to the group."

"Thank you so much," said Lily, feeling as if she'd just joined some kind of exclusive club.

CHAPTER TWO

ROSE

Using the golf cart set aside for her, Rose headed to the Desert Sage Inn full of optimism. The Blaise Group had agreed for her to work with Hank Bowers developing a PR campaign for the inn as the foundation for an upscale group of hotels she'd titled The Corona Collection of Fine Hotels. It pleased her to begin this work, allowing her to help shape the future for the hotel as Alec Thurston had hoped by hiring her, along with Willow and Lily.

Rose had worked for several years as a consultant to small businesses, helping them create a presence on social media. She also ran her own blog called "You Deserve This," where she wrote about various places to dine or visit, showcased different items for sale, or explained topics of particular interest to her growing audience, who were too busy to investigate on their own.

She couldn't wait to see Hank. Though they'd recently become engaged, she'd chosen not to move in with him as long as she was working for Alec. The sale of the inn would be concluded in another two months' time. She just hoped Alec would survive long enough to see it through. The thought of his dying brought a sour taste to her mouth. She loved Alec, always had, always would, though not in the same way she loved Hank. Finding unexpected love with him had been the biggest gift of leaving Las Vegas to come to Palm Desert.

As she drove through the inn's property, she gazed at the landscaping along the golf course. Palm trees, cacti, and other desert plants accented the ground carpeted with green grass. She loved the variety of cactus plants, their shapes, even the needles protecting them. Nature could be so beautiful.

She parked her golf cart in the employee parking lot and went around to the front of the inn. Approaching it through the front entrance always gave Rose a sense of satisfaction. She'd been part of the inn's growth years ago. To see it now filled her with pride. Alec had done an amazing job of creating an upscale property that was as warm and inviting as it was beautiful with everything a pampered guest might desire.

While walking through the front courtyard, she paused to admire the statue of a Native American woman holding out her arms as if to welcome people. As she entered the lobby of the hotel, her gaze was drawn as always to the sliding-glass doors leading out to the large patio beyond. The view of the palm trees and hedges of bright-colored hibiscus sent a wave of peace through her. The lobby, decorated in neutral tones with pops of purple, gray, and green was restful. Guests sat in chairs reading the newspaper or gathered in groups ready to begin their day.

Rose waved to the staff at the front desk and entered the elevator to go to the suite the Blaise Group had reserved for Hank. Though he now was renting a house, his daughter Sam and her family were staying there for a while so Sam could rest during her pregnancy. She'd lost one baby and didn't want anything to happen to another. Leah, Sam's three-year-old daughter was adorable but active. Rose admittedly loved that little girl. At fifty-two and never having had children of her own, she'd embraced Leah as her own, to Hank's approval. Hank was as devoted to his granddaughter as any man could be. It was a joy to see.

The elevator stopped at the second floor and Rose stepped off, a smile already forming. She was as giddy as a teenager around Hank Bowers, the man she'd thought she'd dislike with all his baseball slang and self-confidence. But he was one of the nicest, kindest, sexiest men she'd ever met. In his sixties, he was in great shape and had proved it to her.

She knocked on the door. Hank opened it and drew her into his arms. "I missed you. Are you sure you want to continue staying at Alec's house?"

She wrapped her arms around him and hugged him close, inhaling the aroma of his lemony aftershave with a happy sigh. "For the time being, that's best. I'm sure Sam and Rob wouldn't want us sharing the house with them. It's cute to see how much this time there has enhanced their romance."

"Yes, you're right. I suppose I could move into this suite for a while."

"No, Leah is counting on you to be there with her," Rose said. "We've waited all this time to find one another. We can enjoy our time here until your family leaves."

He cupped her face in his broad hands and lowered his lips to hers. "Mmm. Can't wait 'til they leave," he murmured when they'd pulled apart.

Knowing better, Rose chuckled and shook her head. Hank would be distraught not to have his family around. It was one thing she loved about him. Having lived through an unhappy childhood with parents who rarely showed her love, that meant a lot to her.

"Come on in," said Hank. "I've been working on logos and log lines for the new collection."

Rose's attention was immediately drawn to the work desk covered with papers. She hurried over to see. After studying several examples, she lifted a sheet of paper. "I like this a lot." The design was of a crown over a large C with a smaller c inside. "It both tells the story but keeps it simple."

A smile crossed Hank's face. "That's the one I thought

you'd choose. It's my favorite, too. A real home run!"

Rose laughed at the baseball lingo. "I think Alec will love it." Though it wasn't Alec's choice to make, she wanted to please him with the ideas they were creating for the future of the Desert Sage Inn after he was gone. Hank, bless his heart, understood that.

They worked on blurbs, circling around the concept of the Corona Collection of Fine Hotels. When they moved on to suggestions for notifications to guests and former guests of the inn of the changes that were about to take place, Rose went on high alert. Alec didn't want his loyal guests to think he'd sold out to a company that would reduce the quality of the Desert Sage Inn. Though the Blaise Group had been hesitant to entertain the thought of making the inn the prototype of a new upscale collection within their group of hotels, she'd finally won them over to consider testing the idea. But she understood how important it was that the news reflect a public relations opportunity for both the Blaise Group and Alec's beloved inn.

They worked until noon and then Hank said, "Come back to my house for lunch. Leah was asking when 'Wosie' was going to visit."

Rose's heart warmed. Leah had taken to calling her Wosie, a name she thought was adorable. "Well, then, I guess I'd better go with you. I wouldn't want to disappoint her."

"My family has really fallen in love with you, Rose," said Hank grinning at her.

She returned his smile. "I didn't think it was going to happen, but I'm glad it has. I know how important they are to you."

He wrapped his arms around her. "Well, I wasn't going to let them ruin what was happening between us. You're too special."

They gazed at one another with silly smiles. They'd both been surprised by their instant connection.

CHAPTER THREE

WILLOW

Willow gave her mother, Juanita, a kiss goodbye and left the kitchen to go to the hotel. It was weird living in Alec's house where her parents worked for him, but Alec had insisted she be treated as a guest, like Rose and Lily. He'd always been her champion, believing in anything she wanted to do, which was one reason her interest in the hotel business grew from the time she was a child.

Outside, she waved to her father, Pedro, who was checking the sprinkler system, and climbed into her golf cart. Alec's house was in the corner of the hotel property away from the inn's activity and away from the site of the original house that had been on the property when he'd bought it. The house where his wife and unborn child had died.

Feeling the cool morning air against her cheeks, Willow sighed with satisfaction. She loved being able to spend time away from her desk, especially when she had to share office space with her nemesis, Brent Armstrong. His cousin, Trace Armstrong, was much nicer, but was just as eager to oversee their transition team. The fact that Trace's father, Mitchell Armstrong, majority owner of the Blaise Group, had handed her the job ate at them both. It made Willow more determined than ever to do a good job.

Willow, Brent, and Trace were all working under the hotel's resident manager, John Rodriquez, to learn all they could about the unique operating and service characteristics of Desert Sage Inn that would form the nucleus of operations of the Corona Collection. There were many procedures followed at the Desert Sage Inn that were new to the Blaise Group.

Willow stopped the golf cart and allowed a golfer to cross the cart path to find his ball off the course. She loved the game of golf, but hadn't played it on a regular basis for years while living in the Northeast. Now that she was home in the Southwest, she hoped to begin again. In high school, she'd won the state championship in her senior year.

She admired the mountains in the background. Their bulk and height added texture to the desert landscape around her. A hummingbird, attracted by the red blouse she wore, hovered in front of her and then darted away. Such interesting little creatures, and so territorial.

As she moved forward, she thought of Alec. She'd do anything for him. He was her mentor and a second father to her. She'd tagged along with him for years, learning as much as she could about the hotel business. It was he who'd helped her get into the hotel school at Cornell University.

Willow parked her golf cart in the employees' parking lot at the inn and went in through the service entrance, stopping to get a cup of coffee in the kitchen before heading to the staff offices. She hoped a jolt of caffeine would sharpen her mind. She was about to face Brent, a man as dangerous as a rattler.

When she entered the room set aside for her and the two Armstrong cousins, she was surprised to see Trace.

"Morning! You're early!" she said cheerfully. Trace was as nice as Brent was mean. He was also easy on the eyes with his blond hair, rugged features, and bright-blue gaze.

"Hi. Brent is off today, so it's just you and me."

Taking a seat at the far end of the work table, she couldn't stop a smile from spreading across her face. Without Brent, it was going to be an even better day.

Willow was immersed in her review of a preliminary

budget for next year, when the inn would be under the umbrella of the Blaise Group, when she heard a disruption in the hallway and looked up.

Brent appeared at the doorway. He looked awful. Hungover.

"I decided I'd better come in. I can't trust either one of you," Brent said, stumbling into the office.

Trace got to his feet. "Whoa! What's going on? You look sick."

"Yeah? Well, you don't look so hot yourself," Brent responded, on the defensive as usual.

Willow remained seated and quiet. She'd faced Brent's meanness before and wanted no part of this exchange. Brent was a spoiled brat who'd thought he'd automatically be appointed to the position Willow now held.

Trace walked over to Brent. "C'mon. I'll walk you up to your room."

Brent's shoulders slumped. Much to Willow's relief, he allowed Trace to lead him away.

Long after they'd left the office, Willow sat thinking about them. Brent's father, Duncan, was the younger brother of Mitchell, who owned a greater percentage of the company. Whereas Mitchell was quietly proud of Trace, Duncan coddled and then pushed Brent forward, as if Brent could somehow end up owning more of the company than Trace. It was a family squabble that could only hurt not help those involved because Brent wasn't a nice person. He was spoiled, felt entitled, and was ultimately insecure.

Willow's thoughts flew back in time to when she and Brent were both attending the Cornell School of Hotel Administration. Brent was two years ahead of her and very popular among his white, privileged group. He'd called her "Enchilada," laughing at and demeaning her for being on scholarship. She'd never forget the hurt she'd felt. That's why she felt it was so important for her to prove she was well able to handle any task she was given.

When Trace came back, Willow gave him a questioning look.

"Brent's father told him he'd failed, and should've been given your position. He's taking it hard."

Duncan himself was to blame for Brent's shortcomings. How did he expect his son to stand on his own two feet when he'd spent all this time propping him up? She pushed aside thoughts of them, allowing nothing to interfere with her success. She owed it to herself and Alec.

CHAPTER FOUR

LILY

Lily returned to Alec's house from lunch with Bennett and hurried to tell him about the job offer she'd accepted. It was even better than she'd hoped.

When she arrived at Alec's private quarters, he was sleeping. Disappointed, she headed back to her room to change. She checked her computer for any missed messages and found an email from one of the girls on a local high school track team, asking Willow, Rose, and her to come talk to the student body about empowering women. They'd met them during a team building exercise that Dan McMillan, head of the fitness center at the hotel, had set up for them.

Lily responded to the email saying she was free to come but she'd have to check with Rose and Willow to see what time they could fit into their schedules. It felt great to feel as if she was already part of the community. She was looking forward to sharing some information she'd learned at an employee seminar called, "Dare to Say No." She'd been thinking about it a lot lately. It wasn't until she decided to come to Palm Desert that she'd put some of that learning to use by quitting her job.

Too excited to sit around the house, Lily headed out for a walk. Things were falling into place for her at last. As soon as her condo sold in New York, she'd purchase a place in Palm Desert. She hadn't talked to her sister lately, but Monica was usually pretty busy. Still, on a whim, she decided to call her. Monica was due to go to work in twenty minutes or so, but it would give Lily time to give her the good news.

She punched in the number for her sister and waited. After several rings, Monica's voice came through. "Hi, Shisss! Whazzup?"

Lily's stomach knotted at the slurring of Monica's words. "What's up with you?"

"Nothin'. Jeremy has returned to town and we're tryin' to work things out."

Lily came to an abrupt stop, her heart pounding so hard she couldn't breathe. "Jeremy?" she finally choked out. "I thought you said he was trouble. And, Monica, you sound drunk."

"Aw, Lily, we're just celebratin'. No worries."

Lily's heart sank. Jeremy O'Neill, Monica's ex-boyfriend and father of her three-year-old daughter was a troubled young man who'd been a problem in the past. "Where's Izzy?"

"In bed. It's her naptime."

"Monica, she's usually up by now. What's going on?"

"Nothing to worry about. I've got to go. Jeremy's gonna take me out to dinner as soon as the babysitter arrives."

"What about work?" Lily asked, feeling faint. Having had a mother who was an alcoholic, she knew all about attempts to sound normal and how they sometimes failed.

"I'm taking today off. Jeremy says I owe it to him after all the effort he made to come back. Look, I've gotta go." Monica clicked off the call, leaving Lily gripping her phone so hard her fingers turned white. Monica may think she had nothing to worry about, but Lily knew better.

Lily turned around and headed back to Alec's house with a new plan. During this down time, she'd make the trip back home. She couldn't bear to think of Monica or darling Izzy in trouble. Her sister and Izzy were the only family she had.

###

That evening Lily sat outdoors with Rose and Willow and explained what she was going to do. "As I told Alec, I'll be gone for only a few days. While I'm there, I'll work with my real estate agent to discuss an offer on my condo and make arrangements to ship my car out here. Most of all, I have to talk to my sister about her situation and see that Izzy is all right. The baby sitter I've been paying to take care of my niece is reliable, but she was as concerned as I when I talked to her about what's going on."

"I'm sorry," said Rose. "I know how much you love that little girl. And seeing how vulnerable Leah is at that age, I understand your worry."

"You're doing the right thing by going back to check on the situation," Willow agreed. "Are you sure it's only alcohol that's a problem with your sister?"

Lily shrugged and shook her head. "That's something I'll find out. On a brighter note, I heard from one of the girls we met on the high school track team. She and a number of other students want the three of us to come and talk to them about empowering women as soon as we can schedule it. I'm free most days, but I told them I'd have to let them know if that's something you two can do. What do you say?"

"I'm free to set up an appointment with them," said Willow.

Rose nodded. "Me too. It should be interesting."

"Okay, then, I'll get back to her and tell her to give us some dates and we'll let her know when we can be there." Lily smiled at them both. "Women working together is so important."

"Yes," said Willow, "especially because I'm competing against two guys determined to bump me out of my job."

"How's that going?" said Lily.

"Not as well as I'd hoped. Trace is trying to be cooperative, but Brent is fighting me all the way. It seems so silly when we're all supposed to be working toward the same thing."

"Watch out for Brent," Rose said to Willow. "He's used to having his own way."

"Yeah, well I'm determined to break that old pattern. After all the crap he gave me in college, I'm more than ready to prove I'm better."

Lily lifted her coffee cup in a salute. She'd meant it when she'd said women had to stick together to get things done. Someone like Brent didn't understand the strength of that.

The next morning, bright and early, Pedro drove Lily to the airport. From Palm Springs she'd fly to Denver and on to New York. It was a long day of travel, and she was anxious to get there.

The flight gave her time, too much time, to recall how life had been growing up. Ten years older than Monica, she'd worked hard to protect her as much as possible from a mother whose affections ran hot and cold, leaving them to wonder whether it would be a good day or bad. Lily realized now that perhaps she should have allowed Monica to see more of what addiction could do to a person. Jeremy had always shown signs of being unstable, but until he'd ditched her sister, he hadn't appeared to be severely addicted to alcohol or drugs. He'd just been a total ass.

Now she wondered if she'd missed some signs of it. Bottom line was that Monica's being with Jeremy wasn't a great idea. Monica had always been on the wild side, no doubt in reaction to her upbringing. But now that Izzy, precious little girl, was part of her life, Monica had a responsibility to be a better mother than her own had been.

By the time Lily arrived in New York she was exhausted physically, mentally, and emotionally. Though she'd told Monica when she was arriving, she'd said she'd find her own way back to Ellenton from the city. At this late afternoon hour, Monica should be getting ready to go to work.

In the cab on the way home, Lily called to make sure the babysitter was at Monica's. After talking to her and knowing all was on schedule, Lily decided to go directly to her condo. Monica had promised her it was being refreshed from time to time so that it would show well to any realtor. A part of Lily was sad to see the sale of the home she'd worked hard to have, but she knew life would be much better for her out west.

The taxi driver was, thankfully, not a chatterer. In the back seat, Lily closed her eyes and drew deep breaths. The gray skies and colder air were depressing after the color and warmth of the desert. She hadn't realized she'd fallen asleep until the driver announced in a heavy-accented voice, "We're here."

Startled, she sat up and rubbed her eyes. She paid him, unloaded her suitcase, and rolled it up to the front door of her building. Now that she was here, she couldn't wait to see her condo and all the furnishings she'd carefully chosen for it. The larger pieces of furniture would be shipped out to California after the sale of her condo went through.

From habit, she checked her mailbox. Empty. She almost felt like knocking on the door to her condo, then chided herself for feeling that way after being gone for less than two months.

With a flourish of excitement, she opened the door.

The gasp from her throat hung in the air like the cry of a mourning dove. She blinked in confusion and stared with dismay at the mess inside. With growing horror, she glanced at the dirty dishes on the coffee table and the blanket thrown across the couch. Empty beer cans were tossed on the carpet. She went to the kitchen where an even bigger mess cluttered the counters, dirty dishes filled the sink, and a pot on the stove still had rotting food inside. She gagged and reached for her cell.

Heart pounding, she punched in Monica's number.

"Hello?" Monica said cheerily. "You made it!"

"Yes, I made it all the way back to my condo. What's going on? Who's been staying here?"

"Oh, Jeremy needed a place to stay. I said he could stay there if he kept it nice and clean."

"Have you seen it?" Lily's voice shook with anger.

"Not recently. Why?"

"It's a total mess. My condo is up for sale and needs to be clean and orderly at all times," Lily said. "I thought you understood that. You should've asked me first before you allowed him to stay in my home."

"Oh, Lil, I wouldn't worry about any mess. It's a beautiful place," said Monica. "Anyone can see that."

"Not like this, it isn't. You tell Jeremy he's not to set foot in my condo again. Is that clear?"

"Where will he stay?" Monica asked. "He can't stay here. The babysitter told me you wouldn't allow it, and it would make things easier if he wasn't here."

Lily fought to find words. Had partying with Jeremy addled Monica's brain? "Monica, he shouldn't be staying with you or staying here at my condo. What is he doing back in town anyway? Does he have a job?"

"Listen, we'll talk later. I'm on my way to work. It's going to be okay. Jeremy and I are working things out."

"In the meantime, Jeremy will have to find a different place to stay. If he's left anything here, I'll box it up and put it outside the door, but he's not coming in again."

"Gee, Lily, that doesn't sound like you," said Monica.

"It's me, all right," Lily said. "The new me that's done allowing people to walk all over me. Make sure he understands."

"Okaaay," Monica said. "See you later."

Lily clicked off the call realizing Monica sounded surprised she'd stood her ground and said no. She clasped her head in her hands and let out a shaky sigh. Things had gotten out of hand during the two months she'd been gone. Maybe she shouldn't have taken the job in Palm Desert. She straightened, her body rigid with anger. *No! It was time for her to set boundaries and let Monica grow up and be responsible.*

Lily checked the time and, hopeful, hurried to the manager's office. He was not only the manager, but a very handy man.

He was closing up when Lily burst through the doorway into the office. "I have an emergency situation. Can you please change the locks on my door?"

He glanced at the clock on the wall. "I suppose so. Let me grab my tools and I'll be right there." He shook a finger at her. "I wouldn't do this for just anyone, Lily, but you've always been really nice to me."

They walked back to her condo. When the manager saw the mess inside, he said, "I thought you were away."

"I was," Lily replied grimly. "That's why I want the locks changed on the door. My sister's boyfriend has been staying here without my permission."

He nodded. "Okay, give me a little bit of time and I'll take care of this."

While he worked on the front door, Lily went into her bedroom. Though her bed was still made neatly, clothing and a backpack were scattered across the bedspread. Lily picked up the clothes, shoved them into the backpack, added toiletries from the bathroom, and checked the rest of the rooms for anything of Jeremy's.

Assessing the mess, Lily realized she'd have to scrub the

bathroom, vacuum, and dust, before the condo would be presentable for showing. She'd do it. Now, more than ever, she wanted to get top dollar for it, and as the real estate agent had told her, first impressions were important.

The manager finished his work, billed her, and left with a suggestion to let him know if she needed his help in the future.

She closed the door behind him, gathered Jeremy's backpack and a bag of other items she'd collected, including the beer she'd found in the refrigerator, and set them outside the door with a note that said, "There must have been a misunderstanding. This place is not available for your use."

As tired as she was, Lily went to work cleaning. She had one offer to review that was lower than she wanted, but the more she thought about it, the more willing she was to seriously consider it. She called her real estate agent and left a message asking her to meet in the morning.

She'd just finished cleaning the bathroom when she heard pounding at the front door. Certain she knew who it was, she went to the door and peered out through the peep hole.

Jeremy, looking older and more bedraggled, stood there, his face flushed, his nostrils flaring.

"Hey, Lily! I know you're in there. What's going on? You can't throw me out. I'm here to see Monica and the baby. She won't let me stay with her. So, I gotta stay here."

No way would she open the door. She stood next to it and called out, "No, Jeremy. The condo is up for sale. No one else is allowed to stay here. You'll have to make other arrangements."

"You always were a bitch, Lily," he snarled. "Don't worry. I have lots of old friends who'll let me stay with them. Fuck off."

She waited until he'd gone before she opened the door. Everything of his was gone, including the beer. Sighing, she went back inside and locked the door.

After everything was as straightened as she wanted, she left the condo to head over to Monica's apartment. She couldn't wait to see Izzy.

Excited, she hurried to her car. She opened the car door and stepped back. Someone had been smoking in her Honda, her precious car, the one she'd worked so hard for. Tears stung her eyes. She knew it might seem materialistic to some people to be so upset, but out of gratitude, she'd always taken care of it.

Climbing in behind the wheel, she started the engine and opened all the windows. Then while the car idled, she cleaned up the papers and empty food bags that had been crumpled up and tossed into the back. Placing them into an outdoor bin, she vowed to take back any personal keys from Monica. She was usually more considerate, but then Monica's relationship with Jeremy had always brought out the worst in her.

CHAPTER FIVE

LILY

As she drew closer to Monica's apartment, anticipation threaded through her. Photos and text messages couldn't compare to the real thing, and she was dying to see Izzy in person. In many ways, Izzy was like her own daughter. Lily had been hands-on with her from the beginning when Monica claimed she needed her rest and time to recover. Looking back, Lily realized how much she'd babied Monica, but she'd loved being part of Izzy's life because she was a substitute for the baby she wanted of her own.

Lily parked outside the apartment in Monica's spot and hurried inside. The babysitter, Norma Sutton, greeted her at the door. An older, well-cushioned woman with a pleasant personality, Norma had won over Lily the first time she'd met her and had seen how Izzy reacted to her sweet smile.

"There you are, Lily," said Norma, giving her a quick hug. "I know one little girl who's going to be thrilled that Auntie Lee is back. She's asleep now. But I left the nightlight on bright so you can see her. She's growing so fast."

Lily returned Norma's quick embrace and hurried toward Izzy's room, her fingers itching to hold her. At the doorway, she stopped and on tiptoes moved inside, her gaze never leaving the sleeping child who meant so much to her.

Soft light illuminated Izzy's pillow, exposing her sweet, little face. Hair the color of butterscotch spread across the pillow. Her eyes were closed, but her lashes curled up and away from her cheeks. Izzy's body was sprawled across the bed, looking longer than the last time she'd seen her.

Lily knelt beside the bed to get a closer look. She leaned in to kiss Izzy's cheek and jumped back when she opened her eyes and stared at her. Blinking rapidly, Izzy sat up.

"Auntie Lee?"

Lily sat up on the bed and pulled Izzy into her arms. "It's me, sweetheart."

Izzy wrapped her arms around her. "Don't go away."

At the pleading in Izzy's voice, tears filled Lily's eyes. She sat on the bed and rubbed Izzy's back in comforting circles. "I'm staying right here until you fall asleep."

Izzy nestled closer and closed her eyes. When her breathing deepened, Lily lay Izzy down and spread a light blanket over her. Silently, she left the room. She and Norma needed to talk.

In the living room, Lily sat in a chair opposite the couch where Norma had spread her knitting beside her.

"Norma, what can you tell me about Monica's activities since Jeremy returned. I need to know as many details as you're willing to give me." Lily gave her a steady look.

"Well, I normally don't talk about my clients, but since you're paying me, I will. At first, Monica was thrilled to introduce me to Jeremy. She said they were trying to work things out and get back together. I suggested to her that she shouldn't allow him to stay at the apartment with her, that it might be confusing to Izzy and that I didn't think you'd like it." Norma shook her head. "She was angry about it, but then she said she'd find a place for him. In fact, I think she was a little relieved."

"Yeah, but that place was my condo which is up for sale. It was a mess when I arrived."

Norma bit the corner of her lip and studied her. "I don't think Jeremy is the right man for Monica. She's become like a rebellious teenager, drinking and staying out late, then lying about it."

"I'm going to have a talk with her. We've been through so much together I'd hate for her to slip back to the old, unreliable way when she was with him before. Most of all, I can't let anything bad happen to Izzy."

Norma nodded. "It will be nice to have you here."

"I can stay for only a few days. I'm going to sell my condo, pack up my things, and try to convince Monica to come to California with me."

Norma lifted a finger in warning. "I have bad feelings about Jeremy. He's already convinced her to do things she normally wouldn't. Things like calling in sick to work, telling me she was okay when I know she'd been drinking, and not showing up here on time."

Lily's stomach clenched. "It's an old pattern. Monica and Jeremy together are trouble." But she knew if she pushed Monica too hard, their relationship would explode and the fallout would hurt Izzy.

Unable to hold back a yawn, Lily stood. "If you don't mind, I'm going home. I'll see Monica tomorrow. There's no sense in my trying to talk to her after she gets off work. We'll both be too tired to do much more than argue."

"No problem. I'm here as always." Norma moved her knitting aside and got to her feet. Wrapping her arms around Lily, she said, "You're a wonderful sister to Monica. You have been since I've known you. Let me know what I can do to help. Monica's a nice person too. Just a little misguided."

Lily stepped back and smiled, grateful for Norma's words of encouragement. She'd always felt responsible for Monica and hated the feeling that she'd somehow failed. But facts were facts. She went to the key rack in the kitchen and removed the extra sets of keys to both her car and her condo.

###

After a restless night of dreams filled with old, painful memories of her mother at her alcoholic worst, Lily awoke in a tangle of her sheet and blanket. She pulled her limbs from the coverings and stretched out atop the bed. Her mind whirled with fragments of her dreams as she stared up at the ceiling. She rolled over and checked her cell phone. Her real estate agent had answered her text, saying she'd be glad to meet with her at the condo at ten o'clock.

Lily hurried into the bathroom. If she was lucky, she'd sell her condo today. After a shower and a quick breakfast of coffee and toast, Lily took inventory of her furnishings. The larger, more-expensive pieces she'd ship to California; the smaller items she'd give to Monica or charity. Having seen the different styles of desert décor, Lily wanted to be free to start fresh. She began sorting through her personal papers. Before she'd left for California, she'd tucked them away in a small metal safe. Not even Monica had had access to them. Now, she'd take them back to Palm Desert with her.

Lily was busy sorting through items in the kitchen when a knock on the door alerted her. She went to it, pleased that the agent was early. Perhaps, Lily thought, she was as eager for a sale as she.

Lily opened the door and stepped back as Monica charged through the entrance. "We need to talk."

"Yes, we do," Lily said as calmly as she could "I'm meeting my real estate agent in a few minutes so our talk will have to wait. How about meeting for lunch, my treat?"

Monica shook her head. "Jeremy is moving into the apartment. I have to be there to help."

"What apartment?" Lily said, already dreading the answer.

"Mine. Since he can no longer use this one, we have no choice."

Just like that, Lily was thrown back in time to a different

place, a different scene. Then sixteen, Monica was telling her she was going to move to the City, that she had a job in a restaurant there. Today, Monica had the same, stubborn look on her face.

Lily sighed. "Will you wait until we've had a chance to talk? There's something I want to discuss with you."

Monica's shoulders slumped. "Okay. I have to get back to the apartment. Jeremy's watching Izzy."

Lily's stomach filled with acid. "You're leaving him in charge of her?"

Monica planted her hands on her hips. "What else could I do? You're no longer here to help me."

"You'd better go back to her. I'll pick you and Izzy up at noon."

"Jeremy won't like it. He doesn't like me to go many places without him."

Feeling even sicker, Lily forced herself to refrain from screaming. "I'll see you at noon."

As Monica left, Nan Bishop, Lily's real estate agent, appeared, carrying a brief case.

Lily forced herself to shift gears and managed a smile. "Good morning. Come on in."

"Got your message," Nan said, giving her a wide smile. "You said you're ready to deal, so I brought papers with me. Let's sit and talk, and we'll come up with an acceptable counter-offer, even if it's not what you'd hoped."

Lily led Nan inside.

Nan glanced around. "This looks much better. I had to explain to another client that normally the place was in perfect order. In the real estate business, staging is very important." Nan walked over to the sliding glass door and peered out. "You have such a nice view. The river, the woods are all so peaceful. It's a big selling point." She turned around. "How is

California? You look well, tan and healthy."

This time Lily didn't need to force a smile. "It's great. Excellent, in fact, though some of the circumstances surrounding my new job are sad. The man who hired me is dying."

"Oh, that *is* sad. I'm sorry."

"But I'm very happy with the idea of moving there. I've already secured a second, part-time position and have looked at housing. I'm hoping to make an offer on a condo out there as soon as the sale for this one is completed."

"Well, now. Let's get started." Nan picked up her briefcase. "Shall we go into the kitchen?"

"Yes. We'll be able to spread out paperwork there," said Lily, feeling hope rise within her.

Nan took papers out of her briefcase and set them on the table. "Lily, I hope you're going to be reasonable. I know this offer is ten thousand dollars less than you wanted to even consider. But it's a substantial offer with financing in place. I say we counter by saying we'd be willing to deal at their number plus five thousand dollars. Any counter offer they make to us will be more money than they originally offered. Does that sound like a deal?"

Lily nodded. "Having the financing in place means less worry for me. I say let's go for it."

"I think it's reasonable for both the seller and the buyer. Their agent is pretty confident it'll work because the young couple love the location."

Lily went through the paperwork with Nan, signed in all the right places and sat back and waited while Nan called the buyer's agent.

While they were sitting sipping coffee, Nan received a phone call saying the buyers agreed with the new number and they were sending the paperwork to the office.

Nan stood. "That was easy. It helps to have friends in the industry. We can make things happen quicker." She smiled. "I'd better get back to the office. Why don't you drop by this afternoon and we can complete all the final paperwork?"

"I'll see you in a few hours," said Lily. Though she spoke in a normal voice, she felt like shouting with joy. She was on her way to a new life. Now all she had to do was to convince Monica to leave Jeremy and come to California with her.

Lily waited outside Monica's apartment building for her to show up with Izzy. It was disturbing to her that Jeremy wanted to know Monica's every move. Abusers did that.

She looked up as Monica, carrying Izzy, approached. Seeing her, Izzy squealed with joy and held out her arms to her. Lily took her niece in her embrace and squeezed her, loving the feel of her.

Monica looked on, smiling at the two of them. "She really loves you, you know?"

Lily felt the smile that stretched across her face. "And I love her. Right, Izzy?"

"Wuv you," Izzy said seriously, bringing a sheen of tears to Lily's eyes.

"Where do you want to go to lunch?" Lily asked, buckling the little girl into her car seat.

"How about Sadie's? I'm hungry for some tasty old-fashioned food." Monica patted her stomach. "I'll probably just order salad though. Jeremy says I need to watch what I eat or I'll blimp up even more."

Lily straightened and faced her sister. "And what else does he tell you?"

Monica shrugged and lowered her chin. "I don't know."

"Look, Monica. It's terribly hurtful for someone to tell you something like that. I don't like it."

"Aw, that's just how he is." Monica glanced at her and looked away. "How'd you do with the sale of your condo?"

Lily grinned with satisfaction. "The sale is going through. I got less for it than I wanted, but it's still a lucky deal considering the slow market. And I'm ready to move to the desert. I feel at home there. In fact, I want to fly you and Izzy out for a visit in hopes that I can convince you to move there."

"What? I love my job here. And now with Jeremy back, I don't see that happening." Monica shook her head. "He'd never agree to it."

"What are you talking about? He doesn't have to agree to anything. He gave up his parental rights long ago."

"Well, now he's telling me he wants them back, that if I don't cooperate, he'll take Izzy away from me." Monica climbed into the passenger seat and sat staring straight ahead.

Lily slid behind the wheel and turned to her. "I can't believe that in the few weeks I've been away, so much has happened to change your life. He'd have a huge legal fight on his hands if he tried any such move. You realize that, don't you?"

"I like that he's back. He says he made a huge mistake by walking away four years ago. Now he wants to make things right."

"Does he have a job?" Lily asked.

Monica turned to her. "Not yet. He's looking."

"What kind of work is he looking for?" Lily asked as she drove out of the parking lot.

"Stop asking so many questions," snapped Monica, her tone defensive. "I told you we're working things out."

Lily knew enough about her sister to realize if she kept pushing, Monica would retaliate by limiting her time with Izzy. She'd done it before when they'd argued. She glanced at the rearview mirror and smiled at the sweet little face who was looking at them.

"Izzy, look! See the dog? What does the dog say?"

"Erf! Erf!"

Lily chuckled, delighted with the response. She was one smart little girl.

She pulled up to the red-brick building housing Sadie's Restaurant. Lily got Izzy out of her seat and they headed inside. More like a diner than a restaurant, booths lined the large front windows. A huge breakfast bar offered seats to eighteen people. In between, tables for four filled most of the space.

Today, like most days, the place was busy. A waitress came over to them. "Just the three of you?"

"Yes, please," said Lily. "A highchair for this little one." She jiggled Izzy in her arms, smiling at her with pride.

The waitress smiled at Izzy. "Hi, cutie."

"That's my baby," said Monica. "My sister likes to pretend she's hers."

Lily felt heat rush to her cheeks and tried to find a suitable response.

The waitress smiled at her. "Who wouldn't want to pretend something like that. She's a beautiful little girl. Come this way. I have the perfect table for you."

Lily followed her to a table in a secluded spot and waited while a high chair was found and brought to the table. She placed Izzy into the chair, buckled her in and sat beside her. After the waitress left with their usual orders, Lily turned to Monica.

"I may love Izzy, but I'd never do anything to interfere with your relationship with her, Monica. You're her mother."

"I'm sorry. It's just that Izzy loves being with you. It sorta makes me mad because I'm the one who takes care of her."

"Yes, I know. You and Norma."

They were silent as a young waiter filled their glasses with water and walked away.

"I understand you like California, but I think you should stay here. I know the law firm would take you back in a minute. They've hired a friend of mine who says the place is in shambles without you."

Lily fought a tempting smugness. "As flattering as that sounds, returning to that office is something I'm not going to do. Isn't there a way I can get you to come to California?"

Monica looked torn. "I'd like to come for a visit." She sighed. "If you buy the tickets, I'll make arrangements to come."

"Just you and Izzy. Okay?"

Monica frowned then nodded. "Deal."

Feeling better, Lily glanced at the salad the waitress placed in front of her and suddenly felt hungry.

CHAPTER SIX

ROSE

Rose entered the house Hank had rented, eager to see Leah. The little girl had wormed her way into Rose's heart. She thought of how lucky she was to have found not only Hank, but his family. An only child growing up in a household with little love, she now realized how lonely she'd been through the years.

Samantha, Hank's daughter, walked into the kitchen. "Hi, Rose. Nice to see you. I'm setting up lunch out on the pool deck. That way we can keep an eye on Leah." She turned as Leah raced by her and over to Rose.

"Hi, Wosie. Wanna come for a swim?" Leah took Rose's hand and jumped up and down beside her.

Laughing, Rose bent over to give her a quick hug. "Maybe later. We're going to have lunch now."

"Papa B?" Leah said, giving Hank a pleading look.

He picked her up and hugged her. "We'll go in the pool later. Right now, it's lunch time."

Leah squirmed to get down, and once her feet touched the floor, she was off and running.

"I don't know what I'm going to do with two," said Sam, shaking her head and patting the bulge that was just beginning to show in her abdomen.

"You'll do fine," said Rose. Sam was a strict mother who'd once made it a point to correct Rose on how to handle compliments to a pretty child, like Leah.

"Thanks." Sam gave her a grateful look. "I'll never be the

mom my own mother was, but I try."

Rose nodded agreeably. She recalled how unfriendly Sam had been to her when they first met earlier that year when Rose and Hank also had first met. The meanness in Sam that was once there was gone now that Rose and Hank were engaged. Rose hoped it would continue that way.

Sam's husband, Rob, came into the kitchen. "Is anyone going to join me? We've got everything ready."

"I will," Rose said. She liked Rob. He was as easygoing as Sam was not. Between them, they had an understanding about Sam's protection of her father and her need to worship the memory of her mother.

Outside, beneath the protection from the sun provided by the covered porch, Sam had placed sandwiches on a platter atop a long table that sat at one end of the porch. A pitcher of iced tea, a plate of cookies, and a bowl of potato chips completed the luncheon spread.

Rose took a seat on one of the benches by the table and sighed happily. She relished these family times. Especially when Leah insisted on sitting next to her.

"Sorry for the lack of choice," said Sam. "I made only egg salad sandwiches today. I'm trying to keep things as simple as possible."

"No apologies necessary. The important thing is for you to get your rest. This is such an important time for you," said Rose.

"I'm hoping to carry this baby to term," said Sam. "It's been such a heartbreak trying over and over again." Tears filled her eyes. She glanced at Rob.

"That's why we're here for such a long time. Thanks to Hank, we can stay as long as necessary. With me able to work from home, this is a perfect place to nurture a little one."

Observing the loving look exchanged between Sam and

Rob, Rose's heart warmed. This was the kind of family she'd always dreamed of having.

Hank caught her eye and smiled before turning to Sam. "I've been thinking I could move into my suite at the hotel to give you two more privacy. What do you think?"

"Actually," said Sam, "I was going to ask you and Rose to babysit Leah for a couple of days while Rob and I make a short trip to San Diego and the Hotel Del Coronado. An early anniversary trip."

"We won't be able to do anything like that little break until after the event. At least not for a while," said Rob quietly.

Rose understood his secrecy. Leah's parents hadn't told her about the baby.

"What do you think, Rose? Are you willing to move in here for a couple of days?" Hank's grin was a tease.

Feeling heat rise to her cheeks and then telling herself that was ridiculous, she nodded. "I'm sure I can arrange that with Alec and the Flowers."

"I love the story of how Alec calls you and Lily and Willow the Desert Flowers. It's such a cool thing, like the television show with the guy and his three angels."

Rose smiled. "That's where the idea came from. We're on a mission to save the inn."

"Okay then," said Rob. "I'll make reservations today for the following week. If you start doing workouts at the gym, you might be ready to take on Leah."

Rose laughed with the others. Leah might be only three years old, but she was a whirlwind of activity. Rob swore she talked and constantly moved even in her sleep.

CHAPTER SEVEN

WILLOW

Willow gamely headed to the office, knowing the day ahead would be difficult. Today, she, Trace, and Brent were going to meet with Brian Walden, the consultant the Blaise Group had hired to oversee the 90-day transition period from the time of the signing of the sales agreement to closing of the actual sale of the Desert Sage Inn to the Blaise Group.

In another time and under different circumstances, Willow might be attracted to Trace, but there was too much political maneuvering between them to make that happen. Besides, she wasn't really interested in dating anyone. Dan McMillan, the head of the resort's fitness program was a nice guy she was attracted to, but he didn't show signs of any interest in her beyond friendship.

Rather than trying to find a man, Willow was using all her energy to work for Alec in the hotel manager's office, learning as much as she could about the inn's operations. She'd use that information to promote having the inn become the basis of an upscale collection of hotels. After all Alec had done for her, this work was the least she could do for him.

Willow's thoughts were still on Alec as she parked the golf cart in the employee parking lot.

"Hey, watch it!" came a cry beside her.

Startled, she turned to find Brent driving a golf cart approaching the narrow slot next to her. She stepped back as Brent whizzed by her, intent on getting the parking space.

Once he was parked, he hopped off the cart and approached her. "Hey, I've got tickets to a show at the McCallum Theater. Do you want to go with me?"

Surprised, Willow shook her head. "No, thanks." She would never consider dating Brent Armstrong, not even to keep peace among the three of them working together. She started walking to the employee entrance.

"Wait up!" said Brent, hurrying to her side.

Willow kept walking. She didn't know what game Brent was playing, and she wasn't about to join in.

"Why the brush off?" he asked. "We're working together. We might as well enjoy ourselves for the next couple of months."

Willow studied him. He was well built, had classic features, blue eyes, and a head of thick blond hair. But he held no appeal for her. He was arrogant and spoiled. She'd seen how his father had manipulated and humiliated him. One reason he could be so mean.

"It's not smart to 'fish off the company pier,' as they say," she said. "I'll meet you in Brian's office." She hurried ahead of Brent toward the ladies' room, glad for an excuse to get away from him.

When she walked into Brian's office, he looked up from his desk and smiled. "Good morning, Willow. How are you?"

"Fine. And you?"

"Puzzled, frankly. I find it odd that your report and Brent's match almost perfectly, word for word. Are you two collaborating?"

"What? No!" Clenching her teeth, she turned to Brent. "Are you copying my reports?"

Brent shrugged. "Just taking your information and weaving it into mine for a complete summary."

Willow shot Brian a helpless look. If she opened her mouth, she'd end up shrieking in anger.

He let out a sigh of frustration. "Okay, instead of the three of you working together, I'm suggesting that Trace and Brent continue reviewing the Desert Sage Inn's operating policies and procedures and how to best modify them for the Blaise Group and the new Corona Collection. And I suggest that you, Willow, continue your work alone."

"Then, I'll be in charge of what the Blaise Group comes up with," said Brent, his face bright with expectation.

"No," said Brian. "Neither you nor Trace will be in charge. You'll need to work together on this. Questions, anyone?"

Hurt and confused, Willow remained silent. *Did Brian think she'd copied Brent's work?* The thought stung.

"Okay, Brent and Trace, you guys can go. I need to talk to Willow alone." Brian indicated the doorway with a flick of his hand.

Trace looked unhappy as he rose to his feet and headed for the door. Brent reverted to his old self and glared at her as he left.

After they'd gone, Brian shook his head and turned his attention to her. "I don't like the situation any better than you do, Willow, but we have to move along. From now on, you'll report directly to me. After discussing procedures with John Rodriquez, the resident manager for the inn, you and I will develop an implementation plan. At the moment, that's the best I can do."

"But I was given the responsibility of overseeing the management transition team," Willow protested.

"I know, but I'm sorry to say it's not working out. You have two young men eager to take over for you. Eager enough to hurt the project."

"So, you're allowing them to ruin a chance for me to prove

myself?" Though Willow kept her voice low, it shook with anger.

He shook his head. "Absolutely not. You've already proven yourself up to the task. We have to give the other two a chance to work things out between them. One of them will be going home."

"But Trace ..." she began and stopped. It wasn't her business to say more. She exchanged a meaningful glance with Brian.

Brian smiled and leaned forward. "Now, let's talk about your findings. I was intrigued by some of the ideas that I'm certain came from you."

After they discussed what changes in operating procedures might be required to upgrade the two hotels in the Blaise Group being considered for the Corona Collection, Willow left the office troubled.

Back at the house, she talked to Alec about it.

"Brent copied my report and tried to pass it off as his own. He's the kind of person who would do it."

"How did he see it?" Alec asked in a deceptively calm voice.

Willow sighed. "He must've looked at my computer when I left the room. That's the worst part of it."

"Best to know your enemies," said Alec. "It's a strange situation, but a problem the Blaise Group will have to resolve. I think Brian was right to separate you."

"But I thought it was an honor to be chosen to lead the group," said Willow, unable to hold back a frown.

Alec's smile was reassuring. "Believe me, it was. Mitchell Armstrong is no dummy. When he asked you to do that job, he knew very well who he was dealing with. No worries. John says you're bright and eager to learn all aspects of management. That will do you well, Willow. Trust me."

She nodded. Alec had always been a terrific supporter. But

would it be enough?

CHAPTER EIGHT

LILY

Lily filled with excitement as she sorted through her things and packed up her apartment. The buyers had requested to purchase her larger pieces of furniture and Lily eagerly agreed. It was time to make a clean break. With Monica's promise to visit, Lily felt as if she could move forward. Luck finally seemed with her.

She decided to make a visit to her old office before she left. The woman who'd replaced her had many questions that needed to be answered. Lily had given away a lot of her old work clothes and happily dressed in one of her favorite desert outfits before heading to the office.

Pulling up to a parking space in front of the building, she felt her spirits plummet. It looked the same and she felt the old sense of depression beginning to creep inside her. She brushed at a speck of dust on her navy pants, pulled her paisley-print jacket closer to her, and drew a deep breath. Her life had changed; she had changed.

Inside the office, she was greeted with looks of surprise.

"You look ... well, very ... well, terrific," said David Bakeley, her old boss, looking as if he wanted to hug her as he hurried toward her.

"Thank you," she replied. "The change has been great for me."

"Yes, I can see that. Did you meet Sally, your replacement?"

"We said hello as I came in," Lily said. They both turned as Sally approached.

"I'm so glad you're here, Lily. There's so much I need to ask you," said Sally, looking as frazzled as Lily had always felt.

Grateful that her life had changed, Lily took her arm. "Let's go talk."

"Thank you, Lily, for stopping by. We all appreciate it." David gave her a little salute and returned to his office.

Lily smiled at Sally. "Things seem just the same."

Sally shook her head. "I don't know how you did all the work. We've hired an assistant for me and we're still too busy."

"I love living in Palm Desert and working there," Lily commented. "I'm moving there permanently in a few days, but I'm happy to help you while I'm here."

"Thank you," said Sally. "I appreciate it."

Lily's heart went out to her. She knew how hard Sally was working.

That evening, as Lily fixed dinner, she studied her sister out of the corner of her eye. She seemed to be doing well. Monica was a pretty woman of thirty-two, with natural streaks of blond through her light-brown hair and brown eyes that used to sparkle with happiness but now looked dull. No question about it. Jeremy was bad for her. It had taken all of Lily's strength to insist on having dinner without him. But, as she told Monica, she'd be around for only a couple more days, and it was important they spend time together.

Lily served the chicken casserole that was one of Monica's favorites and tossed the salad before sitting down at the kitchen table. "Once I get a place to live and get it set, I'll send you and Izzy tickets to come see me."

"I can't wait," said Monica, exhibiting some of her old excitement. "Jeremy says it's time for a move."

Lily held up a finger in warning. "Jeremy isn't going to be invited for a visit. And, Monica, don't say anything to him about this yet. Promise?"

Monica's brow furrowed. "I don't know. Jeremy won't like it."

Lily reached across the table and gave Monica's hand a squeeze. "It's going to be our secret. A special surprise for Izzy. For her birthday," said Lily, wanting to reinforce the idea.

Monica nodded. "Oh. He doesn't need to know about birthday surprises. Then it wouldn't be a surprise. Right?"

"Right," said Lily. If she could get Monica away from Jeremy, she didn't care what the tickets cost. In the meantime, she needed to find a place to live.

Two days later, Lily sat on a plane heading for California. Every limb in her body was aching. But the biggest ache was in her heart, which now seemed empty after saying goodbye to Monica and giving Izzy one last kiss.

What a conniving, destructive person Jeremy was. Worry gnawed at her. She hoped Monica could keep her wits about her until Lily was in a place where Monica and Izzy could stay. She'd asked Monica to give her notice at work, but Monica told her she couldn't do that until she had the tickets to fly to California.

At the Palm Springs airport, Lily's spirits rose. One step at a time, she reminded herself as she entered the terminal looking for Pedro. Rose had made arrangements for him to pick her up.

She looked but didn't see his smiling face. Hiding her disappointment, her gaze swept the baggage claim area again and stopped in surprise at the sight of Brian Walden. He saw her and waved before striding toward her.

"Hi," he said smiling. "At your service. Pedro is with Alec and was unable to pick you up, so I agreed to do it."

"Thank you," said Lily, more than a little pleased about the turn of events. She'd had a crush on him from the first time they'd met. A former military officer who'd lost the lower portion of his left leg in Afghanistan, Brian was a tall, fit man with craggy features, brown hair just beginning to gray at the temples and warm, light-brown eyes that missed nothing. Seeing him in a crowd like this, he seemed taller, fitter, more handsome than ever.

He smiled and took hold of her carry-on. "I parked in the lot right outside. We'll pick up your bags and go there."

"Okay. I appreciate all you're doing. I could've taken a cab."

"No, Alec called and asked me to pick you up. Like I said, I was happy to do it." Brian smiled down at her, and her heart skipped a beat.

While they waited for the luggage to arrive, he turned to her. "I'm glad you're back. Mitchell Armstrong is in town. We're going to hold a meeting later this afternoon. Hope that isn't rushing you."

"It's okay. I'm just happy to be here. I sold my condo and will be looking for housing immediately."

"I've been looking at condos in Indian Wells. They've got some really nice places there."

"I'm thinking more like Rancho Mirage. My sister and her daughter will be staying with me for a while. That is, if I can convince them to move here."

"Nice. I only have my mother but she's living in Florida."

"No one else?" Lily asked.

He shook his head. "I was engaged once, but it didn't work out. She didn't like waiting around while I was away fighting in the war."

Lily blinked rapidly at the sadness she heard in Brian's voice. They'd walked and talked together many mornings but he'd never mentioned family or a previous relationship. Now she knew why. She'd always thought he was a strong person from the way he managed his injury, but she understood that, like her, he'd been hurt badly and kept an emotional distance.

Her suitcases arrived on the luggage carousel. Brian easily picked them up. He extended their handles, handed one to her, and, together, they walked to the parking lot.

She expected to find him parked in a handicapped space, but he walked right by an empty one to the back of the lot.

"Why didn't you park up front?" she asked, curious.

"In a handicapped spot?" He shrugged. "I don't need it as much as some others."

She remained quiet but thought he was one of the most thoughtful men she'd ever known. He showed his character to her in so many little ways.

Once they made their way down Highway 111 through Cathedral City and Rancho Mirage, they headed into Palm Desert and drove on to the turnoff for the hotel.

As always, the long drive leading to the hotel filled her with a sense of homecoming. The tall palm trees, their fronds swaying gently in the breeze, the colorful flowers and lush greenery edging the road sent a warm welcome to her. She loved these grounds and would always feel grateful to Alec for introducing her to them when she'd worked as his assistant. Eleven years later, she still loved the place and was grateful to be asked to return. It had already brought her happiness. Sadness, too. She hated the thought of Alec dying from cancer far too soon. He'd not only been good to her; he'd been wonderful to all the Flowers.

At Alec's house, Brian helped her inside with her luggage and then gave her a little salute. "See you at the hotel in two hours. As I said, we'll have a meeting and then a dinner with Mitchell Armstrong."

She nodded and smiled. "Okay. Thank you for the ride and

everything else." She headed to her room.

Willow came in from outside. "Lily! You're back!"

"Yes. And glad to be here." She grinned as Willow gave her a quick hug. "It's great to be home."

"Nice to have you here. Since you've been gone, there've been a lot of changes. The Blaise Group is threatening to back out of the deal, saying they don't like having to put in more money in some of their properties in order to make the Corona Collection happen. Both Rose and Hank are upset. They've stopped working on any plans until the issue is resolved. In fact, Rose is staying at Hank's house while his daughter Sam and her husband are away on vacation. But she and I have already discussed all the pros of the Corona Collection."

"Wow! I haven't been gone that long and look what's happened. No wonder Brian wanted to pick me up at the airport. To warn me about a meeting. He didn't tell me what the meeting was about, though. I wonder why?"

"I heard Mitchell Armstrong didn't want the rest of the team to know what's happening. Rose found out from Hank. That's how I know. It's all supposed to be hush, hush."

"How's Alec?" Lily said, almost afraid to ask. "Is he aware of the Blaise Group's possible withdrawal from the Corona Collection plan, which could jeopardize the sale itself?"

"Yes, he knows about it. Otherwise, he's the same," said Willow, a serious expression washing over her face. "Good days and bad. It's so difficult to watch him go through this."

Lily nodded. "Guess I'd better unpack and get ready for the business meeting. I have careful notes from previous meetings that might prove beneficial."

"I have the budget material, and Rose has all the benefits of promoting the Corona Collection. I'll meet you at the front door. Rose will meet us there," said Willow. "We Flowers will be well-prepared."

Lily hurried into her bedroom, ready to do her share of protecting Alec's wishes.

Later, dressed in one of her more conservative business outfits, Lily headed to Alec's private quarters before meeting Willow.

She knocked on the door and entered to find Alec stretched out atop a reclining chair, reading. He looked up at her and smiled. "Glad to see you. How was your trip?"

"Both up and down," she answered truthfully. "I sold my condo and had a number of items shipped here. But my sister's old boyfriend, Jeremy O'Neill, is back in her life, and he's trouble. I worry about her being with him. Most of all, I worry about Izzy." She felt her eyes sting and blinked away the emotion that gripped her whenever she thought of her niece being in harm's way.

"I'm sorry," he said.

"I hope to convince Monica to move here, where I can help her. We'll see how successful I am. She's pulling away from me. I'm not one of Jeremy's favorite people. I think he's trying to isolate her."

"You can't live her life for her," Alec said calmly.

She nodded. "I know. But, I still feel responsible for her." She drew a deep breath. "I came here to see how you were doing."

He lifted a bony shoulder in a slight shrug. "Today is a good day. That's all I can ask for."

She took hold of his hand. "I'm glad." Her lips trembled. "I'm wishing every day is nice for you."

He smiled. "You've always been such a caring person. I appreciate it." He glanced at her outfit. "Ready for the meeting?"

"Willow told me what's going on. It doesn't sound good."

A smile crossed Alec's face. "All part of the game. Do your part and take detailed notes. The meeting will be recorded, I'm sure. But your notes can capture expressions and emotions that might not show up. Anything I can use for ammunition to make my case."

"I'll do that for you," Lily said with quiet determination.

Alec chuckled softly. "The three of you Flowers are going to bring them down."

Lily grinned. "Yes, sir. That's exactly what we're going to do." She rose, gave him a kiss on the cheek, and hurried to meet Willow.

CHAPTER NINE

WILLOW

Willow knew she'd done a decent job with her research, but she still couldn't hide her nervousness as people gathered in the small boardroom at the hotel. Mitchell Armstrong, though kind, was an intimidating man. And, once again, she'd be facing off with Brent and Trace, who most assuredly had the advantage of being the owners' sons.

Rose saw her and gave her a discreet wink of encouragement. Willow smiled and headed over to her. Lily followed, and the three of them sat together. Willow noticed Hank talking to Mitchell and wondered how Rose and Hank would do on opposing sides.

Trace noticed her and smiled. Brent walked over to her.

"Guess it's showtime," he said. "We'll see who wins this one."

Willow nodded stiffly, trying not to show her dislike of the man.

Brian walked into the room, and talk quieted. "Have a seat, everyone. Lily, will you please sit by me. I understand you're taking notes of the meeting, but we'll also record it."

Hank, Trace, Mitchell, John Rodriquez, and Simon Nickerson, the attorney for the Blaise Group joined Duncan, Brent, and Bennett Williams at the large table, found chairs, and sat down. As tension in the room grew, Willow studied Brian. She liked how calm and cool he remained even when tempers grew hot.

"Okay," said Brian. "We're here to discuss differing points of view over the formation of the Corona Collection of Fine Hotels. It is the wish of Alec Thurston that the Desert Sage Inn become the foundation for forming this group of upscale hotels. Willow, Trace, and Brent have been working on scenarios to defend their positions." He turned to Trace. "Will you begin?"

Trace nodded, and after glancing at her, began to speak.

Willow listened carefully as he went down a list of reasons why he thought the project was premature. Not giving anything away, she made careful notes so she could respond.

"We'll hold all questions until all three presentations have been made," Brian said when Trace was finished. "Now, Brent, let's hear your report."

Brent straightened in his seat. 'I disagree with Trace. I think we shouldn't even be considering forming such a group."

The silence in the room was interrupted when Brent began his reasons why. "As most of you know, my father is opposed to such a move. I reviewed the pros and cons with him and we've come up with a number of issues that convince us it is a bad idea."

Willow stirred restlessly as Brent stated one damning fact after another by reading a paper in front of him. Dismay turned to anger as she realized, as usual, Brent hadn't come up with any original thoughts. Worry about costs of upgrading, not wanting to spend money on changing procedures were all things the transition team had discussed and eliminated from consideration earlier. She glanced at Mitchell and noticed the way his lips had tightened, but other than that small sign of irritation nothing showed on his face.

"Thank you, Brent. Willow, time to hear from you," said Brian.

Willow clutched her report in her hands and let the sheets of paper fall to the table top. She knew her facts by heart.

"You've all heard the negatives of forming this group as Alec Thurston desires. I'm here to add common sense to the equation. I have the numbers to prove that it can work. By investing money to upgrade two of the Blaise Group's existing hotels and adding them to the Desert Sage Inn for the formation of a group of upscale hotels, business can be not only maintained, but improved. In fact, with the publicity campaign already in place at the inn, we can show how much more can be done with the Arizona properties designated for upgrades."

Willow nodded to Lily, who passed out a small report she'd put together after working on projections, showing all the benefits she'd mentioned.

She waited while the others at the table leafed through the reports. When murmurs slowed, she spoke. "I've learned in business one should never be satisfied with the status quo. The Blaise Group has an opportunity to be on the cutting edge, to make money in a new way through the Corona Collection. I don't see why they wouldn't."

Mitchell studied her. "You've heard all the reasons why the company might not want to form such an upscale group. Why do you persist?"

Willow swallowed hard. "Because, as our report clearly shows, and it is based on very conservative and realistic assumptions, it's an excellent opportunity for the company. A side benefit is it also satisfies Alec's wishes. One of my personal, strong guiding principles is if asked to explore an idea, I will respond with total honesty. We all know numbers can be tweaked to make them show what you want, but that's not how I taught my students at Boston University. Intellectual and professional integrity is essential when analyzing proposals or ideas that could make or break a business. When I see that adopting a particular course of action would generate greater returns for a business and increase guest satisfaction as well, I would be dishonest if I didn't mention it or feel strong enough to stick by it." She glanced at Brent and back to Mitchell. "My parents taught me better."

Mitchell's cheeks flushed, but he nodded calmly.

Brent rose from his chair. "This isn't about what your parents taught you. It's about business."

"Exactly," said Willow.

Rose started to clap. Soon others joined in.

Brian stood. "I think we'll take a break. Everyone back here in fifteen minutes."

Willow, Rose, and Lily stayed behind as others left the room.

Rose hugged her. "Great job. I'm so proud of you."

Lily joined in and the three of them stood together, three women from different backgrounds who'd forged a bond working to make Alec's wishes become a reality.

At the sound of a knock at the doorway, they turned.

Mitchell Armstrong stood there. "May I see you in private, Willow?"

Willow felt her hands grow cold, but she nodded. "Of course."

She walked toward him wondering what he wanted. His expression was neutral.

He led her to another meeting room and waited for her to enter.

She stood inside feeling vulnerable.

"Please. Sit down," he pulled out a chair and offered it to her before pulling out another chair from the table and lowering himself into it.

On high alert, she sat.

"First of all, I want to say how impressed I was with your presentation. It bordered on theatrical, but it was right on point and very effective. I, too, believe in honesty, which is why I asked to speak to you alone. I'm aware of the problems Brent can cause and has created at times. I'd like nothing better than to take him off this job, but my brother insists that he be given a fair chance to be part of this learning experience."

"I see," said Willow, not certain she understood completely.

A smile lit Mitchell's face. "Please be assured that your message has been heard, even though it might not be readily apparent. We all need to be patient. Understand?"

"I ... I think so," said Willow, wondering if she really did. If so, Brent would stick around even if he wasn't being as useful as his father wanted.

"Okay, then," said Mitchell rising. "We should get back to the meeting. Our conversation will remain private. It's sometimes better that way."

"I understand," said Willow. Brent would be furious if he ever found out about it.

CHAPTER TEN

LILY

During the break, Lily took advantage of the time to make several, private notes of her own. There was no question in her mind that Mitchell Armstrong didn't have a high opinion of his nephew, Brent. She understood. He was nothing but a pawn for his father, Duncan Armstrong, who seemed the total opposite of his brother, Mitchell. *Funny how different some family members were*, she thought, reminded of Monica.

For the duration of the meeting, Lily pushed personal issues aside and concentrated on what was being said. Rose and Hank presented two scenarios for moving forward with publicity campaigns.

When it came time to summarize publicity campaigns for Alec's position, Rose did a fabulous job of explaining it from a business growth viewpoint. "If you look at the increase in reservations the inn has already received through my marketing efforts, the numbers speak for themselves. With Alec's plan, we've found three niches where that can happen for the Blaise Group. As we all know, heads in beds mean so much more than that. If you look at the projected growth in revenues from all areas of the operation, there's no doubt about the rewards of such a move."

Hank then talked about the publicity campaign and its anticipated results he'd worked on with Rose for going forward without the Corona Collection. It lacked the excitement, allure, and returns of what they'd created for that small collection.

"There should be no doubt about the panache and positive impact of such an upscale group," said Hank.

Lily typed as fast as she could to keep up with not only what was being said, but nuance and facial expressions.

When the meeting concluded, Mitchell stood. "Thank you to everyone here for all of your hard work and excellent presentations. We have a lot to think about," he said. "For now, though, I invite you to relax and socialize over cocktails and dinner in Sage. I have a small, private dining area set aside for us."

"Hank and I can stay only a short time," said Rose. "We're babysitting Hank's granddaughter, Leah, while her parents are away. We've hired a baby sitter for the meeting, but we'll need to get back to her as soon as possible." She exchanged happy smiles with Hank.

Willow turned to Lily. "I'll meet you there." She left with the others, leaving Lily alone with Brian.

"Thanks for helping," said Brian. "If possible, I'd like a copy of your notes."

"No problem," Lily said. "I'll send them along after I get them cleaned up." His copy wouldn't mention the nuances she'd picked up for Alec.

"Ready to join the others?" said Brian, winking at her. "It's business, but that doesn't mean we can't enjoy some time together."

Lily blinked in surprise. *Was he talking about the group or her?*

Playful, he held out an elbow.

Smiling, she took hold of it and they walked out together.

Sage, the gourmet restaurant at the hotel, was a favorite spot. Inside, the desert décor was striking. Lily loved the shade of paint on the stucco walls—a light shade of sage green.

The high white ceiling was crossed by dark wooden beams. The tables, covered in crisp white-linen cloths, displayed small crystal vases filled with flowers in bougainvillea pink, deep gold, and bright yellow. Crystal and silverware sparkled at each place.

She gazed at the far end of the room where a gas fire filled a large stone fireplace. Through the glass sliding doors, she observed a wide patio that held more tables set for dinner. Tall heat lamps were strategically placed among them, lending warmth to the outside area.

She and Brian joined the others in an alcove off to one side. Rose and Willow were already there. She waved, excused herself, and walked over to them.

"Nice job, you two," Lily said to her fellow Flowers. "Alec is going to be pleased. It seems like an easy decision to me. But then I'm not Mitchell Armstrong."

Rose and Willow just stared at her.

Sensing trouble, Lily turned and faced Mitchell.

"I thought I heard my name."

"Not taken in vain," Rose said, making Mitchell laugh and giving Lily a moment to recover from her surprise of having him overhear her.

"I'd like to congratulate the three of you women on jobs well done." Mitchell beamed at them. "I will have to get agreement from my partner and other investors, but don't give up on Alec's wish. Personally, I like it."

Lily glanced at the other two and smiled. They looked as happy as she.

Brian came up to them and casually placed a hand on Lily's shoulder. "What do you think, Mitch?"

"I was just telling these women they did a great job. I wish they worked for the Blaise Group."

Lily smiled and glanced at Rose, who was staring at Brian's

hand on her shoulder. Heat rushed to Lily's face. She didn't know what to think of his friendly gesture, but she was enjoying it.

Later, as everyone was finding seats at the table, Brian said, "Mind if I sit next to you?"

She smiled and shook her head. "Not at all."

"Thanks," he said quietly. "I really didn't want to sit near Brent."

"I can't imagine why," she said, teasing him.

"Thanks for being part of the meeting. I know you'd been traveling most of the day."

"No problem. I'd do anything to help Alec," she responded.

"I gathered that from Alec when he called to ask me to pick you up. He told me a lot of nice things about you." His smile was warm.

Caught off balance, she simply said, "Thanks."

Willow, on her other side, leaned over and whispered, "What's going on with you and Brian?"

Lily shrugged. She wasn't sure what was up with the change in him toward her, but she liked it. A lot.

Dinner was a pleasant affair. Mitchell was a congenial host, steering conversation away from business, telling stories of interesting places he'd visited along with other anecdotes about the Blaise Group and its history.After dessert was served and eaten, he rose, thanked everyone for joining him, bid them good night, and left the dining room.

Lily, feeling exhausted by her long day, quickly rose. "'Bye, everyone. I'm off, too."

As she prepared to leave, Brian came up to her. "I'm ready too. Need a ride anywhere?"

"No, thanks. I'm going to take my golf cart home. The paths throughout the property are well lit. I shouldn't have any trouble."

"Are you sure? I'd be happy to drop you off at Alec's house. It's pretty dark out."

Lily smiled up at him. "Actually, that sounds nice. I can pick up the golf cart tomorrow. It's locked and should be fine in the employee lot."

"Well, then. Come with me."

Lily saw Willow talking to Trace, gave her a little wave, and left with Brian.

He led her to a silver BMW. After he held the door open, allowing her to slide into the passenger seat, he went around the car and got behind the wheel.

"How's it been, staying at Alec's house? It's a beautiful home," he asked her.

"It's lovely, but Rose, Lily, and I are devastated about the circumstances. Alec is a wonderful man who's very special to each of us."

Brian glanced over at her. "I like Alec a lot. We talk over the phone frequently, and he's a straight shooter. That's why I was so interested in what he had to say about you."

She quirked an eyebrow at him. "Such as?"

He chuckled. "All very complimentary." He pulled into the front circle of Alec's house and came to a stop. Turning to her, he said, "Like I told you earlier, I hope to get to know you better. Our first date turned out to be a business thing, but I wonder if we can give it another try."

A rush of warmth filled her. "I'd like that." She reached for the door handle.

"Hold it! I'll get it," cried Brian.

Lily waited patiently as he opened his door, got out, and hurried around the car.

Grinning, Brian opened the door, offered his hand, and helped her onto the pavement in front of him. "Thanks for that, Lily."

"For what?" she said, puzzled.

"From the first time we met, you've never been anything but accepting of my injury. Right now, some people would feel bad about me having to move and would've refused to let me do this simple task for them. It's one thing I admire about you."

Smiling, they stared at one another.

Lily wondered if he was going to try to kiss her, but then he stepped back. "I'll give you a call." He started to walk away and turned back.

Reaching for her, he drew her close. Smiling down at her, his hazel eyes told her so much. "I can't leave. I've wanted to kiss you all evening. May I?"

Already feeling the tug of desire in his arms, she nodded and closed her eyes as his lips pressed down on hers, sweet and gentle.

She responded, and his kiss deepened, sending waves of need through her. She realized he was as turned on as she, and a sound of contentment escaped her.

"Ah, Lily," he murmured, pulling away to cup her face in his hands. "You are such a special woman."

He lowered his lips to hers once more, and this time his kiss made everything around her disappear in a haze that became a need within her.

When they pulled apart, they stared at one another, breathing deeply. She returned his smile of satisfaction, aware of the chemistry between them.

"As much as I hate to, I guess I'd better go," Brian said with obvious reluctance.

She nodded, aware of her surroundings once more.

Still dazed by his kisses, she waited until he was in the car and ready to drive off again before giving him a little wave and going to the front door. She didn't know what Alec must have said about her, but she loved the idea that Brian was definitely interested in her.

Lily had just relaxed in her room when she heard a knock at the door. She opened it to find Willow grinning at her.

"Can I come in?"

"Sure," Lily said. "Have a seat. What's up?"

Willow walked over to one of the two overstuffed chairs in the small sitting area, lowered herself into one of them, and looked up at her. "What's going on with you and Brian? I thought he was all about business and you'd decided to play it cool with him. Is it one of those 'absence makes the heart grow fonder' kind of things?"

"What do you mean?"

Willow smiled at her. "At the gathering, Brian was really into you tonight. Very ... I don't know ... almost protective."

Lily plopped down on the edge of her bed and faced Willow. "Alec asked him to pick me up at the airport and said some nice things about me." She felt a broad smile stretch across her face. "I really like him. He's asked me, and I've agreed to go out with him." It was too early to say much more.

"Sweet," said Willow. "He's a great guy. I have all the respect in the world for him. I just wanted to make sure you're all right."

"Thanks. We'll see how it goes. It'll be our first real date. Not like the time at Tico's where everyone from the transition project ended up having dinner together." She was still dealing with the feelings he'd awakened in her and needed time alone to think about what had just happened between them before she was willing to share it with anyone else.

CHAPTER ELEVEN

ROSE

Rose returned to Hank's rented house pleased by the outcome of the business meeting and dinner with Mitchell Armstrong. Unlike his brother, he seemed a reasonable man. It was sad that Duncan's son, Brent, had inherited his father's belligerent ways. Neither had embraced going forward with the Corona Collection but had fallen in line only with Mitchell's insistence.

When they entered the house, Leah ran over to them, holding up her arms. Hank swept her up and hugged her for a moment before Leah reached for Rose. Pleased, Rose took Leah from him and wrapped her arms around the little girl who meant so much to her.

"Did you have fun with the babysitter?" Rose asked.

Leah shook her head. "No!"

Chuckling, Julie, the babysitter Sam had used once before, approached. "We had a lovely time playing with her dolls. Little Leah is going to be a strict mother."

Rose laughed. She could well imagine where Leah got that idea.

"No! No!" said Leah, pointing a finger at a doll that lay on the floor where Leah had left her.

"She's going to be a tough big sister," said Hank, his features softening with affection. "I can see it now."

Leah wiggled to get down.

"I'll take you home," said Hank to Julie. "Thanks so much for staying with Leah. We really appreciate it."

"She's a darling child," said Julie. "I'm happy to babysit anytime." She held out her arms to Leah. "Want to say 'bye?"

Leah hesitated and then ran over to her. "You're going?"

Julie nodded. "But maybe I'll see you again. Be good."

Leah ran back to Rose and took hold of her hand. She waved to Julie. "'Bye, 'Bye."

Smiling, Julie waved and followed Hank out the door.

Left alone with Leah, Rose sat on the couch. "Do you want to show me your dolls?"

"No!" Leah said. "I want to go swimming."

"Okay. We'll do that after Papa B comes back. Right now, we need to get you in your swimsuit. Then, I need to change before that happens."

Rose held out her hand.

Leah took it, and skipped down the hallway with Rose to her bedroom.

As Rose helped Leah get changed, she marveled at how much pleasure she received from doing this simple task. She'd never considered herself a maternal person, hadn't wanted children so much she'd really pursued it, but now, given this chance of being part of a family, she discovered she loved it.

With the upcoming birth of a sibling for Leah, she found herself looking forward to that time when she'd know Hank's grandchild as a newborn. She thought of Leigh, Hank's deceased wife, and promised herself she'd enjoy the children for her, too.

"I'm ready. Let's go," said Leah, dashing out the door.

Rose hurried to catch her. "No, you have to wait for me to get changed. Then, when Papa B gets back, we'll go swimming."

Leah's face crumpled.

"It won't take long. You'll see," said Rose, amused by how quickly Leah's expressions changed. A future Academy Award winner, for sure.

Back in the bedroom she shared with Hank, Rose quickly took off her business clothes and faced Leah. "You sit right there while I go into the bathroom. Let's count together. One ... two ..."

Leah chimed in. "Three ..."

Rose finished as fast as she could and hurried back into the bedroom.

EMPTY!!

Heart pounding, Rose looked at the sliding glass door. OPEN!!

"Leah!" she cried as she ran outside.

Leah was face down in the pool, her limbs still.

Rose jumped into the pool, grabbed hold of her, and squeezed her tight as she lifted her face from the water.

Leah coughed and started to cry.

Her arms shaking so badly she could hardly hold onto Leah, Rose managed to get to the shallow end of the pool. On legs that felt like butter, she climbed out of the pool with Leah in her arms. Sitting on the edge of the pool, Rose patted Leah's back as she vomited up some water. As thoughts of what might've happened raced through her mind. A tidal wave of nausea hit Rose. She gagged as Leah, recovered now, began wailing.

"What's going on?" Hank looked from Rose, still in her underwear, to Leah clinging to her, her knees drawn up in a fetal position.

Seeing him, Rose began to cry in great gulps. The sudden lack of adrenaline made her too weak to stand. "I told her we'd go swimming when you got home... I ... We were counting ... I ... I had to go to the bathroom."

"Oh, my God!" Hank took Leah in his arms. "There, there, sweetheart. You're all right. Papa B is here."

Listening to his words, Rose cried harder. Sam would probably never allow her to be alone with Leah again.

Once everyone had calmed down and Leah was lying on the bed resting, Hank said, "I think it's best if we all get in the pool. Sort of like climbing back on a bucking horse."

Rose nodded. She'd apologized over and over again to Hank, but nothing would ever make her feel better about what had almost happened to his precious granddaughter.

Hank wrapped his arms around Rose and whispered, "With kids, accidents can happen. Don't keep blaming yourself. I'm just so very, very glad you got to her in time."

"Will Sam ever trust me?" she asked, her voice wobbly.

"Yes. You saved Leah."

"But ..."

He kissed her gently on the lips. When he pulled away, he said, "Lesson learned. One of many when you're around kids. Let's just be thankful."

Later, after they'd both changed into bathing suits, the three of them got into the shallow end of the pool. Leah wore water wings and, with encouragement, was soon laughing and splashing in the water.

Watching her, Rose filled with such tenderness she couldn't breathe.

"Everything all right?" asked Hank, giving her a look of concern.

"Yes," she answered, but she knew it would be a long time before she'd forgive herself for almost losing Leah.

CHAPTER TWELVE

LILY

The next day, when Lily heard Rose's story about Leah's almost drowning, she was horrified for her. She could well imagine how she'd feel if that had happened when she was watching Izzy. "I'm so sorry to hear this. But you can't keep blaming yourself. Things like this can happen. One time, Izzy shook off my hand and ran into the street to get to a dog on the other side. I about had a heart attack. Just thinking about it still makes me feel sick, with the possibilities of what could've happened."

"I guess it's best I never became a mother," sighed Rose, sounding very unlike her usual self.

Lily reached across the kitchen table where they'd been sipping coffee and squeezed her hand. "Don't let that one incident destroy the happiness you've known with Leah. Sure, be careful, keep an eye on her, but enjoy her too."

Willow came into the kitchen. "Morning, Flowers! What's up?"

"Nothing, except Leah almost drowned because of me," said Rose, making a face.

"What? What happened?"

While Willow helped herself to a cup of coffee, Rose gave a summary of what had happened when she and Hank were babysitting.

"Wow! I'm sorry to hear this," Willow said. "But she's okay now. Right?"

Rose nodded. "But I don't know if I'll ever get over it." She waved her hand in front of her. "Enough of this. I'm driving myself crazy. Let's talk about something positive. Willow, you did a great job at the meeting yesterday."

Lily smiled when a pretty pink color filled Willow's cheeks. Willow had no idea how competent she was, how beautiful.

Willow turned to her. "Are you going to tell Rose about you and Brian?"

"Yes," said Rose, grinning at her. "What's going on? He's definitely into you."

"I think Brian finally figured out what a great match it could be," said Willow. "Alec asked him to pick her up at the airport. What was that all about, huh?" She wiggled her eyebrows in an exaggerated way that made them all laugh.

"He seemed very caring," Rose said. "Of course, he's that kind of man, but it was nice to see him that way with you."

Warmth filled Lily. The thought of someone watching out for her was such a pleasing one. For most of her life, she'd been the one taking care of others. But it was much more than a sense of caring that had passed between them when they'd kissed. Still, Lily was reluctant to talk about it until she saw Brian again and knew he still felt the same about her.

"I haven't had a chance to talk to you about your trip back home," said Rose to her. "How did that go?"

Lily shrugged. "I sold my condo and am seriously looking at places here. But my sister is back with her ex-boyfriend, Izzy's father, a man I can't trust."

"Oh, no! How is that going to affect the baby?" said Willow.

Lily shook her head. "He terminated his parental rights, but he's doing everything he can to get back into Monica's life. I'm worried. You know those red flags women are warned about? He's already showing signs of abuse."

"Does she see that?" Rose said.

Lily paused and then spoke honestly. "We pretty much

grew up with emotional abuse. Both of us. So, she doesn't get it because he says he loves her, can't live without her, and all that garbage. I've convinced her to come for a visit, but she's resisting moving here. I'm trying to give her time, but I hate to see her back with someone like him. Especially because of Izzy. I'm thinking of the emotional damage she might suffer with him around."

Rose patted her hand. "It sounds like a difficult position for you. I'm sorry."

"Thanks. In the meantime, I'm trying to concentrate on the positives in my life." She smiled at Rose and Willow. "You two are definitely a part of that."

Willow lifted her cup of coffee. "To us, the Desert Flowers."

Lily and Rose tapped their coffee cups and did the same with Willow.

After the coffee chat, Lily took a shower and got dressed. She planned to edit her notes for Brian and deliver them herself. After that kiss, she was eager to see his reaction to her and if their relationship had a chance of surviving.

In the bright sunshine, she headed out to the hotel on foot. She'd pick up her golf cart at the hotel.

As her feet pounded the pavement in a light jog, Lily thought back to the teambuilding exercises Alec had set up for the three women with Dan McMillan, head of the fitness training at the hotel. She'd hated that first day of walking and hiking. Now, she loved it.

The pathway through the golf course to the hotel was lined with flowers and cacti. Hummingbirds fluttered nearby. One dived at her and then hovered nearby, attracted by the bright-pink shirt she was wearing. "Go find something else," she said, laughing at the bird's antics. She picked up her pace to avoid another confrontation.

At the hotel, she went directly to Brian's office only to find it empty. Disappointed, she debated leaving her report on his desk and decided to hold onto it. She was heading back outside to her golf cart when she heard her name called.

Turning, she saw Brian hurrying toward her. "Lily, wait!"

She studied him as he approached. His sturdy body and classic features had always appealed to her. Even now, the smile across his handsome face sent waves of warmth through her. His injury didn't bother her at all. It never had. Since their failed first date, she'd made an effort to act disinterested in him, but, in truth, he was the kind of man she'd been hoping to find one day. And the kiss between them was something she'd never experienced before.

"Were you looking for me?" he asked, stopping in front of her.

She held up the report. "I wanted to give you the minutes from the meeting yesterday."

He accepted the report from her and said, "C'mon outside. We need to talk."

Lily nodded, suddenly scared. She was pretty sure where this was going. Brian would tell her the kiss was a mistake. They were a mistake. He'd link his change of mind to business, of course, but the message would be clear.

She was quiet as she accompanied him outside.

"You going back to Alec's house?" he asked.

"Yes, then I have plans to look at condos today. First, I need to get my golf cart."

"Okay, I'll walk you to the employee parking lot. We'll have privacy there."

Her heart sank at the matter-of-fact tone to his voice. He'd let her down in a nice way.

They walked to the corner of the lot where she'd parked her golf cart. No one else was around, she observed with relief.

She climbed aboard the cart and faced him.

"About last night ..." he began.

She held up her hand to stop him. "I get it. You've changed your mind about dating."

"What? No. Let me explain," he said, his eyes round with surprise. "After our first so-called date, I thought I might've acted in an unprofessional way, putting you in an awkward situation. You made it pretty clear by avoiding me."

"Me? Oh, but ..." she stopped.

"I talked to both Alec and Hank about the difficulty of dating someone at work, but they reminded me that you work for Alec and I work for the Blaise Group, so there isn't a real problem as long as I continue to do the work I was hired to do."

"You spoke to Alec and Hank about me?" Lily wasn't sure how she felt about that.

Brian placed a hand on her shoulder and gazed into her eyes. "I had to talk to someone about it, Lily. From the first time you and I were together on that early morning walk, I've been falling for you."

"Me? You have?" Lily knew she sounded like a dunce, but she couldn't believe the situation ... no, that *he* was real. He was the first man she'd been truly interested in since she left the Desert Sage Inn ten years ago.

Brian leaned over and cupped her face in his broad hands.

His lips met hers, tentative at first, and then with a need that sent fire to her belly. She lifted her arms around his neck and hung on. Beneath her closed eyes, colored lights flickered like fireworks.

When they pulled apart, they simply stared at one another.

"Wow!" said Brian.

"It was real," sighed Lily. Moisture swam in her eyes at the tender look he gave her.

"What's this?" he said, thumbing a tear from her cheek.

"I'm so happy right now," she managed to say. "I thought you were going to tell me that last night was a mistake."

"You did? The only mistake was in my not making it happen sooner. I'm crazy about you. How about dinner tonight, just the two of us?"

She beamed at him, feeling as if she was in a dream. "Is that a promise?"

He chuckled. "Let's skip Tico's and have dinner at the condo I'm renting. I'm a great cook."

"Sounds like a plan," she said, happier than she'd ever been.

Instead of looking for condos, Lily made an appointment at the hotel's spa and another at a hair salon on El Paseo. By habit, she was careful with her money, but this would be worth the expense. It was important for her to look her best for her first real date with Brian.

As she soaked in the small, heated pool in the spa after enjoying only her second facial ever, Lily luxuriated in the warm water, wondering if this is how many of the wealthier hotel guests lived. The thought made her smile. In New York working too many hours, she'd seldom pampered herself.

After climbing back into her clothes and dining at the tiny spa restaurant, she set off for her hair appointment. The shops along El Paseo were busy on this March day, with tourists strolling along the walks, looking into windows, and exiting the stores carrying bundles. She liked having the opportunity to be among them.

The salon, featuring natural organic products, was quietly active. Lily was introduced to her stylist, a young girl named Celia, and eagerly followed her to her station to discuss what she wanted done. Though she was a person who liked control,

Lily announced to Celia that she could style her hair any way she wanted.

They chatted easily while color was applied. Later, after a shampoo, Lily wondered if she'd made a mistake when she saw locks of her hair falling to the floor as Celia chopped away.

"Don't worry," said Celia. "It's going to look great."

Later, Lily stared at her reflection in the mirror. She already looked so different. Celia gave her hair a final lift with her fingers and stood back. "Well?"

"I love it!" Lily said. Her brown eyes, her best feature, looked larger. The even lighter streaks of blond in her hair looked great with the tan she'd acquired.

Celia grinned. "This is a new look, but perfect for you. Carefree and easy. Just finger your hair as it dries and lift it away from your head. The rest will happen on its own, falling into place at your jawline perfectly."

Lily gave Celia an impulsive hug. "Thank you."

Leaving the salon, she saw a sale sign in the shop next door, and on a whim, she went inside. In the back, lying on a table were several styles of lacy underwear—panties, thongs, and bras. Taking a deep breath, telling herself it was time to make a few more changes, she selected a few items her old bosses in the law office in New York would never suspect she'd choose. Smiling at the thought, she carried her items to the checkout counter and paid for them.

CHAPTER THIRTEEN

ROSE

Rose stood with Hank and Leah at the airport to welcome Sam and Rob. Leah was especially excited to see her parents. Rose, not so much. She was nervous to tell Sam about Leah and the swimming pool accident. But both of Leah's parents deserved to know, especially because she and Hank were working together to make sure Leah wasn't afraid of the water.

The Palm Springs International Airport was small and, though busy, its size made it easy to see Sam and Rob walking down the hallway with the other deplaned passengers.

"Mommy! Daddy!" cried Leah, all but jumping out of Hank's arms.

Laughing, Hank did his best to wave and hold onto his granddaughter. Observing him, Rose felt a smile spread across her face. She loved him so much.

Sam approached and swept Leah into her arms, hugging her tightly. Her eyes welled with tears as she looked at Hank and then turned to Rose. "Thank you so much for taking care of Leah."

"I drownded," said Leah.

"What?" Sam turned to Hank. "What is she saying?"

Hank looked uncomfortable. "Leah had an accident in the pool, but she's okay. Rose and I have been helping her get accustomed to being in the pool again so she's not afraid."

Sam handed Leah to Rob and faced them. "Exactly what happened?"

Rose gulped and stepped forward. "It was me. I left Leah in the bedroom while I used the bathroom. She escaped through the sliding glass door and fell in the pool. I jumped in and pulled her out. She swallowed some water." Rose couldn't prevent her eyes from filling. "I'm sorry. I didn't mean for anything to happen. I was just a moment in the bathroom."

Sam placed her hands on her hips and studied her. "I see." She faced Hank. "And where were you?"

"I was taking the babysitter home," he said, looking like a chastised schoolboy.

"I thought I could trust you two ..." Sam began.

"Hold on," said Rob. "You know what it's like trying to have a moment to yourself, Sam. What are you going to do when this baby comes along? You'll have two to watch."

Sam's stern posture deflated. "Oh, God! Rob's right. I often have to scoot into the bathroom. Especially now. Things like this can happen. But maybe we better remember to use the locks on the door or put a gate around the pool. It's a pain, but necessary now that Leah is moving so quickly. This is a wake-up call."

"I truly am so sorry," Rose said.

Hank put his arm around her. "It's okay, sweetheart. Leah's safe, and that's the important thing. Like Rob says, Leah will be harder to keep track of with a new baby."

"Baby?" Leah asked. "What baby?"

The four adults looked at one another.

"Let's wait until we get home to tell her about the baby," said Rob quietly.

"No! No baby! I'm the baby," said Leah, patting his cheek for attention.

Rose glanced at Hank. He gave her a surreptitious smile. This was one crisis Sam and Rob would have to handle on their own.

CHAPTER FOURTEEN

LILY

Lily walked toward the entrance of Brian's condo building with uncertain steps, well aware of the items she was wearing beneath the sundress she'd chosen for the date. She wasn't used to all the lace on her bra and matching lavender panties. Self-conscious now about her decision to wear them, she considered herself foolish. She was attracted to Brian in a way she'd hadn't been to any man since Alec.

Brian answered her knock at the door and grinned at her. "Hi! C'mon in. I decided on doing something simple for tonight. Grilled steak, home fries, and salad."

"Mmm. Something smells delicious," she said, stepping inside.

"It's the potatoes. Olive oil, parmesan cheese, and garlic. How about a glass of red wine? I have a bottle of a nice syrah open."

"That sounds wonderful."

Brian poured her a glass of wine, filled one for himself, and lifted his glass. "Here's to a great evening!"

"I'll toast that," she said smiling at him. He seemed so relaxed that her previous nerves disappeared.

"Did you do something to your hair? I like it," he commented after swallowing his wine.

Pleased, she patted her head. "Something new."

He nodded. "Looks nice." He led her out to a small patio outside his first-floor condo where a grill had been set up.

"Have a seat. I won't start the steak until the potatoes are done. It's going to be a while."

She sat in one of the two chairs stationed next to a small round table and set down her glass of wine.

He did the same and then asked, "So, tell me about yourself. I know you're from New York State, have been a legal secretary for a number of years, and that's about it. You've never married?"

Lily shook her head. "No. Never have found the right person."

"No children then," he said, studying her.

"I've always wanted them, but it may be too late. Having a baby at my age can be a problem."

He nodded. "Yeah, I'm not interested in having children. At fifty, I don't think it would be fair to any child I might have. My father was sixty when I was born, and it was difficult. I was an only child and he was always an old man to me."

Lily started to say something comforting but stopped. Though she'd told him she was a little old for childbearing, she wasn't quite ready to give up on the idea.

"How about you? Do you have siblings? A happy childhood?"

"Yes and no," Lily answered honestly. "I have a sister who's ten years younger. She has a three-year-old daughter whom I adore. Our childhood was difficult. My mother was an alcoholic, and I had the care of my sister from an early age."

"It's hard to imagine family life in the 1950s television shows being real today, huh?" he said, leaning back in his chair. "Such an idyllic time."

She shrugged. "Maybe not. Everyone, it seems, has had issues to deal with."

He held out his prosthesis. "Guess overall I'm lucky. So many guys have been lost to wars."

"No matter when or where, war's ugly," Lily agreed.

Brian got to his feet. "Let me check on the potatoes and grab the bottle of wine."

After he left, Lily stared out at the planted landscape, thinking about what he'd said. The setting sun spread fingers of red, yellow, and orange in the darkening blue sky, making her think of rainbows. It was disappointing that he didn't want children, but the reality was it would be foolish for her to try for children at her age of forty-two with no marriage prospects in sight. Being a single parent was difficult. She'd seen it for herself. *For once, just think of having fun with no personal agenda. That way, you won't get hurt.* In the past, a date had once told her she was too intense. This time she'd go with the flow.

"Ah, sorry it took me so long," said Brian, appearing with a bottle of wine in his hand. "How about some more wine?"

Lily held out her glass. "I'm ready. Thanks."

He filled her glass and then his own before sitting down. "Thanks for coming here for dinner instead of going out. I'm getting sick of hotel food, even if it's delicious. Being on my own for so long, I've grown accustomed to putting together quick meals and even some gourmet ones on the weekends. It's become a hobby of mine."

"What a wonderful way to impress a date," Lily said, smiling.

He chuckled. "Hey! When you've been single so long, it's either that or eat crap food. Do you cook?"

"I can," she said, "but, honestly, I'm not used to fussing at mealtime. The truth is I've been working late for so long, that until I came here, I'd forgotten what it was like to enjoy quiet evenings and nice, relaxing meals. Of course, living at Alec's with Juanita making a lot of our meals has been fabulous. Unrealistic for the long term, but nice."

"So, what was it like working for Alec all those years ago? He seems like a great guy. Smart, but someone who lets you find your way."

Lily nodded, hiding the tender emotion she felt. Alec was and always would be a man who'd shown her what decency was, in both word and action. Through him, she'd learned to value herself. "Alec is an incredible man. To know he's dying has been difficult for me and Rose and Willow."

"The Desert Flowers, as Alec calls you."

Lily smiled. "We're sort of like his angels, only we're all flowers. He loves it!"

"You three are impressive. I'll say that," said Brian, tipping his head to her.

"It's been such an interesting time for me. I'm very glad he trusted me to help. Rose and Willow feel the same way."

A buzzer sounded. Brian got to his feet. "I'm going to pull out the potatoes and start grilling the steaks. Would you be willing to throw a salad together?"

Lily stood. "That I can do."

Brian lit the gas grill and walked into the kitchen with her. "Make yourself at home. I set out the salad bowl and the dressing. Clean lettuce is in the refrigerator."

Brian left the kitchen with the steaks.

Lily looked around. The kitchen was small but well-laid out. Dark-green marble countertops were offset by white cupboards and stainless-steel appliances. She took a moment and walked to the dining area and peeked into the living room and noticed a gas fireplace. She liked the arrangement of space, the easy flow of it. It was the kind of condo she was interested in.

"Nice, huh?" said Brian, causing her to whirl around with surprise.

She clasped a hand to her chest. "Oh, you scared me. I was

looking around thinking this is something I might like. How many bedrooms?"

"Two plus a study," he said.

"Maybe, after dinner, you'd show me," said Lily and felt her face flush at the thought he might think it was a signal to go to his bedroom for sex.

He chuckled and lifted a hand to her cheek. "Great idea!" He turned and left before she could say anything else.

Later, after the meal, Lily sighed with pleasure. "That was delicious."

"Would you like dessert? I have ice cream in the freezer."

"Thanks, but no. Maybe another time."

"I'm glad you agreed to go out with me. It's been a great evening. Now, how about me showing you the bedrooms?"

Lily paused. *What exactly was he expecting?*

"No worries," said Brian, sensing her thoughts. "I don't seduce women with dinner and then expect something in return."

"Oh, right," Lily said, wanting to pinch herself silly for acting like such a fool.

Smiling, he rose and took her hand. "The office and guest room are a nice size, and the master suite is even better."

He showed her the office and what he'd called the guest room and then led her to the master suite. Curious to see if it was as nicely but plainly decorated as the rest of the condo, she followed him inside. A king-size bed easily fit into the space. In addition to the bed, two bedside tables, a large bureau and an easy chair were in place. A bathroom was off to one side. On the other side of the room, a sliding glass door led to another small patio surrounded by hibiscus bushes.

"This is perfect!" Lily cried. "Do they have condos for sale in this complex?"

"I don't know," said Brian. "I'm renting this furnished on a short-term lease. I'd be glad to give you the name of the agent who handled this."

"Wonderful!" said Lily. Already she could see Monica and Izzy living here until Monica got a place of her own.

Brian slid open the door and stepped out to the small patio. "It's nice to sit here in the morning and have a cup of coffee."

She followed him outside. The bushes around the patio gave her a sense of privacy. She looked across the center courtyard to another building of condos, thinking that of all those she'd seen, this complex was the best. Smiling, she turned to Brian.

"Thanks for showing me around."

He gazed down at her. "My pleasure." He continued studying her to where she was desperately trying to hide the sexual pull he was creating. He was the most captivating man she'd ever dated.

Reading her correctly, he pulled her close and bent down to kiss her.

Her heart skipped a beat and then raced to catch up.

When their lips met, she couldn't hold back a soft moan of pleasure. His kiss was tender but thorough. She reached her arms around his neck, drawing him closer. She wanted more. Much, much more.

Apparently, so did he, because she felt his readiness.

She reminded herself to simply enjoy the moment. It was a gift to find someone who made her feel so wanton, yet so treasured.

When he drew her inside to the bedroom, she eagerly followed. She needed this, him and all he made her feel. She wanted to weep with the longing that was an incessant demand within her.

He picked her up and laid her down on the bed. "Are you

sure this is what you want, Lily?" he asked, his face flushed, his body ready.

"Yes," she answered simply, and held out her arms to him.

Groaning softly, he stretched out beside her, stroking her body with competent, strong hands that seemed to know where she liked to be touched.

After some time, he sat up. "Let me get rid of this damn thing." He took several moments to take off his prosthetic and lay it on the floor. Then he put on protection.

Curious, Lily watched him silently.

He turned to her and drew her closer. "Now, where were we?"

She grinned. "We were at the point where you were driving me crazy."

"Ah, yes," he said playfully before kissing her again.

He unhooked her bra and helped her out of her panties. And then, they continued to learn what brought the other pleasure. She couldn't hold back a cry of satisfaction. He quickly followed.

Later, lying beside him, Lily felt the sting of tears. Making love with him had been spiritual as well as physical, as if it was something that could only happen between the two of them. Perhaps because they'd each shown a vulnerability that made them open themselves to one another in a new way. Whatever, the reason, Lily had never felt like this before.

She turned to him and brushed back a curl from his forehead. Usually he looked so put-together, so military-like in his stance, even with his prosthesis. Now, he was rumpled in a way that pleased her.

He opened his tawny-gold eyes and smiled at her. "That was ... I've never ..."

"Me, too," she said, planting her lips on his, sensing his satisfaction. No more words were necessary. She pressed against him.

CHAPTER FIFTEEN

WILLOW

Willow finished her workout at the gym, feeling great. Working out was a therapeutic way to handle the stress of working for Alec in competition with Brent and Trace. But she was determined to win. Especially because of her negative past with Brent. His father might want him on the job, but few others did. Still, she'd do as Mitchell had requested and give him the opportunity to do his work while trying to maintain peace and patience. But it wasn't easy.

Dan walked over to her, smiling. "Feel better?"

She laughed. "Was I so obvious?"

"Let me put it this way. If that rowing machine was real, you'd be half-way across the Pacific Ocean by now." He grinned and patted her back. "Want to grab something for dinner? It's too late to call up a date."

She cocked an eyebrow at him. "Oh, so as long as you can't ask anyone else, you want me to go with you?"

"No, no," he said. "I didn't mean it that way. You're the one who's always so busy, I don't dare ask."

A warm feeling threaded through her. "Oh, well, in that case. Let me take a shower and I'll join you out front. No more clients this evening?"

He shook his head now. "It's late and the usual rush of people is gone."

"Okay. I won't be long."

Willow hurried into the ladies' locker room and into one of

the showers. She liked Dan. A lot. Though she'd never let him know. He was a fine specimen of a man who had many admirers. Even happily married women who came to the gym flirted with him, ignoring the fact that if their husbands weren't successful, they wouldn't be using the Desert Sage Inn facilities.

After showering and tying back her long, dark hair, Willow applied mascara, eye shadow, and lipstick. She didn't need anything more. She pulled on the skirt she'd worn to work and changed out the blouse for a cotton T-shirt, converting her business outfit into a fun, casual look, enhanced with the Native American Indian silver and turquoise squash blossom necklace she'd taken to wearing.

When she emerged from the locker room, Dan gave her a low whistle. "Lookin' good, Willow. C'mon, let's go. You can outshine everyone at Saguaro's."

Willow smiled, though she wished Dan would see her more as a girlfriend than a gym buddy. But at this stage in her life, working with young men she had no interest in, she was happy that she even got asked out by Dan.

Saguaro's was a cool little bar on El Paseo with outside seating and the best Southwestern pizza in town. When they arrived, the after-work crowd was thinning out. Relieved to find a small high-top table for two away from the door, Willow hurried to it and claimed it for them.

Dan headed for the bar. "Beer?"

She shook her head. "No, I'd like red wine, pinot noir, please." She liked beer on occasion but preferred red wine. At the hotel school, she'd learned to like a lot of different varieties, but pinot noir suited as both a sipping wine and a nice accompaniment to a meal.

While she waited for Dan to return, she studied her surroundings. The wooden paneled interior was brightened with paintings of desert scenes. On the tables, plastic cactus salt and pepper grinders matched candle holders of the same design. Funky but cute.

Tourists sat among the regulars, unsuspecting how easily these snowbirds and tourists stood out. Even so, they were welcomed. After all, they were the ones who kept businesses flourishing. Being acquainted with the inn from a young age had taught her that.

Dan returned with his beer and her wine.

Once he was seated, he lifted his glass. "Here's to another day!"

"A better one," she said, clicking her glass against his.

They'd just taken sips, when an attractive woman approached their table.

"Hi, Dan! Lucky to find you here," she said, fluttering her eyelashes at him. "I was thinking you might like to drop by my house. For private sessions."

"Hello, Sylvia. How are you?" he replied, his tone neutral.

"Fine. A little lonely these days. Truthfully, I really do need a workout. It's been a while since we had private training sessions at the gym. I talked to Meredith Evans the other day, she mentioned how well she was doing with them."

"Yes, well, she is a regular at the gym," he said, looking uneasy.

"I'm going to sign up as soon as I can, but I don't want to be in a class of any kind. I want personal attention from you." Sylvia slung an arm around him. "What do you say?"

"Call the hotel and make the arrangements," he said stiffly.

"Okay, that's a deal. Me and you," she said, before weaving her way from the table toward the restrooms.

"Wow! Do you have to put up with that shit all the time?" Willow said.

Dan shrugged. "I figure it's part of my job. You can't believe the tips I get when all I do is be nice to a woman like her. Their rich husbands are away and they're desperate for attention."

Willow lifted an eyebrow and studied him. "You're just nice to them?"

He waved a hand in dismissal. "Don't get me going. If I ever stepped out of line, I'd be out of one of the best jobs I've ever had."

"But you've had the chance to do so?" she said.

He nodded. "You wouldn't believe the offers I get. That's why I made a promise to myself to never date anyone from the hotel." He smiled at her. "This isn't a real date. It's just friends meeting for a drink. Right?"

"Right," she managed to say, hoping the hurt that was stabbing her didn't show.

CHAPTER SIXTEEN

LILY

Lily crept inside Alec's dark house feeling like a teenager sneaking in after being late for a curfew, still filled with excitement and a bit of wonder. Her evening with Brian had been magical. Even if a carriage drawn by horses had dropped her off, she couldn't feel more like Cinderella discovering her prince. She'd almost made it to her wing of the house when a voice called out to her, "Is that you, Lily?"

She jumped and twirled to find Alec sitting on the living room couch. "Yes, I'm sorry. Did I disturb you?"

"Not at all. I've been wandering the house, too restless to sleep." He patted the couch next to him. "Tell me what you're up to."

Even in the shadows of the one dim light on in the living room, Lily was sure Alec could see the way her cheeks had colored as she sat down next to him.

"Is there anything I can do to help you feel better?" she asked, reaching for his hand.

He shook his head. "No, thanks. Aren't you up late for you?"

She smiled. "Brian and I had our first official date."

"Ah, I see from your smile that it went well. I'm happy for you, Lily. I especially like Brian."

"It's been a long time since I found someone like him." She glanced at Alec but didn't say anything more. She could tell he was remembering their time together too.

"When is this sister of yours coming to visit?" he said. "I'm anxious to meet her and little Izzy. I know how much they mean to you."

Lily let out a sigh from deep inside her. "I'm hoping to get her here as soon as I find a place for them to stay. In fact, the condo where Brian is staying is just what I've been looking for. I'm calling tomorrow to see if they have any more units in the complex for sale."

"They'd be welcome to stay here," Alec said.

"Thanks, but I don't think that would be the best. I want Monica to see how it could be if she moved here, staying with me until she gets on her feet. At the moment, I'm very worried about her. Her old boyfriend is back and, believe me, he's a controlling jerk."

"Do you need my help for anything?" Alec asked.

Tears stung Lily's eyes. Alec was such a kind man. "No, but thanks. I'll work it out on my own. You've done so much for me already."

"You know I'm happy to do so," Alec said, smiling at her.

She wrapped her arms around him, careful not to squeeze too hard because of his frailty. "I do know that, and I appreciate it more than you know."

Alec patted her back. "Well, then, I guess I'll go back to my apartment and see if I can get some sleep, even though it seems I'm doing that most of the time."

"Do you want me to walk you back there?" Lily said, getting to her feet and offering him her arm.

He gripped it and rose to a standing position. "Thanks, Lily. That would be nice."

Together they walked through the house to his wing, each quiet, each, she suspected, remembering another time when she might've gone to bed with him. Her thoughts skipped to Brian, chasing those memories away.

###

When Lily walked into the kitchen the next morning, Rose and Willow were already there, sitting at the table, sipping coffee.

Rose grinned up at her. "You had a late night. How did your date with Brian go?"

Lily stopped. "How'd you know that? I thought you were staying at Hank's place."

"Actually, Alec told me. He's really happy about it. I'm not sure what's going on, but sometimes I think he purposely chose to have us work with someone he thought was special. Look what happened to Hank and me."

Willow cocked her eyebrow. "Then what does that say about me. He knows I'd never have any interest in Brent."

"And he wouldn't know what I was looking for," said Lily. "Besides, Brian and I have had only one official date. Who knows where it's going?" Her spirits drooped at the thought of a bad ending. Last night had been a dream come true for her, but she had no idea if a relationship was what Brian was looking for on a permanent basis.

"Okay, okay," said Rose. "It was just a crazy thought of mine."

"You've moved back in here after taking care of Leah?" said Lily.

"Yes," said Rose. "Even though Rob and Sam and Leah are leaving soon, I don't feel right about being there with Hank while they're there. Especially when we three all agreed to stay here at Alec's house for the duration, except for special occasions."

"I'm concerned about Alec," Lily said, unable to hide the sadness that crept into her voice. "When he and I talked last night, he seemed so fragile."

"I think he wants to hang on until the sale goes through," said Willow, shaking her head sadly. "In the meantime, we're all part of his plan to make the sale go the way he wants."

Lily shared looks with Rose and Willow, seeing their pain, understanding completely what they were feeling.

"Have you had any luck finding a place to live?" Rose asked her.

"Not yet, but there's hope. It's not a day for me to work at the law firm, so, I'm going to see if there are any condos for sale in the same complex as Brian's."

Willow elbowed Rose playfully. "That sure would make a late-night rendezvous easier for Lily. Right, Rose?"

"Yes. Maybe, if she gets a condo there, we should think of buying her a big flashlight to use between places."

Lily laughed. "One date, ladies. That's all we've had." In truth, she loved being teased about Brian and her. It made it seem so real.

"So, tell me about his condo and his complex," said Willow. "I know I can't stay here in Alec's house forever. And as much as I love my parents, no way am I moving back in with them."

As Lily described the layout of the condo, the top-notch kitchen, she grew more excited. "It's in Indian Wells, but close to the border of Palm Desert, which makes it convenient to all the shopping." She turned to Willow. "Do you want to go with me to talk to the sales people there?"

Willow beamed at her. "I'd love it. After seeing what's happening to Alec, I want to stay close to family for a while. Living on the east coast sometimes was too far away."

"I know the feeling," said Lily. "Every time I try to call my sister, the three-hour time difference becomes an issue."

"Have you heard from her recently?" Rose asked.

An unsettling worry embraced her. She checked the kitchen clock. "No, but I think I'll go call her now."

Lily grabbed a cup of coffee and took it to her room. Even if she worked late, Monica should be up with Izzy.

Sitting on a chair, looking out at the landscape, Lily set down her coffee cup and clicked on Monica's cell number.

After several rings, Monica picked up. "Hello."

"Monica? It's Lily. How are you?"

"Not so good. I've been sick."

Alarm caused the pitch of Lily's voice to rise. "What is it? Something serious?"

"Not unless you call pregnancy serious," said Monica. "Remember how sick I was with Izzy? Well, it's the same with this one."

"Oh, my God! Is Jeremy the father?"

"Yes! Of course! Who did you think it'd be? You know I don't fool around," snapped Monica.

"I'm sorry. I didn't mean to make it seem that way. What does Jeremy say about all this?" Lily managed to say calmly though she wanted to scream at her sister.

"Jeremy? Ha! He doesn't know. I'm not going to tell him until I have to," said Monica. "When I do, he'll be concerned about my working. He doesn't like it when I call in sick. He says we need the money."

Anger, like a flash of fire, filled Lily. "Does he even have a job yet?"

"He's still looking. It has to be just right for him," Monica said with little emotion.

"Okay, Monica, I'm looking at a place today. As soon as I get it set up for you, I'm sending airline tickets for you and Izzy."

"No. I need you to come back here, like you did when I was pregnant with Izzy," said Monica with a distinctive whine.

Lily's heart fell. "I can't. I have work in California. It's best if you come here to Palm Desert. But, Monica, whatever you do, don't mention this plan to Jeremy. I'm not paying for him to come here."

"I won't. I promise." Monica's voice cracked. "I'm just so damned tired."

"Hang on. I'll work on things as fast as I can. Talk to you later. Give Izzy hugs and kisses from me and a hug from me to you."

"'Bye," said Monica softly, and clicked off the call.

Lily went back to the kitchen to find Willow. "Okay, you're welcome to join me, but, fair warning, I'm going to try to find something suitable today. I'm not waiting. My sister needs a new home and I'm giving it to her. Ready to go?"

Willow shook her head. "I'm sorry, I got a call and can't go with you. Brent and Trace want to talk about the cost of renovating the Arizona properties. It's going to be more expensive than we'd thought."

"I'm sorry, too. I was looking forward to spending time with you," said Lily. "But don't worry. We'll work something out."

"Thanks for being so understanding. I asked if we could delay the meeting but they said no. I had no choice but to agree."

"Such bastards," said Lily. "I don't see how you can stand to work with them."

"It's just Brent who wouldn't agree. It's a power play for him. I'll end up beating him at his own game, but the process might kill me."

"I'm counting on you to win," said Lily. "I'll catch up with you later."

Disappointed, Lily headed out by herself. Maybe it was just as well nobody else got involved with her small, troubled family. Getting Monica out here was only the first step in fixing things. A lot more work would be required to get everything right again. She thought of Jeremy. What was it about him that made Monica like putty in his hands?

CHAPTER SEVENTEEN

ROSE

Rose looked at the graphics and script for an ad campaign Hank had created on his computer and was silent.

"What do you think? Do you like them?" Hank waited expectantly for an answer, a look of pride on his face.

"From Alec's point of view, not so much," said Rose honestly. "Your words have made it seem as if being elegant is something new for the Desert Sage Inn when it's always been that way. If anything, it's a totally new direction for the Blaise Group."

"Really? That's your response?" Hank's cheeks were flushed with emotion.

"Look, Hank, we're working together on this, but I still have Alec's wishes to consider. That's something I was worried about when we became engaged—this rivalry thing. My feelings for you aren't going to influence the job I'm doing for him. He knows I'll be forthright." She lifted her gaze to his. "I pride myself on my honesty. That's one reason our relationship works."

He rubbed a hand through his graying hair. "That's the hell of it. I want you to be upfront, but I hate having us constantly battling one another on fine points."

"The graphics are great. We just need to tweak them a bit, along with the copy."

"Most people would be satisfied with what I've done. A word here or there isn't going to make much of a difference."

"Really? That's your response?" she said, teasing him with the duplication of his words.

They looked at one another stiffly then Hank burst into laughter and drew her to him. "Rose, my wonderful Rose, you're not going to let me get away with anything, are you?"

She smiled at him. "Absolutely not."

CHAPTER EIGHTEEN

LILY

As Lily drove into Brian's condo complex, memories of the night before assailed her. Titillated by how easily she'd become wanton in bed, she couldn't stop a smile of satisfaction from creasing her face. She'd loved every minute of making love with Brian, even the awkward, getting-to-know-you moves. He was a generous man.

Her thoughts flew to her sister. Did she have that kind of relationship with Jeremy? Lily doubted it. He was much too selfish, much too demanding.

Lily found a parking spot outside the sales office and before getting out, murmured a soft prayer that everything would work out. She was anxious to get settled for many reasons.

Standing beside her car, Lily studied her surroundings. The two-story, tan-stucco buildings were well maintained. In her research, she'd learned they were only six years old. Time enough for landscaping to grow and young enough that a lot of building maintenance wasn't required.

Palm trees swayed in the breeze. Bright pink blossoms on bougainvillea plants were offset by the white flowers of nearby oleanders, providing both a lush and colorful texture to the landscape.

Inside, an older woman with short, gray hair smiled at her from behind a desk loaded with pamphlets. The name plate on her desk said "*Billie Thompson*". "Hello! Sorry for the mess. I'm working on mailing out brochures. How can I help you?"

"I'm wondering if any condos here are available for sale?" said Lily. "I've been in a ground-floor unit and really liked it."

Billie smiled up at her. "At the moment, we don't have any condos available. But we usually have a few for sale come summer months. Try us then."

"Okay, thank you," said Lily, her spirits flagging. A condo like Brian's was too good to be true.

She left that complex and tried another in Rancho Mirage that she'd liked, and was told the same thing—come back after May 1st.

Determined not to give up, she entered the Desert Isle complex in the country club area and parked outside the sales office. Like Brian's complex, the grounds were well maintained and the two-story, stucco-faced buildings were in excellent shape. A large pool and attractive clubhouse were within view.

She got out of the car and went inside the sales office.

The man behind the desk listened to what she wanted and said, "Hold on. Let me check." He studied his computer. "We have a ground-floor unit coming available on April 1st. It will officially be on the market then. Number 401. You can drive by it or walk around the property to see it from another angle. Let me give you a map of the complex and a sales brochure for it that we just completed. If you're seriously interested, I can give you a tour."

Lily eagerly accepted the paperwork. After studying the photos, description, and price of the unit, hope filled her. "I'd definitely like to take a look at it."

They walked to a corner of the grounds. Building #4 overlooked the property line populated with tall oleander bushes and other plantings behind the cluster of buildings. The patio for the unit, she noted, would have a nice view and some privacy. Not far away, a small picnic area with outdoor grills designated a safe place where she could grill her own food if she desired.

Inside, the open space housed a living room, a kitchen nook, a newly refurbished kitchen, three bedrooms and two baths, plus a small office area. Though the unit was spotless, the walls, painted a light green, would have to be repainted in a color she liked, and the carpeting in the master bedroom was something she'd want replaced. Other than that, the condo was just what she'd been looking for. If she could make a quick offer, the owner might consider the one she had in mind.

Crossing her fingers for luck, she said, "Do you have a standard sales agreement I could look over?"

The man smiled and nodded. "Of course. But's it's my responsibility as an agent to suggest you find a lawyer or someone else qualified to help you negotiate any contract."

Lily couldn't hold back the grin she felt spreading across her face. "I know the perfect law firm. Thanks so much. Have there been other offers or signs of interest?"

"No, because we haven't advertised it yet. The owner wanted to wait until the last renter was out and she had time to sort through her things. But I should warn you that these condos don't stay on the market very long."

Lily left the complex feeling as if she'd won the lottery. Maybe, for once, her timing would be right.

When Lily entered the law offices of Williams and Kincaid, Jonathan smiled at her from behind the reception desk. "Hi, Lily. What are you doing here? It's not your day to work."

"No, but I'm wondering if either Bennett or Craig are around. I need their advice on something."

"Bennett's out of the office, but Craig's here. Let me buzz him to let him know you're here and would like to talk to him."

Lily waited, and in a few minutes, Craig entered the

reception area. "Hello! Couldn't stay away, huh? Your training session isn't for another week."

She laughed. "I need someone to look over a contract for me, and I couldn't think of a better place to come."

"Oh? Come back to my office and we'll discuss it."

She followed him to his office. He indicated a chair for her to sit in before taking a seat behind his desk. "What's going on?"

"I've found a condo I'd like to buy. It isn't even on the market yet, which is why I thought of having someone here look at it, rather than a real estate agent."

He smiled and nodded. "I'll be glad to look at it for you. Why don't you leave it here and we can discuss it tomorrow, if that's not too late?"

"That would be wonderful," she said. "I know enough about contracts to realize a second pair of eyes is always wise."

"Smart thinking. How's everything else going?"

"All right," said Lily. "The reason I'm anxious to find a place so quickly is so I can have my sister and my niece come for a visit. I'm hoping she'll then agree to move here."

"I've found it's not always easy to have family around, but given a choice, it's better than not having them here," said Craig. "What time do you want to meet tomorrow?"

"I'm free until three o'clock. Willow, Rose, and I are meeting with young women from the high school to talk about female empowerment."

A smile curved his lips. "The Desert Flowers, as Alec calls you, are going to be great at doing that. Good luck! Why don't we meet for lunch at the inn? I'll go over any details with you then."

"Thank you. Craig, I really appreciate your help on this."

"No problem. Now that you are part of the family, I'm happy to do it for you, *gratis*."

"That's even better!" she said, more and more excited about the way things were going. She couldn't wait to tell Willow about the condo. She might want to look there, too.

The next day, Lily joined Willow in Rose's car and told them all about the condo she wanted to buy. "In fact, Willow, I think you might be interested in the complex. It's only eight years old, is beautifully maintained, and the condos are as nice as any I've seen."

"Thanks. I'd love to look at whatever information you have." Willow let out a long, soft breath full of emotion. "It's been a bad day for Alec. I'm really worried about him and what it's going to mean for all of us when he's gone."

"I can't bear to think of him leaving us," said Rose. "I know it's inevitable, but no matter when it happens, it's much too soon."

"Yes, just knowing he's around has been so comforting to me," said Lily. "If I am able to buy the condo, like you, Rose, I won't move out of his house. I want him to know we're all here for him."

"All right, ladies," said Rose, speaking into the gloom that had filled the car, "we've agreed to wing it with the high school girls. Right? We'll each tell something we've learned along the way that's job related and then answer questions."

"I won't mention my time here at the inn, but I have a lot of other material," said Willow.

Lily smiled. "I intend to talk about the power of saying no, not limited to intimacy, but to business." She still couldn't believe how she'd let other's expectations take over her life.

"I'm going to spend some time on empowering yourself in business by making sure your work is impeccable," said Rose, with an edge to her voice. "I've been screwed so many times by others in business."

Lily filled with satisfaction. The young girls who wanted advice were going to get an earful.

When they walked into the library/media center, Lily was surprised to see so many girls waiting for them. They looked young and eager and so innocent that tears stung her eyes. Had she ever been that young? After the stress of dealing with her mother and doing her best to take care of Monica, she'd been forced to grow up much too soon.

The tall outspoken girl Lily recognized walked up to them. "Hi, I'm Caroline Norris. Do you remember me from our race?"

"Yes," said Lily. "And I'm Lily Weaver." She held out her hand.

Caroline shook it and turned to Rose and Willow. "We're all so glad the three of you could come and talk to us. Some of us are facing college; others are going right into jobs."

"Then it's time we talked," said Rose, with a bit of humor.

Caroline grinned. "We have three chairs set up for you, facing the crowd."

Caroline led them to the chairs and turned to the group. "Here they are – The Desert Flowers, Rose Macklin, Lily Weaver, and Willow Sanchez."

After the applause had died down, one girl called from the crowd. "Desert Flowers sounds so flirty, so feminine, almost as if you need the talk more than we do."

Caught off guard, Lily looked to Rose.

"Women don't need tough names or rough manners to project a sense of strength. To the contrary, soft words, pleasant manners can be as powerful as harsh words or a pushy manner. The secret is to be aware of your own strength, your own power, and use it. Be yourself. Isn't that why you brought us here?"

"Still, Desert Flowers sounds too sweet," the girl protested.

"I can respond to that," said Lily. "We came together because of our friend who is dying. We're working together to carry out some of his last wishes. Each of us has a special talent to do that. We could be called Angels, like that old television show, or anything else. It doesn't matter. I'm Lily. My friends are Rose and Willow, names of desert flowers. It's a term of endearment, and we're proud of that code name."

"Code name? It sounds like some kind of war," said another girl.

"Less a war than a constant battle to be heard and to be recognized for our work," said Willow.

"The need is not as apparent as one might imagine," said Rose, "but empowering yourselves with knowledge and self-confidence will make a difference in what you do with your lives."

"Once you are aware of your strengths, you will be better able to make the best choices for you," said Willow.

"And learn to say no, not only in your personal lives but in business, too," added Lily. "For instance, it took me a while, but I finally learned to say no to a work situation that was ruining my personal life. I needed a sense of empowerment that came from knowing I was doing an excellent job and had a right to make some limits on my time. I've always been a people pleaser but am now learning to set boundaries."

"Yeah, it might be easy for someone like you, older and more experienced. But what about people like me, trying to even *find* a decent job?" said a young girl with thick glasses. "Everything out there is menial. I want a better job than that."

"Dream jobs rarely come along," Rose said. "Starting at the bottom and working your way up is how most people succeed, no matter the level at the beginning." She held up a finger. "But, let's say you've found a job that you and two others are interested in. How are you going to make an impression?"

Lily brainstormed with Rose and Willow about possible job scenarios, all designed to give the young girls insight into the importance of knowing who they were and how they could make those strengths work for them.

"Most of all, you need to like yourself enough to understand who you are and what you need or don't need from your job, from friends, from family," said Rose.

"And don't be afraid to be who you are," added Willow.

Lily thought a moment and added, "Be honest with yourself."

"Thank you so much for all your insights. Now, let's open it up to questions. I know you all have a lot of them," said Caroline.

The next hour and a half passed in a blur for Lily. The girls were intelligent, persistent and sweet in their quest for more information. As she listened to their questions and the discussion that followed, she thought of Monica and wished her sister could be here to listen. She needed to have a better sense of self, but she doubted that would happen if Jeremy continued to chip away at what remained of her self-confidence. Lily wished there was something magical she could do to make Jeremy disappear.

It was almost five o'clock when Lily followed Rose and Willow out of the building.

"I don't know about you, but I'm ready for a margarita and a chance to let my mind relax," said Rose.

"Let's go back to the house," said Lily. "I want to show you the pictures of the condo I'm thinking of buying."

They quickly agreed.

###

Lily sat with Rose and Willow, sipping her cool drink with a new appreciation of the comfortable companionship. In discussing their arrangement with the high school girls, Lily felt an even deeper connection to the other two women.

Willow looked through the photos Lily had taken of the condo and the complex itself and handed Lily's phone back to her. "It looks fabulous for the price. I'm definitely interested in looking there. But don't mention it to my mother. She thinks I should stay with them until I find the man of my dreams."

Lily shared a laugh with the others.

"What about Dan?" Rose said. "I thought you were interested in him. He'd look perfect in shining armor atop a white horse."

Willow made a face. "Don't I know it! But, honestly, he's not interested in me. I have yet to meet anyone else I'd want to date." She turned to Lily. "You and Brian together? I think it's perfect."

"We'll see," said Lily. "Before I get too involved, I have family issues to take care of. Honestly, I wish my sister could've been at the meeting with the high school girls. She needs a talk like that to wake her up. I haven't mentioned it, but I just found out she's pregnant."

"Oh, no!" said Rose.

"Is Jeremy the father?" Willow looked as shocked as Rose.

Feeling sick at the thought, Lily nodded. "Monica doesn't want to tell him about it yet. I need to get her out here before he finds out. He's already complaining about her taking time off from work when she feels too sick to go in, and he doesn't even have a job."

"You weren't kidding when you said it was a bad situation," said Rose.

Willow gave Lily a sympathetic look. "What can we do to help?"

Lily shook her head. "If Monica won't listen to me, I don't

know what I or anyone else can do." She thought of Izzy and turned away to hide her tears.

CHAPTER NINETEEN

LILY

Lily was just about to have dinner with Rose and Willow when her cell phone chimed. She smiled. *Brian.*

"Hello! I was wondering if I'd hear from you today," she said happily.

"Sorry to be so late in asking, but are you free for dinner?"

"I'm just sitting down to dinner with Rose and Willow," she replied.

"Okay. How about meeting at my condo after dinner? There's something I need to discuss with you. Something I haven't mentioned before. It's important." His voice shook with emotion.

Lily's stomach squeezed into a knot. "All right. I can do that."

"I'm leaving the hotel now. Come as soon as you can." Again, he sounded shaky.

More certain than ever that things were not good, Lily swallowed hard. "I'll get there as soon as possible." She hung up and faced Willow and Rose. "I don't know what's going on with Brian, but he's very upset." Her vision blurred. "I'm going to skip dinner to meet him at his condo."

Rose and Willow gave her sympathetic looks.

"Can we help?" Do you want us to go with you?"

Lily shook her head. "No, thanks." There was no point in even trying to eat. She grabbed her purse and headed out to her car, her pulse racing in nervous beats.

Though, in truth it felt like hours, she made it to Brian's place in record time. He was standing in the parking lot, briefcase in hand, when she drove in. He looked up at her with surprise.

She pulled into a parking space and got out. "Hi! I got here as quickly as I could."

"Thanks. Come on inside. We need to talk." He let out a long sigh and ran a hand through his hair. "Life can be so damn complicated."

Observing the parallel stress lines across his forehead and the tightness of his jaw, she was surprised by this new image of him. Even during the most difficult moments in meetings, he'd always retained his cool.

She waited while he unlocked the door to his condo and then followed him inside.

He waved her to the couch. "Have a seat. I'll be right there." He headed into his bedroom.

When he returned, he sat on the couch beside her and turned to her. "I haven't been completely honest with you regarding past relationships. I told you that though I'd dated, nothing had worked out. While that was true, I was engaged to one of those women, Becky Davis, who suddenly ended our relationship. That was ten years ago. At the time, I couldn't blame her. I was having issues with post-traumatic stress problems. That, the fact that I have this situation with my leg, and the fact I didn't want children pretty much scared her off. Her ex-boyfriend and she quickly got married. That should've been the end of it. And, in truth, it was except for something I just found out today. She's divorced and is in the final stages of pancreatic cancer. She has a nine-year-old boy who she claims is mine after having blood testing done. He and I have the same relatively rare blood type, AB Positive. Only now has she told me about him."

"Oh my God! What are you going to do?"

"First off, I'm going to Austin to see Becky and the boy and to take a DNA test. Then I'll try to work out something for him. If he's mine, I'll bring him back here and go from there." Brian looked as sick as Lily felt.

She took hold of his hand. "What can I do to help? Do you want me to travel to Austin with you?"

"No, thanks. But you can help me at this end. If he's mine, I'll need to find a babysitter for him, get a list of the best schools, doctors, and all that."

"I know just the person to talk to. Sarah Jensen will know all of that."

"The part-time Assistant Manager?" said Brian. "Perfect. Her family has been here a long time and she'll have the information we need." He reached out and cupped her cheek with his broad hand and gentle fingers. "I know we're just getting to know one another. I don't want that to stop. If all this might scare you away, please let me know now."

She caught her lip and then smiled up at him. "I'm not that much of a scaredy-cat. I love kids and have always wanted them. Let's take everything one step at a time."

He drew her to him. "Lily, you made me happy last night and now, this sweet gesture. If I hadn't already fallen for you, I would right now."

When his lips met hers, Lily felt the vulnerability in them and responded with tenderness. She felt a commitment to him that would seem much too early under different circumstances.

"I've fallen for you, too," she said honestly. "From the moment you walked into the very first meeting at the inn, a man in charge."

"Well, I don't feel in charge now. I've never wanted kids, don't know much about how to be a parent, and don't know what I'm doing at this moment except trying to react."

"Reacting in a nice way," she reminded him. "Do you have pictures of him? What's his name?"

"His name is Oliver." He handed Lily his cell phone. "Here are a couple pictures of him."

Lily took the phone from him and eagerly studied the shots of a small boy with dark-brown hair and green eyes that peered through round, horn-rimmed glasses with uncertainty.

"He's adorable!" Lily exclaimed. "But, Brian, there's no question about his being your son. He looks just like you!!" It was uncanny. Though he looked a little small for his age, Oliver had the same facial features as Brian.

"Yes, that's what my mother said. She's thrilled she might have a grandchild." His eyes grew moist. "I'm just not ready for this." Lily knew from conversations they'd had on their early walks together that Brian was an only child and his mother was still alive, in her late seventies.

"You'll be ready for Oliver after you get through the shock of it," said Lily, quietly but firmly. "From our many conversations and seeing you at work, I know what kind of man you are. Just give yourself time to breathe."

He leaned back against the couch and stared up at the ceiling. "His mother hurt me deeply, but it's awful to think of her dying so young. She's about your age."

"Why didn't she tell you about Oliver before now?"

"She said she honestly didn't realize he was my son because she and her ex had already gotten together before she broke our engagement. And he and I look somewhat alike. I was such a fool I didn't even realize they were ..."

Lily leaned over and kissed his cheek. "Now you do. And by the looks of the photo, Oliver is a darling little boy. No doubt he'll be frightened by all that's happening. But your presence and time for him to get to know you is all important now. Especially if his mother is close to dying."

"She's talking about days." Brian's eyes filled. "She recently moved back to Austin to be with her sister, Susannah, who promised to take care of Oliver. At the last minute, Becky called me and asked me to take him, saying she couldn't rest in peace if I didn't know the truth."

"Understandable," said Lily. "And if Susannah has had the care of Oliver, she can help you with the transition."

Brian nodded thoughtfully. "Of course. I hadn't considered that. God! I don't want the boy to be frightened of me."

"The boy?" she chided softly.

He gave her a sheepish look. "Oliver. I guess they call him Ollie."

"How do you want to handle having him living with you? You've got another few weeks' of rental here. Right?"

"Right. I've been looking at small condos, but now I'll have to consider buying something a little bigger. There's a dog involved too."

"Oh, my! You're actually getting a whole family all at once."

"It looks that way." His face lit up with a smile. "Ollie does kinda look like me, doesn't he?"

She nodded and smiled at the way Brian was already reacting to having Ollie in his life. Yes, there would be ups and downs, but Brian Walden was a very special man, and she bet he'd make a very good father.

"What do you say, I cook something to eat," she said. "If you have eggs, I could whip up an omelet, make a simple meal."

"Sounds terrific," said Brian giving her a grateful smile. He reached for her again.

Lily nestled up against him, needing his comfort as much as he needed hers. Life was throwing them a big curve that would make or break their relationship.

"One day, one thing at a time," Lily said, telling herself to stop projecting for the future. Their relationship was new, but no matter what, she'd be there for him. For Ollie too, if needed.

After their meal, Lily and Brian worked together to clean the kitchen and then Lily said, "I guess I'd better go."

"Thanks for coming, Lily. It means a lot to me." He drew her to him and lowered his lips to hers.

She closed her eyes, letting his kiss tell her how important she was to him. But even if he asked, she wouldn't stay any longer. He had an early morning flight and they both needed time to themselves.

When he pulled away, he smiled at her. "I'll call you tomorrow night, after I've met Ollie and spoken to Becky."

"Okay, good luck with everything."

Lily left his condo wondering how life could get so mixed up, so quickly. One thing she was sure of was the special feeling she shared with Brian. But would that continue with a little boy and his dog in the picture?

Thinking of his possible new family, Lily decided to check in with Monica and realized it was too late to call.

CHAPTER TWENTY

ROSE

Rose finished dinner with Willow and decided to go visit Alec. It hadn't been one of his better days. She was hoping to find him in better spirits.

She knocked on the door to his private wing and waited until she heard him respond.

At the sound of his voice, she stepped inside his living area. He was stretched out on a lounge chair, listening to classical music. His lips curved when he saw her and he lifted his hand in greeting.

Smiling, she went to his side and pulled up a chair beside him. "Hi! How are you doing this evening? I heard you had a rough morning."

"One of those days when I wonder if it's worth hanging on, but I'm not ready to go just yet. How are you and Hank doing?"

"We're fine. Working together and being together. If you'd told me a few months ago that all this was going to happen, I'd call you a liar. But here we are, both facing challenges." Her vision blurred. "It's hard for me to be so happy when I know your circumstances."

"Well, now, there's no way you can change that," said Alec, giving her a tender smile. "The best thing you can do for me is to be happy. It gives me great comfort to know that you and Hank are being given a second chance at love."

Rose shook her head and poked him playfully, gently. "I get the feeling you had this planned all along."

He chuckled. "You know that isn't true. I've never met two more independent people. It should make for some interesting times ahead."

She smiled. "Yes, we don't always agree on particulars on the campaign for the inn but we're pretty much on the same page when it comes to how we want to live. He's thinking of selling his house in Atlanta and buying something smaller nearer the kids. And we're both looking for a place out here to live during the winter. We'll see."

Alec took hold of her hand. "I'm sure you'll work it out. Hank is a generous man, a great guy. And now he has you. I think how happy I was years ago with Conchita. I'm thinking of her more and more, getting ready, I suppose, to see her again."

"I wish I'd known her," said Rose. "She must have been a lovely person."

"She was," he said simply as tears rolled down his cheeks.

Rose stayed with him until his eyes closed. Then she rose and quietly moved away.

CHAPTER TWENTY-ONE

LILY

When Lily returned to Alec's house, all was quiet. Relieved to have some time to herself to think things over, Lily went out to the patio and sat in a chair in the dark. Gazing up at the stars twinkling above her, Lily felt a calm wash over her. She was pleased Brian had reached out to her. Their relationship was new but there was an underlying tie between them that made it seem so much stronger.

She'd always wanted a large family, a family unlike her own growing up. Having Izzy in her life had been a blessing, but as Monica had reminded her, Izzy was her niece, not her child.

Now, considering all possibilities in her future, maybe it would be best to rent until her future was more secure. She needed to find something with enough space to have Monica stay with her until she was able to find a job and housing of her own.

Tired of thinking about all that was happening, Lily went inside and to bed.

At breakfast the next morning, Lily told Willow and Rose the news of Brian's son and how she'd help him with the transition.

"Poor guy! He must be totally shocked," said Rose.

"Now I know why Brian cancelled the meeting this morning," said Willow. "He's scheduled a virtual meeting for tomorrow afternoon."

"He said he'd call me and let me know how things are going," said Lily. "I told him I'd help him however I can. He's thinking I might want to sub-lease his condo if he finds something more suitable for Ollie and his dog."

Rose hesitated, cleared her throat, then said, "I know you and Brian are dating and you're helping him, but he isn't about to take advantage of you, is he?"

Lily clapped her hands to her cheeks and then lowered them with confidence. "No, Rose. I don't believe that at all. It's hard to explain, but we have a stronger connection than that."

Rose nodded and gave her a look of satisfaction. "That's all I wanted to hear. I like Brian a lot, but if I thought he was hurting you, I'd speak up, like now."

"Thanks, Rose," Lily said. It felt wonderful to have a friend like her.

After breakfast, Lily called Craig and cancelled their luncheon. "I'm having second thoughts about rushing into anything."

"I understand," Craig said. "There will be a whole slew of condos coming up for sale in the next month or two. Are you all set for your training next week?"

"Yes," Lily said, wondering how it would work if Ollie returned to Palm Desert with Brian. Thinking of it, she decided to speak to Sarah Jensen.

Lily clicked off the call and phoned Sarah, who agreed to meet her at the hotel.

Sitting in The Joshua Tree, the informal restaurant at the inn, Lily waited for Sarah to appear. Sarah was an assistant manager to John Rodriguez and was someone she, Rose, and Willow were friends with. She was a petite, pretty blonde who was the mother of a two-year-old boy, Henry, and had opted to move back home to Palm Desert while her husband, Eric, served in the military. She was a delight and a source of useful information because her grandparents had moved to Palm Desert years ago, soon after the area opened up with the arrival of the ventriloquist and puppeteer, Edgar Bergen, and others seeking refuge in the desert from Hollywood.

Seeing her now, Lily lifted a hand to wave and felt a smile spread across her face. Sarah was someone who seemed to bring cheer wherever she went. To everyone, that is, but Brent Armstrong. She would not let him get away with any of his underhanded tricks.

Wearing her uniform of a black skirt and sage green blouse, she looked much younger than thirty-two as she slid onto a chair opposite Lily.

"What's up? You said you needed to talk to me about a private matter? Is it something to do with the hotel?"

Lily nodded and leaned forward. "It's a personal matter of Brian's. He asked me to reach out to you for information." She quickly explained the situation to Sarah. "I've made a list. We thought we'd ask you first about doctors, babysitters, and schools."

"What a shock this must be to him," Sarah said. "When you have a child in the normal way you get a few months to get used to the idea. Poor guy! He must be so overwhelmed."

"That's putting it mildly. I'll know more information after he calls me tonight. In the meantime, let's talk." In her customary efficient way, Lily drew out a paper and began checking off information as Sarah gave it.

"A babysitter? Why don't I ask Nita, who babysits Henry, to give me a couple of recommendations?" Sarah grinned. "But Nita is mine."

Lily laughed. She knew how difficult it could be to find a babysitter. It had taken her months to find a babysitter she liked for Izzy.

When they were through with questions from Brian, Lily asked about condos in the area. Like Craig, Sarah recommended waiting a few weeks before signing up for anything, but when she heard about Brian's condo, she perked up. "If you can get into that complex, it's a well-respected one, with value that will always be there because of its prime location."

Feeling better about her decision to hold off on purchasing anything at the moment, Lily thanked her.

"What do you hear from your husband?" Lily asked her.

Sarah's eyes sparkled. "Only a few more months and then he'll be discharged. I'm not sure what he's going to do, but he's agreed to live here until we can figure it out."

"What about you? Have you decided anything about staying at the Desert Sage Inn?"

Sarah made a face and shrugged. "I don't know if I will. Brent and I don't get along. It shouldn't matter, but if he's going to stick around, I'm not sure I want to."

"Working for family businesses can be difficult," Lily said, commiserating with her. She'd once been forced to leave a small law office because the two brothers owning it couldn't agree on anything, making her life miserable.

"You're right. For all the glamour, it is still a family business." Sarah's cell buzzed. She glanced at it and got to her feet. "Gotta go. I'll be back in touch with you regarding babysitters. Talk about family business. I'm pretty sure Nita has a family member who might be interested in working for Brian. I'll call you later."

They exchanged quick hugs and then Sarah went on her way. Lily finished her coffee and headed back to Alec's house satisfied. She wanted to be able to give Brian a full report when he called that evening.

Too restless to sit still after a busy morning, Lily decided to check out a few things on her list for Brian. The elementary school, the doctor's office and library in Palm Desert were easy to find.

On a whim, she called Nan Bishop, the real estate agent she'd seen earlier, and asked for information on housing in the area.

After agreeing to send her some possibilities online, Nan said, "Have him give me a call if he finds anything of interest."

"Thanks. I will." Lily clicked off the call. She'd done all she could do for Brian for the moment.

When he called that evening, Brian sounded in a panic.

"Things aren't good here. Becky is at home with Susannah with Hospice helping her. Ollie is upset, of course, and doesn't want to talk about the future. Susannah says I need to give him time, and I will. After seeing him, I'm angry Becky didn't tell me when she realized he was my child so I could have been there for him all those years."

"What is Ollie like?" Lily asked quietly, hoping to calm him.

"He seems like a great kid. Very smart, kind of small for his age, and not that athletic, but he loves science and animals. Jake, his labradoodle, is a great dog and a big comfort to him. I have to find a place to live that's suitable for dogs too."

"Speaking of that, I have lots of information to share," Lily said, pleased she'd made the effort.

After going through the list she'd drawn up and talking about the listing of houses Nan had sent along, Lily heard a catch in Brian's voice as he thanked her.

"Thanks, Lily. I appreciate this. It makes the situation easier because of your support. I appreciate everything you're doing for me."

"I'm glad to help any way I can. How long do you anticipate

remaining there?" Lily asked.

"I'll stay until Becky dies. Susannah and I are trying to come up with a schedule for Ollie, but she feels he should be allowed to continue living with her through the school year. That would give her and me a chance to help Ollie with the transition from Texas to Palm Desert."

"And then what?" Lily held her breath waiting for his answer.

"I'm going to move my consulting business to Palm Desert. I'd already begun discussions about it. First, I have to get my mind wrapped around the fact that I've got a son." A dog barked in the background. "And a dog."

"I'm so sorry about Becky, but pleased her sister is looking out for Ollie and you. She sounds nice."

"Yeah, she and I knew each other years ago. We've always liked one another. She and her husband have three kids of their own, so I think she's relieved Becky finally told me the truth. We'll be sure that Ollie stays in touch with her after he's moved in with me." He sighed. "I promised her I'd do my best with him. That's all I can do."

"That's all anyone can do. I'm happy things seem to be working out, Brian. I can't wait to meet him."

"You will, I promise. It just won't happen for a while. He's got to get used to one new thing at a time."

He was right. If their relationship was going to continue to grow, they all had to take one baby step, then another.

"When the time comes, Becky doesn't want a big funeral, but there will be a small memorial service. I'll stay here until that happens. It could be any day."

"Take care, Brian."

"You, too, Lily."

"I'll be here waiting for you," said Lily.

"That makes everything seem better." He clicked off the

call before she could say anything else.

CHAPTER TWENTY-TWO

WILLOW

Once her job at the Desert Sage Inn was over, Willow needed to find something new. She wanted to stay in Palm Desert and continue working in the hotel business. With the meeting cancelled at the inn, she decided to spend some time looking at other hotels. She was looking for a small, upscale inn with a fine reputation. The two such hotels she immediately thought of were The Chateau at Lake La Quinta and the Hotel Paseo in downtown Palm Desert. She pushed those thoughts aside and instead drove to a small inn not many visitors knew much about.

The Premio Inn was less than three miles away from the Desert Sage Inn, hugging the foothills that stretched along the backside of Premio's property. The entrance to the inn was very subtle, just a small sign indicating a driveway off Route 111 in Indian Wells. She'd heard rumors that the owner/manager of the small inn was getting ready to retire, and she hoped to have a conversation with him.

Willow made her way down the driveway. The natural landscape was lovely, though she thought the addition of a few flowering plants would make it even better. She pulled in front of a large hacienda that served as the main building. The beige, stucco-faced building with a red-tile roof welcomed her with a wide front porch lined with rocking chairs and small seating areas that begged her to have a seat. Bougainvillea softened the edge of the porch with green leaves and colorful flowers. The Spanish feel to the place felt like home to her. A valet hurried out to greet her.

Smiling, Willow got out of the car and gave him her keys. “I won’t be long. I just want to have a look around and maybe grab a bite to eat.”

He bobbed his head. “Of course. I’ll park the car for you. Just tell the staff at the front desk when you’re ready to leave and someone will bring the car to the entrance.” There were no other cars parked in sight.

“We don’t like to keep cars in front of the building,” he explained. “It makes it seem too commercial. I’ll park your car off to the side.”

“Thanks,” Willow said, impressed by the idea of keeping the view of the inn unimpeded by cars.

She walked inside. Polished Mexican tile spread on the floor before her, their reddish-brown color broken by thick woven rugs of American Indian designs. Dark wooden beams crossed the high, off-white ceiling. Turquoise pots holding a variety of flowers, green plants, and cacti were strategically placed around the lobby/living area. Brown leather couches and chairs offered comfortable seating.

Willow walked over to the front desk. “Hello, I’m wondering if the manager is in. If so, I’d like to speak to him.” She handed the staff member one of the business cards Alec had had made for her, stating her management position at the Desert Sage Inn.

The young man studied the card and nodded. “Let me see if he’s available.”

Moments later, a short, stout, white-haired man appeared. He smiled at Willow and held out his hand. “George Hartmann. What can I do for you, Ms. Sanchez?”

“I’m wondering if I might talk to you privately. I will be completing my job for Alec Thurston at the Desert Sage Inn and I’m looking for other opportunities.”

He blinked in surprise. “I heard Alec was sick. Is it bad?”

Willow nodded. “I’m afraid so.”

“Come with me,” said George. “Alec is an old friend. I want to know more.”

He led her to an office behind the front desk and urged her to sit down in one of the two chairs facing his carved oak desk. “So, it’s true? Alec is retiring?” George said, taking a seat behind his desk and looking at her with concern.

“I’m afraid he’s dying, Mr. Hartmann,” Willow said, unable to hide the tears that stung her eyes. “Alec called two other women and me back to the hotel to help him with the forthcoming sale of it. After that, I’ll need a new job. I’ve taken the liberty of bringing my resumé.” She handed it to him.

He took it and looked it over. “Now I remember ... Alec sponsored you for the hotel school at Cornell, one of the best. I know how highly he thinks of you, and to bring you back now speaks volumes. You say he’s selling the hotel?”

“Yes,” said Willow. “I can’t say more about it, but it’s true.”

George studied her. After a few minutes he spoke. “I’m getting close to retirement, but I’m not ready to move on that yet. Why don’t I keep your information and call you should I be ready to think of making changes?”

“That would be wonderful,” Willow said. “I haven’t approached larger properties because after being at the Desert Sage Inn, I can’t think of moving in that direction. “

“Understandable,” said George. “We have a lot of hotels in the area, but none quite as fine as some of these special operations. I’m sure you understand managing a property like this is a lot like having a bed and breakfast.” He chuckled. “With a whole lot more to it. But knowing your guests and pampering them is the same. We limit our advertising because our guests are friends of friends and repeats of all ages.”

“For good reason. Before I go, I’d like to look around.”

"Be my guest," said George, getting to his feet. "Some of the smaller guest houses in the back are meant to be very private because of the prominence of our guests. I'm sure you understand."

"Of course," Willow said, more intrigued than ever about the property. Hollywood stars and government officials liked the privacy at The Premio. She shook hands with George. "I appreciate your taking the time to see me."

"You're welcome. Please remember me to Alec. He's a fine man, a gentleman. He and I discussed joining forces at one time, but he went on to grow his property while I've kept mine smaller."

George walked her to the lobby and left her there to rediscover the little inn she already loved. She reminded herself that the chance to work here would be slim. George had a reputation for being old-fashioned and had always had a male as his assistant. Still, as she walked through the public spaces and outside to the private cottages tucked in among foliage here and there, she vowed if the opportunity arose to work at The Premio, she'd take it.

CHAPTER TWENTY-THREE

LILY

Lily was awakened by a call from Brian. "Morning," she said sleepily. "Is everything all right?"

"Becky died last night."

Lily sat up, alert now. "I'm sorry, Brian. I really am. Where's Ollie?"

"He's still asleep and has no idea what's happened. Any suggestions for what I should say to him?"

"I don't know what her family's religious beliefs are, but I've found after spending so much time with Izzy that the truth is always important. Right now, he probably needs to know he's not alone, that he's going to be with you in the future. You know how much he loved his mother, and it's okay to be sad about her death."

"That's pretty much what Susannah said. She and I are going to tell him together. I'll stay here for the memorial service, then come back to Palm Desert."

"Alone?" asked Lily.

"Yes, I've agreed to do what Susannah suggested. Ollie will stay with her until school is out. We'll Skype or do FaceTime as often as we can. I'll come visit every couple of weeks. She'll continue working with him on the idea of living with me and leaving her."

"That sounds like a healthy plan. He needs to know he can trust you with the next phase of his life."

"Yes, I know. I won't let him down," said Brian.

Lily smiled at the determination in his voice. Brian would

be there for Ollie.

"I've been looking through the listings the real estate agent sent you," he continued.

"Oh, good. Do you want me to follow through on any for you? I know how anxious you must feel about the situation, and I'm more than happy to help. It gives me a chance to look over different areas."

"Are you sure you don't mind doing this? I suppose I could wait, but Nan said other buyers were interested."

"It's no trouble. I wouldn't offer if I wasn't sincere about helping you."

Brian let out a sigh of relief. "Okay, there are two I'd like checked out. I want to be sure either place would be suitable for a family with a dog."

"Which ones are you talking about?" Lily reached for the notepad and pen she kept at her bedside. She jotted down the listing numbers and addresses as he gave them to her. "I'll do that today. Nan said for me to call her if you had any interest."

"Thanks. It means a lot to me. Talk to you later. The family is beginning to stir."

She clicked off the call, please by his confidence and trust in her.

That afternoon, Lily gamely walked through two properties that would definitely house a young family and dog, but she wasn't excited about either one.

"Do you have anything else in this location?"

Nan leafed through one of the sales books she carried and paused. "Here's one you might like. It's a little more expensive, but there's wiggle room in the price because it needs to be repainted and needs new carpeting throughout the interior. It does, however, have an updated kitchen and a nice, fenced-in, outdoor pool area. It's been empty for a while now."

As soon as Nan pulled her car into the driveway, Lily's interest grew. There was something intangible about the white-stucco, one-story house that appealed to her. A small courtyard was part of the front entry. Double wooden doors painted green welcomed people inside.

"Nice, huh?" said Nan, opening the front gate.

"So far," Lily replied, working to remain noncommittal.

Nan unlocked the front door and motioned her inside.

Lily stepped into the house and emitted a soft gasp. Bold, primary colors on different walls in the open living area were shocking. "Oh, my! You were right. The colors are awful. It's going to take a competent painter to cover them up."

Nan nodded her agreement. "That's why the house hasn't sold. But if you put that aside and look at the bones of the house, and mentally replace the color on the walls and the worn carpeting, this house is a gem."

Nan led her to the kitchen. In contrast to the colors elsewhere, the kitchen was charming with its black and white theme. From there, they went into one wing of the house where the master suite and a small office were located. In the opposite wing, three bedrooms and two and a half baths were more than enough for Brian and his family and would allow visitors if he wanted.

Outside, the pool area reminded Lily of a smaller version of the one at Alec's house. Lush landscaping inside a wooden fence made the yard and pool private. A covered patio had enough space for both dining and relaxing. It even had an outdoor grill built in, along with a small refrigerator.

Lily knew in a heartbeat that she'd love a house like this, had felt it from the moment she saw it. But it wasn't her choice. To be fair, she'd include information on all three properties and report back to Brian.

"Thanks for showing me this," said Lily. "I'll be in touch with Brian later today and call you back if he has interest in any of the houses you toured with me."

"Okay," said Nan. "If it's a no, we'll just keep working until we find something he wants."

Lily smiled, wondering what the future was going to hold for Brian and her. She loved being with him, but too much had changed in his life to be sure of anything like that.

Rather than interrupt him, Lily texted Brian, telling him she'd put together information for him to look at regarding houses and asked him to call when he was free.

She was surprised when he responded, *Will call you later.*

At Alec's house, feeling a bit unsure about her relationship with Brian, Lily wandered outside to the pool area. Alec was lying on a chaise lounge under an umbrella.

She walked over and sat down in a chair beside him. "Hi! How are you doing today?"

"Actually, a little better. Something about being outside." He smiled at her. "Juanita said you're house hunting."

"Not for me, but for Brian." She told him about the situation with Ollie. "I've offered to help Brian find a suitable place for Ollie and the dog to live with him."

"So, you and Brian are working together on this?" Alec's lips stretched into a wide smile.

"Yes, but I'm a little confused about our relationship right now because of what's happened. We'd already agreed to see where it would take us."

"Seems to me he wouldn't have you look at houses for him unless he was serious about you."

"I'm not sure. Remember, he's accustomed to my helping him with projects at the hotel."

Alec squeezed her hand with encouragement. "Trust me. I

think he's really interested in you. He and I had a little talk a while back." His eyes twinkled. "All three of you Flowers are looking to make a home here. That makes me happy."

Lily gave him a grateful nod. "I'd forgotten how much I like it here. Working for Bennett Williams is going to be an excellent way to get back into the work force without falling into the rut I was in back in New York."

"Ben's a bit of a character, but a trustworthy man nevertheless. How's your sister?"

Lily shook her head. "I've tried to get in touch with her, have left several messages but still haven't heard from her. If she doesn't call me soon, I'm going to fly back east. I'm really worried about her being with her old boyfriend. It's not a healthy situation."

"She's lucky to have you for a sister. I remember how close you were at one time."

"Yes, well, she's always needed me. Especially after Izzy came." Lily got to her feet and gave him a kiss on the cheek. "Better go check my phone." She hesitated and then blurted, "I love you, Alec."

His eyes filled. "Love you too, Lily."

Lily left him, marveling at the way their relationship had evolved. He was a man she'd once been in love with. Now, she simply loved him.

Lily went to her room and tried to reach her sister once more.

"Hello?" Monica answered right away, surprising her.

"Hi! I've been trying to reach you. What's going on?"

"Nothing. I've been busy." There was an edge to Monica's voice that Lily didn't like. Suspicion crept through her. "Are you alone?"

"No," Monica replied. "Jeremy is here. I'm cooking him

dinner."

"He doesn't know about the pregnancy yet, does he?" Lily asked, praying Monica hadn't told him.

"I've been working a lot lately," Monica replied, ignoring Lily's question. "Why don't I call you later?"

At muffled conversation in the background, Monica added. "Guess I'll text you instead."

"Listen," said Lily. "I want you to come here as soon as possible. Perhaps next week. Do you think you can do that?"

"I'll call you later if I can." Monica's voice trembled. "Or maybe you'll call me." She clicked off the call.

Holding the phone in her hand, Lily suspected Jeremy had been overseeing her calls at Monica's end. She decided to ask Brian if Monica and Izzy could stay in his condo, in case Jeremy tried to follow Monica to California. No doubt Jeremy would know about Lily's connection to Alec's house, but not Brian's.

Later, when Brian called back, he sounded tired.

"How's it going?" she asked sympathetically.

"As well as can be expected. The service is set for tomorrow. Becky's chosen to be cremated so Ollie doesn't have to deal with a casket or a burial service. Susannah's trying to make it a celebration of Becky's life."

"Susannah sounds like a wonderful support for both Ollie and you," said Lily.

"She's been great," Brian said. "But I wish you were here with me."

"I'll come if you want," she said, pleased he'd mentioned it.

"Sometime in the future. Right now, it's too hectic and confusing for Ollie without introducing another person in his life. But, Lily, that doesn't mean I don't have ideas about our future," he added in a teasing way.

Happiness filled her. She'd needed that little bit of

reassurance. "Let me tell you about the houses I saw. There's one I particularly love, but all three have possibilities."

After giving him a description of the different properties, she said, "I'll text you pictures and email you the information I typed up."

"Thanks. I won't make any decisions until I see them for myself, but having you preview them for me is a big help."

"You're welcome, Brian. You know I'll help in any way."

"Yes, I know. It's the kind of person you are. I'm making reservations to come back to Palm Desert in three days' time. By then, Ollie and I would've had a chance to begin to get to know one another. He's been without a father figure except for Susannah's husband, Bill, and seems to like the attention." He chuckled. "He's fascinated by my prosthetic, like his cousins."

"I can see why. Kids that age love robots and bionics," said Lily, smiling,

"Hey, you're right. At least a part of me is bionic." The laughter in his voice faded. "I hope I can be a good dad to him."

"Just the fact that you care so much is a great start, Brian," she said. She couldn't help wondering how her life might've been different with a man like Brian as her father.

CHAPTER TWENTY-FOUR

ROSE

Rose looked up from working on her computer in Hank's hotel suite as he walked into the room. "Did you get the email from Brian?" she asked.

"Yes. That's why I was coming to find you. I just got off a call with Mitch and Duncan Armstrong. They want us to travel to Phoenix to check out the two properties there. Hopefully we can get some worthy shots of the hotel even though renovation is still going on. We can stage various areas if needed."

Hank walked over and kissed her on the cheek. "We can pretend our stay there is our honeymoon."

She laughed. Now that they were engaged, Hank was more anxious than she about setting a wedding date. As much as she liked the idea, she wasn't going to do anything about it while she was focusing on Alec and being there for him during his illness. She wanted her wedding to be a happy time.

"I ordered two rooms for us." She gave him a mischievous grin. "But I'm open to room service."

Playing along, he said, "I've heard it's very good."

They were laughing together as he drew her up into his arms. "Love you, Rose."

Later that day, they walked into the Blaise Group's hotel, The Desert Queen. Work was being done on the lobby, changing the paint color on the walls from a harsh red to a subtle light tan in order to showcase the new furniture that had been ordered. Some of the tall pottery pots planted with a variety of cacti would remain. Others would be replaced for being too garish.

Assessing the situation, Rose was happy the space itself was pleasing. With the new décor, it would become stunning. She bypassed the easel holding a sign apologizing for any inconvenience and telling about exciting news to follow. The sign was something she and Hank had worked on together. Even the smallest detail mattered.

On the exterior side of the room, she looked through the sliding-glass doors to the landscaping beyond where a new fountain was being installed. Brent Armstrong had bragged so much about the hotels in his family, she wondered if he would concede that the "dressing up" on this one really made a difference. But it wasn't the physical appearance alone that would make this hotel more in keeping with the Desert Sage Inn. Staff had to be trained and motivated to do a better job. That was something Willow was going to be working on along with John Rodriquez.

"What do you think?" asked Hank, coming up beside her. "Makes a big difference, huh?"

"Yes. I want a comprehensive tour of the property tomorrow. Today, I want to do pretty much what I did at the inn and act like a guest."

He grinned at her. "Want me to be Papa B?"

Smiling, she shook her head. The first time they'd met, she'd only known him as Leah's grandfather, Papa B. To her embarrassment he'd later been introduced to her as Hank Bowers, the man from The Blaise Group assigned to work opposite her.

After she got set in her room, Rose went down to the reception area and toured the restaurants. The gourmet restaurant needed a change-up of linens, crystal, silverware, and china but was fine otherwise. The main dining room for breakfast, lunch, and dinner was tired. She knew from reports that new furniture and carpeting had been ordered and would be in place soon. The colored-glass window that was a focal point on the outside wall showed a stunning desert scene. She'd seen a color board showing the proposed changes, and the color scheme of the new décor was centered around the colors in the window.

By the end of the afternoon, Rose felt better about including this hotel in the Corona Collection. The basic structure and layout were fine. As part of the staff training program, new uniforms were going to be handed out, eliminating the dark brown colors and shifting to a light turquoise for the tops and khaki or lighter tan for pants and skirts. A subtle thing that would add to the overall effect of making things a little classier.

Hank joined her at the fitness center, where she was taking photos for her blog. "Ready for a glass of wine?"

"Yes, I am. What do you think? Are we ready to sign up a professional photographer to do some shots of the hotel or should we wait? Two more weeks and the lobby and main restaurant should be done."

"I say we wait for the photographer. But after talking to management here, I'm happy with their plans going forward. Duncan and Mitchell are flying in tomorrow. We can talk to them then."

"All right. The printing company is standing by for the new brochures."

"That's settled then. Now, let's agree on where you want to go for dinner. Fancy? Or down home?"

"Hmmm. I was looking at the menu of the gourmet restaurant and saw a fish entrée I'd like to try."

"That's a deal. Let's swing by there to make a reservation

and then head out to the poolside bar to see what's happening there."

As they walked together, Rose glanced at Hank. She liked the fact that a simple thing like making plans for the evening was so easy between them. Though she'd stand firm when it came to defending Alec's wishes for his inn, she was more than happy to accommodate Hank on choices like this.

He turned to her and smiled. "A lot has happened to us since I was last here. I'm so glad you agreed to marry me."

"Me, too." It had taken the support of his daughters to make that happen. She'd always be grateful to them for it.

CHAPTER TWENTY-FIVE

LILY

Lily stood inside the Palm Springs International Airport terminal, her nerves doing a tap dance inside her. Brian and she had talked on the phone every day. She'd listened to his worries and his hopes for the future with Ollie and his dog, Jake. They'd even talked about the house he might like to buy. But they hadn't discussed their relationship. Seeing him now, like this, would tell her a lot.

His flight's arrival was announced. She joined the throng of people gathered at the end of the hallway where deplaned passengers entered the baggage claim area.

She drew a deep breath and waited as several people walked toward her. She saw Brian behind them. He seemed lost in his thoughts, but when their gazes connected, a broad smile stretched across his face and he waved with enthusiasm.

Tears of relief stung her eyes. She hadn't imagined the connection between them.

He walked right up to her, dropped his carry-on bag, and wrapped his arms around her. "I'm so happy to see you, Lily."

She smiled and hugged him. "It's wonderful to have you back home. You look as if you need a rest."

"Yeah." He rubbed a hand across his bristly cheek. "I haven't had a decent night's sleep since before I left."

"It's a lovely afternoon for a nap next to the pool at Alec's house. He suggested I invite you."

"Sounds great," said Brian with a yawn. "Let's drop my bags off at my condo, and I'll grab my trunks." He picked up his bag and took hold of her hand.

She walked alongside him to her car. "It's not fancy, but it's mine," she said, as she unlocked her Honda Civic.

"I appreciate the ride." He struggled to place his long legs in the small passenger side but didn't complain as he immediately slid the seat as far back as it would go.

"How's Ollie doing?" she said as she pulled out of the lot.

Brian nodded thoughtfully. "He's a strong kid and clearly loves his aunt and her family. But I think we connected. He understands that for the next several weeks, he'll be staying with Susannah, but that he's eventually going to be living with me. He's excited about having a house with a pool and," he gave her a sheepish grin, "I've agreed to his getting a pet gecko."

Lily sucked her in breath. "Wow! That's real commitment on your part."

He chuckled. "Wait until you meet Ollie. He's a pretty impressive little guy." He grew serious. "He's a lot like I was at his age."

"Genetics are pretty amazing. I can't wait to see him."

Brian gave her hand a squeeze. "I think you're going to like him. It's important to me."

She pulled into his condo development, parked the car, and turned to him. "It's important to me too."

He unbuckled his seat belt and cupped her face in his hands. Her heart fluttering, she closed her eyes as his lips met hers. His kiss told her how much he'd missed her, how special she was to him. She wrapped her arms around him wanting to hold on forever, then realized she was being held back by her seat belt.

He released the buckle, bring their bodies closer, and continued kissing her.

When they pulled apart, they were both breathless.

"Come on inside. I'll get things set and then we can go. But, first, I want to give you a proper kiss." His smile lit his craggy features, and Lily wondered if Ollie had the same smile.

Later, sitting on the pool deck at Alec's house, Lily watched Brian remove his prosthesis. It didn't bother her to see the stump of his leg. Her gaze swept over every inch of him with admiration as he sat in his blue swim trunks. She remembered what it was like to make love with him and felt a surge of desire. He was a fabulous lover.

As if he knew what she was thinking, he looked up at her.

Heat rushed to her cheeks, and a smile spread across his face. He'd already asked her to spend the evening with him.

He signaled her to come closer.

She stepped to his side and then braced her feet on the pool deck as he stood, using her for balance. Together they made their way to the edge of the pool and there, Brian dove in, leaving her to follow.

Since coming to Alec's house, Lily had made use of the pool. She knew she'd never be as strong a swimmer as Rose, but she'd improved a lot.

Her face broke through the water's surface and she came face-to-face with Brian who'd moved closer to her. Smiling, she stood and wrapped her arms around him. They were just about to kiss when she heard a voice say, "Welcome, Brian!"

She turned to see Alec making his way slowly toward them. She got out of the pool and helped him into a chair. "Thanks for the suggestion to invite Brian here."

Alec's lips curved and a once-familiar twinkle came to his eyes. "Wanted to get some information directly from him." He held up his hand to stop Brian from leaving the pool. "Enjoy your swim. We'll talk later."

Lily dove back into the water and began to do laps in the

pool to work off the surge of sexual energy she'd shared with Brian. She could well imagine what a midnight romp in the pool would be with him. No wonder Rose had taken to talking about nighttime swims with Hank.

After both she and Brian had swum enough, they got out of the pool and made their way over to chairs beside Alec.

"While you two talk, I'm going to change my clothes. Unless you want me here, Alec."

Alec shook his head. "We'll fill you in when you get back. This is unofficial business."

Lily headed inside, then stopped and turned around. "You're not doing anything crazy, are you, Alec?"

He laughed. "Me? No never."

She hesitated and then left them. When she returned a short while later, showered and dressed for a casual evening, Alec and Brian were dozing in their chairs. Studying them, she smiled. She loved both men—Alec as someone who'd accepted the shy, unworldly woman she'd been and had shown her how special a strong relationship could be, and Brian for loving her as she was.

As she approached, Brian opened his eyes and smiled at her. Quietly, she pulled up a chair and sat beside him, hoping not to disturb Alec.

Alec's eyes fluttered open, and he straightened in his chair. He stared at her sleepily and then a smile creased his face. "There you are, Lily. Looking very pretty, too."

"Thanks, Alec," she said, suddenly shy as the men gave her approving looks.

"Brian and I discussed a number of topics while you were gone," said Alec. "It seems both of you are intending to stay in the area. I'm sure Brian will have a lot of options here. As you know, Bennett Williams, is interested in having him come in as a partner because of his previous work as a lawyer."

"But I work there," said Lily. "That might not be a good idea."

Brian shook his head. "Don't worry. I won't interfere with your job. I've got lots to think about and some time to do it." He lifted her hand and squeezed it. "But I do need your help in finding a house. You will go with me tomorrow, right?"

She nodded. "Yes. I'm anxious for you to see the one I especially like."

"I like how the two of you get along," said Alec. "Now, I must make my way back to my room. Lily, dear, will you help me?"

Lily got to her feet. "Of course."

They slowly walked to Alec's wing of the house. On her arm, Alec seemed just a shadow of his former self. Cancer was such an ugly disease.

After she'd made sure Alec was seated comfortably in the lounge chair and she'd notified Juanita as he'd asked, he took hold of her hand.

"Brian is a good man. He's assured me he has real feelings for you. If you want to pursue this relationship, you have my blessing."

Lily clapped a hand to her mouth. "Oh, my God! You sound like a protective father." She didn't know whether to laugh or cry.

"I feel that way. I want you to be happy."

Her vision blurred as she bent over and kissed his cheek for this very sweet moment.

When she returned to Brian, he grinned at her. "Did Alec tell you I passed his test?"

"Test?"

Brian nodded. "Alec warned me against hurting you. I told him I never would."

"I'm sorry ..." she began. "I had no idea ..."

"What's up with you and Alec?" he asked, giving her a puzzled look.

"I dated him for two years several years ago. It didn't work out because I was looking for something permanent, and he'd warned me he wasn't." She took a seat next to Brian. "I was a young, inexperienced, wounded woman. He saw that and befriended me. When it became too serious, he ended it. To be honest, he's the first man to ever show me a supportive, warm relationship. My childhood was a nightmare. You can't know what his caring meant to me."

Brian drew a deep breath and nodded. "If what you've told me about your mother is part of that, I understand."

They gazed at one another silently.

Then Brian said, "I won't hurt you, Lily. I promise." He drew her onto his lap and held her tight.

She leaned against him and felt tension ease from her shoulders. As embarrassed as she'd briefly been by Alec's actions, she loved him for it.

After they left Alec's house, they went to the hotel and into The Joshua Tree restaurant to grab a quick supper. Though neither had spoken of it, they both were anxious to get to Brian's condo and the privacy they'd find there.

Dinner was constantly interrupted by staff members coming to their table to greet Brian. Lily was impressed by their sincere interest in him. He was a nice guy who treated everyone well.

By the time they were ready to leave the restaurant and hotel, she was more than ready for time alone with him. From the sexy look he gave her when they stood in front of his condo, so was he.

As soon as the door was locked behind them, Brian took

her in his arms and moved a hand to her waist to draw her closer. "Sorry dinner lasted so long. I've wanted to have you here alone with me all evening.

"Me, too," she murmured before his lips came down on hers.

As Brian kissed and caressed her, desire shot through her. No man had ever made her feel quite this way, as if two pieces of a puzzle were finally fitting together.

Brian stepped back. "Before we sit and talk, come with me," he said, his low voice thick with passion.

She took the hand he held out to her and followed him into his bedroom. More comfortable with one another, Lily was soon awash in wave after wave of pleasure.

Later, lying beside him, she placed a hand on his strong chest and felt the rapid beat of his heart. And from the smile on his face, Lily knew he was as satisfied as she.

As she lay with him, Brian began to tell her more about his past week.

"Watching Ollie, talking to him, and realizing he was mine was mind-blowing. I'm going to make this work with Ollie. Other fathers have months to get used to the idea. I'll just have to deal with it."

"You're going to make a wonderful father," Lily said, thinking of her own wishes.

He turned to her. "Thanks, but I don't want other children. It wouldn't be fair to them. I'm fifty-two with some limitations."

Lily's eyes rounded with surprise. "What limitations are you talking about? As far as I can tell, you have none."

He stared at her for a moment and then chuckled happily. "I guess I was thinking of one of my ex-girlfriends and how she thought my life was limited because of this stump." He caressed her cheek. "Thanks, Lily."

"I mean it, Brian."

"I know, but I really think one child at this stage in my life is enough. Would you be willing to agree to that moving forward?"

Lily swallowed hard. She'd always wanted children, wasn't sure she could or should have them. "I'm not certain I can have children of my own. At my age, I've been warned it might never happen."

"How about we share Ollie? He'll need a mother too."

She sat up and stared at him. "Are you asking me to marry you?"

"It would make sense, wouldn't it?"

"What!! A marriage of convenience? No, thanks!"

So hurt she couldn't breathe, she hopped out of bed, grabbed her clothes and raced into the bathroom. Tears streamed down her face as she struggled to dress and ignored the pounding on the locked door.

"Lily! Please! Listen to me. Everything came out all wrong. I didn't mean to make it seem that way."

She opened the door and faced him.

Visibly upset, he reached for her.

She stood her ground. "You'd ask me to marry you so I could be a mother to Ollie. That's it?"

"No! I ... Why do you think Alec asked to see me?" He ran a hand through his thick brown hair and gazed at her with the hazel eyes she loved so much. "I asked him for permission to marry you."

"What? When?" She stopped. "You mean while I went inside to get dressed, you and he talked about proposing to me?" Her eyes filled. She recalled her earlier conversation with Alec and knew it to be true.

"This isn't a last-minute thing. It's something I thought of before Ollie even was part of the picture. I've spoken to my mother about you, even picked up a family ring the last time I saw her. I was so sure I was right about you."

Lily sat on the edge of the bed, letting those thoughts run through her head. She looked up at him and saw the misery on his face.

"Come here, Lily," he said softly, drawing her to her feet and up against him. "I know the timing seems crazy, but while I was away all I could think of was you back here and how you fill all the parts of me that I've been missing. I love you, Lily, and I always will. I'm asking you now. Will you marry me?"

She studied him, seeing his sincerity. He'd always been honest with her. Like everyone kept saying, he was a good man. "Yes! Oh, yes!" she cried throwing her arms around him and hugging him tight.

"Wait! Hold on!" With the help of his walker, he moved away from her.

Though there was a part of her that wanted to help him, she waited while he made his way to the bedside table and back to her.

"I'd kneel, but it'd take me a while to get up," he joked. Holding the small, black velvet box open, he said, "Lily Weaver, would you do me the honor of being my bride, my wife, my love?"

Lily clasped her hands and nodded, crying too hard to speak. Through blurred vision, she gazed at the beautiful marquise diamond flanked by two others and felt as if all her dreams were wrapped up in this moment. She'd waited so long for the right man to come along. And now that she'd found him, she couldn't stop her tears of joy.

He hugged her tight. "There, there. Is it all so bad?"

She chuckled and smiled up at him. "No, it's all so right."

He slipped the ring onto her finger.

She stared at it, thinking how perfect the ring looked on her hand. For the first time in her life, she was sure her future would be bright.

CHAPTER TWENTY-SIX

WILLOW

When Willow walked into the kitchen the next morning, she saw Rose and Lily huddled together at the kitchen table.

"What's up?" she asked, still trying to wake up after a restless night.

"Lily's engaged!" said Rose, waving her over. "Come see her ring! It's gorgeous!"

Smiling, Lily held out her left hand. "I wouldn't care what it looked like, but I do love this."

Willow studied the ring and gave Lily a hug. "You and Brian make such a cute couple. I'm so happy for you!"

Rose nudged Lily. "Tell her about Alec."

"Oh, yes. Alec knew before I did. Brian asked him for permission to marry me. Isn't that sweet?" Lily's eyes grew moist. "I was surprised, then very pleased."

"That's very touching. Alec's like a second father to me," said Willow. She glanced at the other two women. "When he says we're his Desert Flowers he means it in the best way."

They nodded their agreement.

"Who would've thought two of us would be engaged?" Lily said to Rose. They turned and smiled at Willow. "You're next!"

Willow held up her hand. "Whoa! Not me. I haven't met anyone I'm that interested in. Besides, work had to come first for a while. I've got challenges to meet for the inn and then I'm going to find a job here. Like you two, I want to stay."

"Do you know where you want to work?" Rose said.

Willow smiled. "I've got my eye on the Premio Inn. I've already talked to George Hartmann."

"Really? What did he say?" asked Rose.

"Nothing much except he's thinking of retirement and would keep my resumé. But I know how chauvinistic he is, so I'm not sure if it's wise to be hopeful."

Rose nodded. "I've heard that, too. He's never hired a woman, not even for housekeeping."

Lily took hold of her hand. "Don't give up dreaming about it, Willow. Look's what happened to Rose and me."

Willow didn't know if Lily was talking about working at the hotel or giving up on the idea of marriage. In either case, she couldn't worry about it now. She was headed to Arizona to help John do some training at the Desert Queen Hotel.

CHAPTER TWENTY-SEVEN

LILY

Lily left the kitchen bubbling with excitement. She knew from her sister's work schedule that Monica should be up by now after working a night shift. Fresh excitement filled her as she picked up her phone to call her. Though she'd left text messages during the last week, she hadn't had a chance for a real conversation with her.

In the privacy of her bedroom, she punched in Monica's number and waited in eager anticipation for her to pick up.

A soft voice said, "hello?"

"Monica, is that you?" Lily listened to the sound of someone walking, then the opening and closing a door, and Monica said, "Hi, Lily!" in a clear voice.

"What's going on?" Lily asked.

"I have to be quiet. Jeremy is sleeping."

"Is he staying over at your apartment now?" Lily asked, trying to keep worry from choking her.

"He had to. He has nowhere else to go," said Monica in a defensive tone.

Lily swallowed hard, though she wanted to scream in frustration. "Have you thought more about coming out to California?"

"I really want to, but Jeremy doesn't think it's wise for me to take time off from my job. He says it's too hard to find work."

"Listen, I want you to at least come for a visit. I'll find someplace for you to stay. Let's aim for next week. But,

Monica, don't tell Jeremy about your plans. He'll try to do something to ruin them."

"Do you think I can sneak away like that? Really? He barely lets me out of his sight." Excitement crept into Monica's voice.

"He has to sleep sometime, Monica. You and Izzy can leave, go to the city for a day or two, then get on a flight."

"Let me think it over," said Monica, sounding more like herself. "Is that the only reason you called?"

"No! Actually, I called to tell you I'm engaged!"

"Engaged? But you've only been gone a couple of months. Are you crazy?"

Disappointment pounded through Lily. "Crazy in love with him. And though it's happened quickly, I'm ready to commit the rest of my life to him. I want you and Izzy to meet him. You'll see for yourself what a decent, kind man he is. In the meantime, I'll send you a picture. His name is Brian Walden. He's older than I am and a war veteran." She stopped and then gushed, "Oh, Monica! He's the best thing that's ever happened to me."

"Great, Lily," said Monica in a monotone. "I gotta go. Jeremy is calling."

The silence that followed told her Monica had ended the call.

Lily tried to tell herself that Monica meant well, but the hurt that coursed through her was real. She realized that in a short amount of time, Rose and Willow were more like sisters than her own.

Deflated by the call, Lily wandered out to the pool. Alec was stretched out in a lounge chair. Happy to see him, she trotted over to him.

"Alec! Just the person I want to see. Brian told me he asked your permission to marry me."

Alec lifted up on his elbows and smiled. "And?"

"And this." Lily held out her left hand. "He asked, and I said yes. I owe you a thank you."

Her eyes filled. "Your approval means so much to me."

He kissed her hand. "I'm happy for you. Brian is a fine man and you're a special lady. I like the thought of the two of you together."

She sat down in a chair next to his. "Some people might think everything happened too quickly, but I know he's right for me."

"There are times we have to ignore others' criticisms, especially when our heart has already spoken. You and Brian are both old enough to know what you want."

"At first, I thought he wanted to rush things because of Ollie and how I could take care of him ..." Lily let her voice trail off.

"I'm sure that's a factor, but knowing Brian as I do after speaking to him privately, I assure you that's not the case. He fell for you early on. As I said, you're a very special woman. He saw that in you right away."

Lily released her breath in a happy puff. Since the first day they'd shared an early morning walk, she'd felt something amazing happen between them. She wasn't crazy like her sister said. She was a woman madly in love with a man who made her feel as if she belonged with him.

She stood and bent over to kiss Alec's cheek. "While we're talking about special people, I want you to know how special you are to me. Thank you for your many kindnesses."

Still feeling emotional, she left the pool area and went inside to check airline information for her sister and Izzy. Somehow, she'd get them out to California. Safely.

Later, as promised, she met Brian at the realtor's office. Nan Bishop greeted her enthusiastically when Lily walked into her office and found Brian already there.

"So glad you could join us." She beamed at Lily. "I understand congratulations are in order. Brian told me he's popped the question and you've accepted."

"Yes," Lily said, smiling at Brian. She kissed his cheek and sat down in a chair beside him.

"Sweet. It's always helpful when I know the woman involved already likes it. But to be fair, I'll show Brian all three houses, as we agreed." She turned to her computer. "I'm showing him the information online and then we'll go visit."

"Okay," said Lily. She sat quietly as Brian was briefed on each house. If necessary, she'd speak up, but she wanted Brian to be able to judge for himself which house he liked best, if at all.

As Nan had done earlier, she drove to the first two houses before taking them to the third house—the house Lily already loved.

As with the other two houses, Brian remained quiet until he'd toured this one. He turned to her. "What do you think, Lily? I like this one a lot."

Lily clapped her hands joyfully. "I *love* this one! The paint colors are awful, but easily fixed. The carpet needs to be replaced, but the rest of the house is in great condition. The outside is perfect for a boy and a dog."

Brian laughed. "I guess you've got it figured out. Okay, let's go through the house room by room and make a list of what needs to be done. Then I want to check out the plumbing and heating and all those sort of things."

"Deal." She gazed at him, feeling such love she thought she'd burst.

"Tell you what? I've got some calls to make. I'll leave you two alone and go to the car."

"Thanks," said Brian, drawing Lily to his side. After Nan

discreetly left the living area, Brian smiled at her. "Can you see us living happily together here? Is this house what you really want? We can look at others."

"Are you pleased by the thought of owning this house? Neither of us has seen the other's previous home, so I'm trusting you to be honest with me."

"If everything else checks out, and the house inspections are acceptable, I'd like to make an offer." They walked outside onto the pool deck. "This fenced-in yard is great for Jake, and Ollie will love the pool. I like the outdoor kitchen area for me. What about you?"

"I love the dining space as well as an outdoor living space."

"Okay. Now let's go through the interior again."

As they stood at the threshold of each room, they talked about how it could be used. The room they picked for Ollie was perfect with a Jack-and-Jill bath that led to a guest room. A third room could be used as a home gym or an office. The master suite was both spacious and private, with a sliding door leading out to the pool and spa area.

"I think that does it," said Brian, nodding with satisfaction. "I'm going to check out the appliances."

Lily waved. "Go ahead. I'm going to jot down notes about paint colors for each of the rooms." After he left her and she'd made her notes, Lily walked out to the pool, slipped off her sandals, sat down at the edge of the pool, and put her feet in the water. Wiggling her toes with pleasure, Lily lifted her face to the blue sky and whispered a soft, "thank you" for the way her life was turning out.

She thought of Ollie, the little boy she had yet to meet, and hoped she'd be a good step-mother to him. He was the only child she'd share with Brian. She wished she could get Monica to understand how important it was for her and Izzy to move California. But she knew if she pushed too hard, Monica would never come. It was a big sister, little sister thing.

At Brian's condo, Lily sat with him at his computer, reviewing the pros and cons they'd made for the house after he'd looked at all the mechanicals. He'd already told Nan he wanted to make an offer. Now they were estimating the cost to make the house the way they wanted. It felt surreal to Lily that in such a short time she'd become engaged, had selected a house with Brian, and had committed to be there not only for him but for his son, Ollie, and Ollie's dog, Jake. Every time she started to feel overwhelmed, she told herself it was everything she'd always wanted. The only thing that made her unhappy was her sister's response to the engagement. Monica didn't even know about Brian's new family.

After Brian and Nan talked about a reasonable offer, he made arrangements to drop off a check as earnest money at her office.

When he hung up the phone, he said, "Nan's pretty confident the owners will take my offer because the house has been on the market for so long. Before we go out to dinner to celebrate, I want to call my mother so she can 'meet' you."

"Oh, my word! What is she going to say? First, you tell her you have a son and now you're going to tell her you're engaged?"

Brian chuckled. "It's not like that at all. You'll see." He set up a FaceTime call on his computer and moments later, a pretty, gray-haired woman with a quick smile and kind eyes answered.

"Hello, son! How are you?"

"Hi, Mom! There's someone I want you to meet."

"Is it Lily? Did she say 'yes?'"

Lily's jaw dropped. She gave Brian a questioning look.

He grinned. "I told Mom about you weeks ago. Said I'd met

the woman I wanted to marry. Say 'hi' to my mom, Irene Walden. Everyone calls her 'Reenie.'"

Lily clasped her cold fingers and sat still as Brian moved the computer so they were facing his mother together. "Hello, Mrs. Wal ... Reenie. It's nice to meet you. I want you to know that though it seems sudden, I really do love your son."

"He's very loveable, isn't he?" she responded. "And what do you think of Ollie? How do you feel about having a nine-year-old boy in your life, along with a new husband? I already adore being a grandmother. I thought it would never happen."

"I haven't met Ollie yet, but I'm excited to do so. I've always wanted a family, so you can imagine how very lucky I feel. And I love the ring. Brian said it's a family piece of jewelry. That means so much to me."

Reenie beamed at them. "I'm so happy you like it, dear. It once belonged to my mother. I can't wait to meet you in person, Lily. I'm planning on going to Austin to meet Ollie the next time Brian is there. Then later, after things are in place with the two of you, I'll come to Palm Desert. Any idea when the wedding is going to take place?"

Lily and Brian glanced at one another. "We haven't talked about it, but not for a little while. I'm here in California to help a friend."

"We'll make sure Ollie is comfortable before making that happen," added Brian.

"Common sense," Reenie agreed. "I'm so happy for the two of you. Can't wait until I can see you in person, Lily. You're lovely."

"You're welcome to visit anytime, Mom. You know that," said Brian.

Reenie laughed. "I've got it marked on my calendar. Next week in Austin. Two weeks later, Palm Desert. Brian, please give Lily my email address so we can chat back and forth. I want to know everything about you, Lily, and I promise to give you all the family history on Brian's side, including all the little tricks he played on me growing up."

"Not that, Mom," groaned Brian playfully.

Reenie laughed. "It's only fair. Hopefully, Ollie will be as much an imp as you were."

"We'll see," said Brian. "Lily loves kids, so that's going to help with the transition."

"Very nice. Well, I have to go. It's suppertime here in Florida. Goodbye, loves."

The screen went blank.

Lily let out a sigh. "Your mother is wonderful."

He nodded. "Yeah, she is."

"And you told her about me several weeks ago? Really?"

Color flooded his cheeks as he took her face in his hands. "Yeah, I told you. I knew even then how I felt about you, but I didn't want to scare you off."

As his lips came down on hers, Lily knew that for as long as she lived, she'd remember this moment. He loved her! He really loved her!

CHAPTER TWENTY-EIGHT

WILLOW

Willow took a careful look around her as she walked into the Desert Queen Hotel in Phoenix, anxious to spot areas for improvement. Though it wasn't part of an assignment, she was using this time working for Alec as a refresher on hotel operations. Now that she'd decided she wanted to get back into that end of the business and to stay in Palm Desert, she was eager to put her knowledge to use.

Behind her, Brent Armstrong's voice was irritating as he bragged to an attractive young front desk clerk that this hotel was in the family and would be his one day. His cousin, Trace, remained quiet though he, not Brent, was the person more likely to run it.

The property was attractive and well-situated in the area, but studying it now, Willow could see how important the upgrades underway were to the overall atmosphere. Brent might tell her that hotels in the Blaise Group were fine, but his uncle and then his reluctant father, principal owners of the company, had agreed with Rose that it was smart to do some upgrading.

The resident manager, a man in his early forties, was due to meet them for lunch. Willow had reviewed the information about him and had seen his photo and was intrigued by the information that Luis "Lou" Molina hadn't attended hotel school but had, instead, worked his way up the ladder from the time he was a teenager who parked cars for the hotel's valet service.

Willow left the lobby and went to her assigned room. She had a short time before lunch to get unpacked and then do a little more investigation.

Her room was on the seventh floor overlooking the pool area. She hung her clothes and stepped out on the balcony. Palm trees swaying in the light breeze partially shaded the figure-eight pool and deck. Hotel guests reclined on chaise lounges and sat in chairs surrounding small tables under colorful umbrellas that provided protection from the sun. The sounds of laughter rose to greet her, and she smiled. Her love for the business came in part from a desire to make people feel happy and comfortable. On a hot day like this, an inviting pool was bound to make that happen.

She checked the facilities in the bathroom, surveyed the amenities, and left her room satisfied by what she saw.

Downstairs, she headed for The Sand Castle, the family restaurant. Lou would meet her there. She hoped she'd have a couple minutes alone with him before Brent and Trace showed up.

No such luck. The three men were standing at the entrance to the restaurant talking.

A look of irritation crossed Brent's face when he noticed her. Trace and Lou turned to face her.

Lou was of average height and build, with brown hair, and twinkling, light-brown eyes that radiated laugh lines, verifying his reputation as an amiable man.

"Ah, there you are," said Lou, holding out his hand to her. "Nice to finally meet you. I've heard excellent things about you." His smile reached his eyes.

Willow shook his hand, admiring his handsome features. "Thanks. I'm excited to be here to help train the staff. John Rodriguez sends his apologies, but a problem at the hotel came up that he had to handle."

"We probably could've handled it," said Brent, "but instead we're here to help Willow."

"It'll be helpful to have fresh eyes on procedures here," Trace said, smiling at her.

Grateful for his support, she said, "We want all hotels in the Corona Collection to have the same high standards of service and care for guests."

Lou took her elbow. "Let's get seated. We'll have lunch, and then I'll give you a tour of the hotel, especially the areas reserved for employees. We've surveyed our staff to see what suggestions they have for improvements."

As Lou led her through the restaurant, she noticed a number of people staring at them. But then, Lou was a striking man. Brent and Trace didn't have his flair but they, too, were attractive.

As soon as they were seated, a waitress came over to them and handed out plastic-coated menus. "Good afternoon. May I get you something to drink?"

Willow ordered iced tea, and the three men followed suit. After orders had been placed for lunch, Lou studied them. "How's it going, working together?"

"I think it's fair to say it's a learning experience for all of us," Willow promptly answered.

"Maybe for you," Brent said. "For me, it's pretty much the same old stuff."

Lou's eyebrows shot up. He turned to Trace. "And for you?"

"As I told my dad, I'm learning a lot. The more I see of the upscale operations, the more I like the concept of a Corona Collection of hotels. In this business nothing is static."

Lou nodded and smiled at him. "You're right about that. Wouldn't you agree, Willow?"

"Yes. That's one reason the industry is so exciting. People and times change, giving us new opportunities, but we have to reach for them. I love the challenges offered by the creation of the Corona Collection. The fact that Rose Macklin and Hank Bowers worked together on publicity materials for it is just one example of how our team has responded."

"Yeah, I was impressed by the imaginative approaches they came up with," Lou said.

"Did you know Willow and I went to the hotel school at Cornell together?" Brent said, grinning at her.

"Actually, not together," Willow said calmly, though anger had her pulse pounding at the thought of Brent trying to subtly poke at her or at Lou. And she wasn't about to let the remark go. "Brent was two years ahead of me. After he left, I was elected to head the student advisory board and was able to give a lot of input that helped the program. We addressed issues like bullying, talked to both faculty and students about the environment at the school, and recommended better ways of communication for such things as job openings at Statler Inn and teaching assistant positions in the school. I was also a TA for one of the Finance and Accounting professors in my senior year."

Brent opened his mouth to speak and closed it.

"It's that kind of leadership the Blaise Group is looking for," said Lou smoothly. "You're an old-fashioned hotelier like me. I understand you started at a young age too."

Willow smiled with satisfaction. "I did. Alec Thurston made sure I had a thorough grounding in the business."

"Mitchell Armstrong took me under his wing back in the day when the company was much smaller. Today, I help him with special intern programs for kids from all backgrounds. It's worked well to find management material."

"I was in one of those programs," Trace said, "before I went to the hotel school at the University of Nevada-Las Vegas. It helped a lot."

Willow smiled at him. Trace was the total opposite of Brent—unassuming, pleasant, nice. Too bad he came from a family full of people like Brent.

Their food came and conversation turned to the food and beverage operations. Willow listened to Lou talk about it as she ate her Southwest Salad—seasoned grilled chicken, corn, avocado, beans, and romaine lettuce all were tossed together in a lime vinaigrette.

When they'd all finished their meal, Lou signed the tab and rose. "Let's take that tour I was talking about. We'll start on the ground floor where a lot of back-of-house space is designated for staff. With over three hundred employees, it's important."

As they got to their feet, Willow ignored the glare that Brent had kept on his face. Brent's father might be one of the owners of the company, but both he and Brent had a lot to learn about people.

The tour was as insightful as Willow had thought it might be. To meet the standards of the Desert Sage Inn, employees and the property needed a lot more attention.

CHAPTER TWENTY-NINE

LILY

After deciding Mexican food was what they really wanted, Lily sat with Brian at Tico's restaurant thinking back to the one other time she'd come here with him. She'd thought it was going to be a date. Instead, it had become a gathering of a group from the hotel staff, with Brian acting as if she was just one of his co-workers.

"Remember last time we were here?" she said.

Brian nodded. "Talk about a date gone wrong. I was already afraid of making my feelings toward you known, and then everyone from the hotel was here."

"That's why I pulled back from you. I didn't know what to think."

He wrapped his fingers around her hand and squeezed it. "Now you do."

"Let's talk about the house," she said. "I've got the list of improvements we drew up earlier."

He laughed. "Okay, list lady. With luck, I'll hear soon whether my offer has been accepted. Nan assured me it would be, but until it's signed off on, I'm keeping an open mind."

"I have a confession to make," said Lily, hoping Brian would understand. "While you were still in Austin, I went ahead and made a list of contractors you might want to use for improvements on any house you might buy. As soon as a decision is made on the house, I've got the information on who to call to have work done."

Brian's features softened as he gazed at her. "I love that

you're so organized, Lily. I want to be able to move fast on getting into a new place."

"I figured as much. And now with your mother coming to visit, it's even more important."

"If necessary, Mom can stay at the hotel, but you're right. She'll want to be able to envision a place where she can visit in the future." Brian shook his head. "I can't believe all that's happened."

When the waitress approached and asked if they wanted another cocktail, both Lily and Brian gave her an enthusiastic, "Yes!"

That evening, as Lily sat with Brian on the couch in his condo, he said, "Are you sure you're happy with the house I'm buying? We can continue looking, if you wish."

She shook her head firmly. "No, I really like it. The house and neighborhood are perfect for a boy and a dog. Did you see the bicycles outside a couple of homes down the street? As I drove by, I checked the kids and I saw a couple of boys I thought might be Ollie's age. And then, when I stepped inside the house, it just felt right. You know?"

Brian grinned and nodded. "I like it too."

"What are you going to do about your job here?" said Brian.

Lily sat up and faced him. "What do you mean?"

"I know you've agreed to work part-time for Bennett, but I'm wondering if we can work something out so one of us is home with Ollie after school."

"One step at a time," said Lily, coolly. "I begin my training in a couple of days. And you already have the name of an available babysitter through Sarah. In the meantime, we'll have the whole summer to work things out. You haven't even found a new job yet."

He gave her a sheepish smile. "You're right. I'm jumping

the gun and expecting you to upend your life to care for Ollie. What an idiot! I'm sorry. I'm not the Neanderthal you might think. I'll be careful about any thoughts like this without talking it over with you first."

"Good, as long as you understand the *two* of us will be raising Ollie together. Though I'm excited to be part of our family, I won't be taking on all the child-rearing responsibilities alone."

"That's only fair." He pulled her closer. "I'm grateful you're such an important part of a family we have together. You were already part of my plans before I even knew about Ollie."

His kiss warmed Lily's insides. She'd always had a lot of responsibility for her sister, and it felt wonderful that, going forward, she'd have someone at her side to face the unexpected when she was helping others. Thinking of her sister, she said, "I can't wait for you to meet Monica and Izzy. In fact, I was wondering if they could stay at your condo for a few days when you are on one of your trips to Austin to spend time with Ollie. I'd stay there, too."

"No problem. There's room." Brian frowned. "Have you been able to convince her to come for a visit?"

"Not really. She wants to come, but she's worried how Jeremy will react. I've decided to fly to New York and get them both on a plane with me. A surprise visit might take care of any problem with her boyfriend."

Brian tipped her chin up and studied her with concern. "Promise me you'll be careful. It's an unstable situation."

"I know," she said softly. "That's what worries me."

Lily felt as if she was in the center of a tornado as the next few days unfolded. Brian's offer for the house was accepted, a home inspector completed his review and, surprisingly, came up with only a few minor issues, she helped line up a painting contractor, and together, she and Brian chose new carpeting to be installed after the painters left. Her training at the law firm began, keeping her days hectic. But both the work and the people there were exactly what she'd been hoping for.

To add to her full schedule, work for Alec continued with a couple of meetings being held to relay updated news to the transition teams. Willow made a great presentation about the training at the Desert Queen Hotel, and Rose and Hank presented samples of printed matter for all three hotels in the new Corona Collection. Things were slowly coming together. Or so it seemed. Both Brent Armstrong and his father, Duncan, were now questioning little bitty details, stalling issues related to changes in policy or how new procedures should be followed.

As Lily finished up her week of training at the law firm, Brian flew to Austin to meet his mother and introduce her to Ollie. While he was gone, Lily made it a point to spend as much time as she could at Alec's house. Being with Rose and Willow kept her grounded, and after all that was going on in her life, she needed that.

On Sunday, Brian called to say that instead of flying back to Palm Desert, he was going to spend the next week in Austin.

"I'll miss you," Lily said, but her mind was whirling. This would be a perfect time for her to fly to New York and bring Monica and Izzy out to California. Though he was concerned about her, and both Rose and Willow had offered to go with her, she knew she had to do this alone.

Aboard the flight to New York, Lily reviewed how she wanted to proceed. If she was lucky, she'd be able to talk to Monica in private before she was scheduled to go to work that evening. If not, she'd have a conversation with her tomorrow. Instead of taking a limo or cab from the airport, she'd rent a car so she'd have her own transportation. She hadn't called Monica to tell her she was coming, too afraid Jeremy would see any message or overhear a call and do something to prevent Monica from seeing her.

As passengers near her dozed off reading a book or watching a movie on the cross-country flight from L.A., nervous energy kept Lily awake. If things were as bad as she suspected between Monica and Jeremy, she had to act fast.

The flight was smooth, but the traffic from the airport to Ellenton was not. Though it was later than she'd hoped, she drove into Monica's apartment complex and parked near the entrance. Monica's car was gone, but the lights were on in her living room. She sat a moment unsure how to proceed when she saw Monica peek outside and quickly step away from the window.

Lily got out of the car, hurried to Monica's door, and knocked.

"Who is it?" Monica said.

"It's me, Lily!" She glanced around nervously.

Monica cracked the door open. "Lily? What are you doing here?"

"I came to see you. Quick! Open up, Monica." Until she knew where Jeremy was, she was scared.

Monica inched the door wider, grabbed hold of Lily's arm, and pulled her over the threshold, slamming the door and locking it behind her.

Lily studied the bruises on Monica's face and felt tears form when she noticed the cast on Monica's left arm. "What happened to you?"

Monica shrugged. "Jeremy says I'm clumsy."

"Bullshit! Where is he now?" Lily's pulse threaded through her in nervous beats.

"He's gone out with his friends. I'm to wait here with Izzy.

He fired Norma."

"Fired the babysitter? Why? Aren't you working?"

Monica shook her head. "Not for a while. He says it makes people suspicious to see me banged up this way."

Lily's stomach filled with acid. She took hold of Monica's shoulders and shook her gently. "Look at me. I'm here to help you. Where's Izzy?"

"She's asleep in her room. I keep her away from Jeremy as much as possible."

"When is Jeremy due back?"

Monica shook her head. "I never know. It could be anytime."

"Okay, you're coming with me! Understand? Grab your purse, any personal papers you can find, and a change of clothes. I'll pack some things for Izzy."

Monica stepped back. "No. Jeremy will be mad."

Panic filled Lily. "Monica, this is your only chance to escape from that monster. Trust me. We have to leave now. Hurry. I'll get Izzy."

Monica clapped a hand to her mouth and stared at her, blinking rapidly as if just coming awake. "Oh, my God! Okay. But we have to hurry."

Lily raced into Izzy's room, grabbed a change of clothes, shoes and socks and stuffed them into her purse. Then she knelt by the bed. "Hi, baby girl. It's Auntie Lee. We're going on an adventure."

She picked Izzy up and wrapped a blanket around her.

Moving as fast as she could, she carried Izzy to the car, quickly buckled her into the backseat and ran back to the apartment.

"Do you have everything you need? Grab all your keys!" Lily said, snatching one of Monica's baseball hats and placing it on her head.

"All set! Let's get the hell out of here!" Monica cried and slammed the door behind them.

They sprinted to the car.

"Get in back and get down on the floor," Lily ordered and slid behind the wheel. Her hands shaking, she started the engine and headed out.

They were at the entrance to the parking lot when Monica's car approached.

Lily tugged the hat down to cover her face and forced herself not to gun the engine as she continued to move forward. Grateful to be in a car Jeremy wouldn't recognize, she spoke softly to Monica, "Stay down. Stay down."

Once they were on the main street, Lily succumbed to the impulse to speed. Seeing Jeremy had shaken the core of her.

"Hey! Where are we going?" Monica cried from the backseat. "Slow down!"

"Sorry, I'm so nervous." Lily drew a breath to steady herself. "We're going to someplace close to the airport."

"Kennedy?"

"No," Lily said. "Jeremy might suspect we'd do that. We'll drive to Newark and find a flight from there sometime tomorrow."

At the sound of crying, Lily checked the rearview mirror. In the backseat, Monica had covered her face with her hands and was sobbing. Izzy, bless her heart, was a deep sleeper.

"Everything's going to be all right," said Lily, her voice trembling.

Monica shook her head. "You say that, but you don't know Jeremy. I'm afraid he'll find us. And if he does, he'll kill me like he's always saying."

"No, we're not going to let that happen," Lily responded with a burning determination. "When we get to California, we'll get help, find some sort of protection. For now, you're no longer under Jeremy's control. We're going to work together to keep it that way."

"Thank you, Lily! Thank you!" Monica started to cry again, deep racking sobs that brought tears to Lily's eyes.

She drew a deep breath. "All right, let's try to relax. I'll drive us into New Jersey and we'll find a motel where we can both get some rest."

"I'm exhausted," Monica admitted. "I feel as if I'll never be able to get enough sleep."

"Better call Norma and tell her what's happening. Even though she hasn't been babysitting recently, we don't want her anywhere near Jeremy."

"Okay. I'll do that now," said Monica.

As Lily drove through the darkness, she prayed they'd all be safe. She knew it wouldn't be easy, but they had to find a way to be free of Jeremy.

The next morning when Lily awoke from a disturbing dream, it took her a minute or two to understand where she was and how she'd gotten there. She turned to the double bed where Monica had been and sat up quickly. It was empty.

Still in her underwear, she jumped out of bed and peered out the window. In the playground to the side of the entrance to the motel, she saw Monica pushing Izzy on a swing. Relief, hot as lava, wove through her, stinging her eyes with tears. They were both so important to her. Telling herself to be calm, she threw on her clothes and went out to greet them.

As she approached, Izzy noticed her and cried, "Auntie Lee! Auntie Lee! We're on a 'venture!"

"Yes, sweetie! That we are!" She lifted the girl in her arms and hugged her tight. "I'm so happy to see you."

"Me too! Mommy said I was asleep when you got here."

"Yes, you were a big sleepyhead!" Lily tickled her, smiling

at the sound of her laughter. This child deserved all the fun of life, not what she may or may not have witnessed or experienced.

"She wanted to wake you earlier," said Monica coming up to them. "But I thought it only fair that you get a chance to sleep in. We haven't had breakfast. Want to go in and get some? Believe it or not, I'm ravenous. Usually, I was too nervous to eat."

Lily had noticed how thin Monica had become. "Is the baby all right?"

Monica nodded and patted her stomach.

Lily set Izzy down, took hold of her hand, and they walked inside.

After they'd eaten all they could of the complimentary breakfast, they returned to the playground so Lily and Monica could talk about their plans while Izzy played.

Lily sat on a bench beside Monica where they could keep an eye on Izzy and turned to Monica. "I figure we'll get a flight to Atlanta and take a flight from there to L.A. in case Jeremy tries to find you. It's a little out of the way and more expensive, but I think it'll be worth it. Once we're in California, the only way he can check on me is through the hotel, and they'll keep any information about me confidential. I have a safe place for you to stay. Someplace where he wouldn't know to look."

Monica gripped her hands together. "He's going to be livid."

"You have your phone, your driver's license and credit cards, don't you?"

"Yes, all except my Mastercard. He took that from me."

"When we go inside, we'll cancel that card. He never should've had it."

"I know," Monica said softly. "But you don't understand

Jeremy."

"I hope to never see him again," said Lily with a deep-seated anger she couldn't conceal. Looking at her sister's bruises, her broken arm, Lily clenched her fists.

CHAPTER THIRTY

LILY

After taking care of cancelling Monica's credit card and making flight arrangements, Lily called Rose, the early riser of the group.

"What's up?" Rose asked her cheerfully.

Lily told her about the abuse Monica suffered and how they'd escaped and then gave her the flight info to Atlanta and on to Los Angeles. "It's scary stuff. I'm calling to ask you for a favor. Will you get word to John Rodriquez at the hotel that no one is to give out any information about my working there? I'm about to call Brian, and I want to be able to reassure him on that matter. He can take care of informing the Blaise people."

"Of course. I'll make that call as soon as we disconnect." Rose let out a long sigh. "Incidents of abuse similar to what's happened to Monica have got to stop. Why do some get off mistreating others in such a cruel way? How is she holding up? And what about Izzy? And the baby?"

"The baby is fine. Monica is outside with Izzy now. When I first spoke to her, she didn't want to come with me because she was afraid Jeremy would be angry. Then, when I insisted, it was as if she woke up from a spell. We got out of that apartment so fast it saved us. Jeremy was driving into the parking lot as we were driving out."

"Oh my God! And Izzy? How much does she know?"

"I'm not sure. We've told her we're on an adventure. It'll be the first time she's on a plane, so we'll keep her occupied with that theme. I'm sure other events will come out later."

"What are you going to do about finding a place here?"

Lily sighed. "I already mentioned something to Brian about Monica visiting, but I need to ask him again if we all could stay at his condo for a while."

"Smart. Jeremy wouldn't have any connection to it," said Rose. "Anything else I can do? I'll let Willow and Alec know too."

"No, thanks. Just knowing you all are there will make it easier for us. Talk to you later."

"Take care, sweetie. Be safe. All of you."

Lily checked the time and punched in Brian's private number.

"Hello?" His deep, comforting tone washed over her.

"Hi," Lily said, and then unable to hold in her emotions, she began to cry softly.

"Lily? What is it? Are you okay?" Brian's voice rang with concern.

"No ... yes ... I'm hiding out in Newark, New Jersey, with Monica and Izzy. Jeremy's been physically abusing her, and I helped her escape from her apartment. We're going to fly from Newark to Atlanta and then on to L.A. hoping Jeremy doesn't try to track us down and know we're headed to Palm Desert."

"Whoa! Are you safe?"

"For the time being we are. We'll drive to the airport soon. Being among the crowd where there's security, we should be fine. I don't think Jeremy would think of finding us in L.A. But when we get to California, we need a safe place to stay. I'm hoping you will let us go to your condo. He shouldn't be able to make any connection to it. Rose is calling John Rodriquez to ask him to inform the staff that no information about me is to be given out. I'm asking you to do the same for the Blaise Group."

"Sure, no problem. But, Lily, do you need me to come there? What about L.A.? I assume you're flying into Ontario. I can make arrangements to have someone pick you up there. I'm still with my mother in Austin and not planning on coming back for another two days. But, if you want, I'll change my plans."

"No, no. I understand how important this time with your mother and Ollie is. You all need to be together."

"I'll worry about you. And when I get back, that bastard better not come near any of you."

Fresh tears filled Lily's eyes. It was such a relief that, for once, someone had her safety in mind. Like it or not, it was going to take a while for the fear that had engulfed her to go away.

"We'll get into Ontario late tonight. If you could have someone meet us, that would be great." She gave him the flight number. "I have the key you gave me to your condo. We'll go directly there from the airport."

"Okay, but, Lily, you have to promise me you'll let me know how things are going. I'm worried about you."

"I know," she said softly, filled with love for him. "How's Ollie?"

"He and Mom are getting along great." He chuckled. "Becky's parents were never around these last few years, so he's liking the fact that he has a grandmother who is more like a fairy godmother than anything else."

Lily smiled at the thought. "Your mother is delightful."

"Yeah, she's really thrilled about my having Ollie and you in my life."

"I am too." Lily looked up as Monica and Izzy entered the room. "I'd better go. Love you."

"Love you, too, Lily. Be safe and play it smart."

"I'll do my best," she replied, wondering at the fresh tears in Monica's eyes.

She clicked off the call. "What's the matter?" she asked Monica.

"Jeremy's sent over twenty texts."

"Wait! I thought you turned off your phone," said Lily.

"I just turned it on for a minute," Monica replied. "What's wrong with that?"

"You need to keep your phone off. You checked to be sure your location won't show up on any of the apps. Right?"

Monica nodded.

"When we get to California, we'll get you a new phone and new number. We don't want Jeremy to be able to trace you." She held out her hand. "Want me to keep the phone for you?"

"No," said Monica. "I'm a big girl."

"Okay. Let's get ready to go to the airport. We'll be safe there."

At the check-in at the airport in Newark, they were asked questions about the lack of luggage for Monica and Izzy, but once through security, they relaxed.

Lily took turns with Monica walking Izzy around their gate area. The flight to Atlanta was short, but the later flight would seem very long with a three-year-old.

Once they were airborne, Lily spent time with Izzy, showing her how the tray table worked, letting her look out the window and generally trying to keep her occupied.

Later, aboard the flight to L.A., Lily felt as exhausted as Monica looked as she covered Izzy with her blanket. Curled up in the seat beside her, Izzy looked adorable and so, so innocent.

Lily leaned back in her seat to rest, but her mind kept whirling. She should've come to New York earlier. As much as she hadn't respected her mother for all the men in her life, Lily didn't remember her having bruises and broken bones. She stared at the movie screen ahead of her seeing nothing until her eyes finally closed.

It seemed no time when the announcement came that they were soon approaching the Ontario Airport. Lily turned to find Izzy staring up at her. Overcome with love, Lily reached over and hugged her. Izzy immediately wanted to get up to go to the bathroom.

Lily turned to Monica in the row seat across the aisle. She was leafing through a magazine. Not wanting to disturb her, Lily unbuckled Izzy and walked her back to the bathroom. Izzy was both fascinated and a little afraid of how everything operated, but cooperated just before it was announced that everyone should stay in their seats.

Lily hurried back to their spot, moving Izzy ahead of her, careful not to bump into the seats along the aisle. Monica turned to her and mouthed, "Thank you!".

"No problem," Lily replied, and buckled Izzy into her seat before buckling her own belt.

Anticipation filled her as they circled in the sky. This was the first time she'd returned to California with a firm thought of a new life with a man she loved. As disappointed as she was by Brian being away, she still knew he was there for her in spirit.

During the deplaning process, Lily was busy tending to Izzy, who having slept most of the trip, was now bursting with energy. Slipping her a cracker, Lily said, "Hold on! It'll soon be our turn."

When at last they emerged from the plane, Lily pretended to run through the terminal holding firmly onto Izzy's hand. Izzy giggled and pranced by her side. Other passengers glanced at them and smiled.

Later, entering the baggage claim area where she'd agreed

to meet their ride, Lily stood apart from Monica and Izzy and scanned the room, searching for someone holding a sign with her name on it. She stopped short and gaped at the tall man holding a sign that simply said, "Lily".She sprinted forward, her vision blurring. "Brian! What are you doing here?"

He grinned and swept her in her arms. "I couldn't stop thinking about you. I had to make sure you were safe."

"Thank you so much," she said, accepting his kiss.

When they pulled apart, Monica and Izzy were standing by her side.

"Brian, I want you to meet my sister, Monica Weaver, and her daughter, Izzy. This is Brian Walden."

"Welcome to California," said Brian, not reacting to the bruises on Monica's face.

"Hi, Brian," Monica said, giving him a tentative smile.

"Auntie Lee, up!" cried Izzy.

Laughing, Lily lifted Izzy into her arms and faced Brian. "There. Now you can get a closer look."

"Hi, Izzy. How old are you?" Brian asked.

Izzy lifted four fingers.

Lily chuckled. "No, not for another month. You're still three."

"Three," said Izzy solemnly, clinging to Lily but giving Brian a broad smile.

"A big girl," Brian said solemnly.

Izzy nodded with satisfaction and wiggled to get down.

"Stay here, Izzy," said Monica. "We have to wait for Auntie Lee's suitcase."

"No others?" Brian asked quietly.

Lily shook her head. "We didn't have time to pack. We'll go shopping tomorrow."

"Okay, let's grab your bag. Pedro is waiting with the car that Alec insisted on sending."

"Oh, how sweet!" Tears stung Lily's eyes and she realized what an emotional toll the escape was taking on her. She turned to her sister and wrapped an arm through hers, feeling the need to know she was fine.

Brian retrieved the suitcase she'd described and motioned them forward. "This way."

They stepped outside.

When Lily saw Pedro standing beside the sleek, black limo the hotel used, she ran forward. "Pedro! How sweet of you to make the trip at this time of night."

Beaming, he nodded. "My pleasure, Lily. Now, who do we have here?" he said bending low as Izzy ran to them.

"That's Izzy, and this is my sister, Monica."

"Welcome," he said, shaking hands with Monica. "We have cold drinks and a few snacks for you in the car. Make yourself comfortable." While he held the door for Monica and Izzy, Lily went around to the other side.

"Here, let me," said Brian, holding the door open for her. In a softer voice he said, "Everything's set at the condo. Rose arranged to have the condo cleaned and fresh sheets on all the beds. She and Willow filled the refrigerator with groceries for you, too."

"Amazing," Lily said, overcome with gratitude.

"You've got a lot of people behind you. Monica and Izzy, too."

Lily's body went weak. She was so used to carrying burdens on her own.

Brian wrapped an arm around her to steady her. "Don't worry. We've got you."

She slid onto the seat of the car and took a moment to gain her composure before turning to Izzy, who was trying to climb onto her lap.

CHAPTER THIRTY-ONE

ROSE

Hope you don't mind," said Rose to Hank, "but before we go to your house for dinner, I want to do one more check on Brian's condo. He's on his way to Ontario, and I need to place a couple of things inside."

"No problem," he replied. "This situation with Lily and her sister is awful. After hearing about a creep like Jeremy, I feel grateful my girls haven't ever been involved with scum buckets like that."

"I like Rob. He's a great son-in-law and is wonderful with Samantha. What about Nikki? She's still not dating?"

"Not that I know of. A year back, a male nurse was interested, but after a couple of dates, Nikki realized it wasn't going to work. Hopefully, she can find someone. I imagine it gets pretty lonely when she leaves her job and goes home."

"And dealing with cancer patients would be stressful," added Rose. Of Hank's two girls, she'd found Nikki to be more easy-going, but Sam and she had worked hard on becoming closer, especially because Sam's daughter, Leah, adored "Wosie" and would require even more attention when a sibling was added in the months ahead.

Hank pulled in front of Brian's condo and looked around. "Nice place."

"Yes," said Rose. "Willow likes it too. She's hoping to stay in the area and would love to find a condo in this complex." She grabbed the bags she'd brought with her, and they went inside, using the key Brian had left for them.

Monica was staying in the guest room, next to the small office they and staff from the hotel had converted to a child's room for Izzy, using equipment provided by the hotel.

Rose opened one of the bags and placed new underpants, a swimsuit, a couple of T-shirts and a pair of denim shorts on top of the bureau for Monica. Lily had once told her that her sister was the same size, and though she knew they'd go shopping on their own, she wanted Monica to have a few things to change into after a day of traveling.

In Izzy's room, she laid out underwear, a bathing suit, a nightgown, and a play outfit on top of the chest of drawers so Lily wouldn't miss them.

"There," said Rose. "At least they'll have something to put on until they go shopping."

"I see you made sure they each had a swim suit." Hank smiled at her. "So thoughtful."

"I'm sure in the morning, one little girl might want to go swimming. Especially if she's on an adventure like Lily and Monica are telling her." Tears stung Rose's eyes, surprising her.

"Are you okay?" Hank said, giving her a look of concern.

"I once had a boyfriend smack me in the face. He said it was an accident, but he'd struck out in anger when we had a disagreement. I dumped him in a hurry. I can't imagine what Monica has gone through. Even now she's afraid of him."

"Do you think it's dangerous for Lily to be involved?" said Hank.

"Enough that we're all keeping tabs on her and her sister."

"You Desert Flowers certainly have grown to love one another."

Rose smiled. "It's true." She could've said so much more, but with Hank she didn't need to. He understood her better than anyone else.

CHAPTER THIRTY-TWO

LILY

As Pedro drove up to Brian's condo and stopped the car, Lily couldn't help looking around. When she saw a man standing in the shadows studying them, her muscles tightened. When she realized the man looked nothing like Jeremy, she drew a calming breath and told herself to calm down.

Brian opened the door for her, and with him standing by, she immediately felt better.

"I'll get your suitcase," Pedro said, pushing a button to release the trunk of the car. It popped open, and he pulled out her luggage.

She went to him and gave him a hug. "Thank you so much for making this trip. It means the world to me."

"I'm happy to do it," he said, smiling.

"Like I've told Willow, she's so lucky to have you and Juanita for parents."

"Yes, thank you," said Monica, joining them. In her arms, Izzy stared at them and rubbed her eyes.

"We'd better get this little one to bed," said Lily. "See you tomorrow, Pedro. Thanks again."

Pedro gave them a nod and climbed back into the car.

As he drove away, Brian turned to Lily. "All set?"

"We'll see. I really appreciate your allowing us to hide here. You've gone from living alone to having three extra people here and more to come."

He smiled at her. "A whole lot of changes, but then,

someone said change is good for the soul. I just hope this works out for Monica and Izzy. Pretty scary stuff."

"I know. Let's go inside."

As they stepped into the condo, Lily noticed it had been cleaned. Surfaces sparkled and a vase of fresh flowers sat on the kitchen counter.

Brian led them to the makeshift room for Izzy. Seeing the new arrangement made the horror of the last couple of days come alive.

"Oh, this is wonderful," said Monica. She lowered Izzy onto the bed.

"Look!" said Lily. "A sweet little nightgown. And there are other things too. Rose and Willow must have left them for her."

Izzy sat up, suddenly awake. She stared at the nightgown in Lily's hands. "Mine?"

"Yes, Izzy. I'll help you put it on."

"Let mommy wash your face and hands first," said Monica. She left the room and came back with a washcloth.

Together, Lily and Monica got Izzy ready for bed.

"I'll see you in the morning, Monica. I think you'll find everything you need in the bathroom," said Brian. "Rose and Willow have made sure of it."

Monica turned to her. "Wow, Lily, when you said you'd made friends here, I had no idea what they'd do for you, for us ..." Her voice broke and she covered her face with her hands.

"Let's help you get situated," Lily said softly, rubbing her back.

"I'll give you two some time alone." Brian nodded to Lily. "See you in a few."

She found Monica's gaze on her as he left the room. "Brian's such a great guy. You deserve someone like him, Lily."

"Thanks, but that doesn't mean you deserved someone like Jeremy in your life. It doesn't work that way."

"I know, but I'm happy for you. How many times have you rescued me?"

Lily draped an arm around Monica's shoulder. "I'll do it as often as I need. You know that. Now, let's get some sleep."

After Lily made sure Monica had everything she needed, she headed into Brian's room.

He was already in bed, waiting for her when she opened the door. She ran over and threw herself into his arms. "Oh, Brian! I'm so glad you decided to leave Austin so you could be here when we arrived. The last couple of days have been awful. I've tried to put up a calm front, but I've gone from wanting to kill Jeremy to just simply crying. No one should be allowed to do what he did to Monica. She was like a frightened little rabbit when I first got there. And that arm and those bruises! Thank goodness, the baby is all right."

He drew her closer. "I had to come. I wanted to make sure everyone was all right. Abuse is a terrible thing. We're going to have to be careful about how we handle this. What's going to happen to her apartment? Her car?"

"You know me. I've already put together a list of things to take care of. We'll have to find someone to pack up her apartment and ship her car out here. The guys I used for my things did a great job. I thought of them right away."

"Ah, Lily. You're such a treasure. Monica and Izzy are lucky to have you in their lives."

A tear slid down her cheek. "I should've gotten them out earlier."

Brian lifted her chin and looked her in the eyes. "Don't blame yourself for any of this. That wouldn't be right. You've offered to help several times. Monica is lucky you cared enough to fly to New York and discover the truth."

A sigh escaped her. "You're right. But I won't rest until she's safe here."

"You've had a rough few days. Come to bed and get some rest. Willow brought some of your personal things here. They're in the bathroom."

Lily managed to get on her feet and staggered into the bathroom. Seeing the nightshirt and all her personal items carefully placed inside a canvas bag, fresh tears filled Lily's eyes. In some ways, this was the worst and the best of moments.

The next morning Lily was awakened by the sound of voices. She rubbed her eyes sleepily and stared at the bedside clock. Nine o'clock. Gasping, she sat upright. She couldn't remember the last time she'd slept this late. She glanced at the empty space beside her and climbed out of bed. As she took care of her morning rituals, thoughts of the previous two days came rushing back, and she hurried to find her sister and Izzy.

In the kitchen, Brian was sitting at the kitchen table sipping a cup of coffee. He smiled at her. "Good morning, Sleepyhead!"

She grinned, walked over, and gave him a kiss. "Where are Monica and Izzy?"

"Outside on the patio. Monica has been trying to keep Izzy quiet, but she's pretty excited to be here. I took them over to the clubhouse to show them the pool. Izzy can't wait to get in that water."

"Have they eaten?"

Brian nodded. "Yes, but Monica didn't eat much."

Lily frowned. She'd have to talk to Monica about eating properly for the baby.

Izzy ran into the kitchen, followed by her mother. "Auntie Lee! I saw a pool! Can I go swim?"

Lily glanced at Monica. "I don't know why not. We all can go, can't we, Monica?"

"Sure," Monica said after hesitating a moment.

"The crowd won't come for a little while so we'll have some privacy," said Brian.

The look of unease on Monica's face evaporated.

"You and I can talk about plans while Izzy plays in the toddler pool," Lily said, grabbing a cup of coffee. "It's important for us to keep busy."

"Yes, otherwise I'll go crazy," Monica said. "I keep looking for him."

"We're safe here," said Lily. "Let's get ready. Willow brought me one of my swimsuits," said Lily. "I'll meet you back here in a few minutes."

She carried her coffee into the bedroom.

Brian joined her. "Do you mind if I don't go to the pool with you? I want to check on a few things at the house. I think I might move in there even while we're finishing up some projects and waiting for furniture to arrive."

Lily paused and nodded. "If you'd rather stay at the hotel, I'm sure they'd find space for you there."

He shook his head. "No, I want to get a feel for the house. We only have a few weeks before Ollie and Jake will join us."

Lily walked over to him. "Thanks for your support, Brian. It means the world to me."

"Anything to help. I'm just sorry this happened."

"Me, too. I thought I'd speak to Craig or Bennett Williams to see what, if any, legal action we can take. I'm worried that nothing can be done from a distance. A restraining order in New York isn't going to help Monica here."

"Let me know if there's anything we can do about the situation."

She nodded. "Will do."

He stood by as she pulled on her swimsuit and grinned. "You're so beautiful, Lily."

She knew better, and yet, he made her feel that way.

Grinning, he kissed her. "See you later."

The community pool was the perfect place to relax, or try to. After putting sun screen on her and making sure Izzy had a hat, Lily and Monica helped each other with sun screen and sat by the toddler pool. A box of toys left at the pool by others contained a plastic pail. Lily gave it to Izzy to use.

While Izzy sat and splashed in the shallow water, Lily pulled out a sheet of paper from her purse and turned to Monica. "I've made a list of things we need to do."

Her cell rang. *Willow.*

"Hi, Lily! I heard you got back safely last night. My mother is offering to help take care of Izzy while you and your sister are busy. I can't wait to meet your family. I'm sorry it's under these conditions, but I want them to know I'm here to help any way I can."

"Oh, Willow, that's so sweet! And thanks to you and Rose for seeing that the condo was prepared and for giving them a change of clothes. Tell Juanita we'd love to accept her offer to help. I've got a whole list of things we need to do today."

Willow laughed. "That's so like you." Her tone grew serious. "We'll be here all morning. Just let us know when you're coming. Rose will be here waiting for you, too."

"Thanks. We're at the pool right now. But after a bit, we'll change and come right over to Alec's house to meet you." Lily hung up and turned to Monica. "My friends are eager to meet you. And Willow's mother, who's Alec's housekeeper, has offered to babysit Izzy while we take care of a few things."

Monica smiled. "Nice to know you have such close girlfriends. Jeremy made me stop seeing mine."

Lily shook her head. "It never should have happened."

Monica sighed. "I didn't realize what he was doing until it was too late. He threatened to run away with Izzy if I didn't do what he wanted. The yelling and name calling became his fists to make his point. Then he was always sorry, and the whole thing became my fault." She shivered. "It was awful."

"We didn't have an easy childhood, but we never had to put up with physical abuse," said Lily. "I'm so sorry."

"Well, it's never going to happen again."

"That's why I want you to begin counseling right away," said Lily. "And I want a doctor to take a look at you and check on the baby to make sure you're both okay."

Monica shook her head to protest.

Lily put an arm around her. "Please. For me. For yourself, for your baby, and most of all, for Izzy."

Monica sighed. "I suppose you'll nag me until I do."

"Let's just take one step at a time. This morning, we need to go clothes shopping for you and Izzy. I want you to meet the lawyer I work for, and we need to know how best to proceed with your apartment and your car. We can let that rest for the moment. I don't want any information to be leaked about where you are."

"Jeremy is going to know I'm in California. He knows I wanted to come here."

"We're safe at Brian's. But we can't go to the hotel. I'm going to rent a car and store my own at Alec's just to be safe."

Monica covered her face with her hands and drew several deep breaths. "Lily, I don't want anything bad to happen to you because of me."

"Don't worry. I'm going to take every precaution I can. We'll find help for all of us." She glanced at Izzy pouring water out of the bucket onto her toes, and her heart welled with love. She'd do anything to keep her family safe.

Driving up to Alec's house, Lily filled with a sense of homecoming. Her desert family, whom she'd grown to love, would help them.

"Such a beautiful house," murmured Monica, staring at the stucco, one-story, two-wing structure that always reminded Lily of a desert lizard sprawling in the sun.

"It's gorgeous," agreed Lily. When she'd first come to Alec's house, she'd felt like she should tiptoe through it, barely making her presence known. Now, it felt like home.

She came to a stop in front of the house and feeling a sense of pride, helped Izzy out of the backseat. She'd already added the purchase of a toddler safety seat to her list.

Lily took Izzy's hand. "Come. You and Mommy are going to meet Auntie Lee's friends."

Izzy nodded solemnly, no doubt aware of the tension that stiffened her mother's back.

Before they reached the front door, it opened and Willow and Rose came rushing toward them.

"Hi, Lily!" Rose cried. She squatted in front of Izzy. "And you must be Izzy. I'm Rose, but my little granddaughter calls me 'Wosie.' You can too."

Izzy giggled and looked up at her mother, who was accepting a hug from Willow.

Rose stood and held out a hand. "Monica, we're happy you're here."

"Thanks," said Monica shyly, shaking Rose's hand.

"Lily, welcome home," said Willow. They hugged and then Juanita stood at the door.

"Come on inside. I've got refreshments ready." Her dark eyes twinkled. "And a special surprise for Izzy."

As they approached, Juanita gazed at Monica with concern. "Hello, I'm Juanita. I'm glad you are safely among friends." She smiled down at Izzy. "And I know Izzy and I will get along great."

They entered the house and moved into the kitchen. As Juanita had promised, a plate of cookies sat on the counter alongside a bright, rainbow-colored bag with a big pink bow atop it.

"Coffee, anyone? Tea? Lemonade?"

Lily turned to Monica. "You have to try Juanita's homemade lemonade. It's very refreshing."

"And her cookies aren't bad, either," said Rose, taking one from the plate and wrapping an arm across Juanita's shoulder.

"Sit down, everyone. I'll put the plate of cookies on the table. And like I said, I have a special gift for Izzy."

Izzy looked up at Juanita with a bright smile. "For me?"

Juanita grinned. "Sit down next to your Mommy. I'll bring it over."

Izzy scrambled up into a chair at the table and watched carefully as Juanita placed the gift in her lap. "For you, *cariña*."

Izzy opened the bag and pulled out a stuffed bunny rabbit in a warm shade of brown. Izzy hugged it to her. "Bunny."

Lily turned to Juanita. "Thank you so much. We left so many things behind."

"That's what I heard." She turned to Izzy. "Keep going."

While they watched, Izzy pulled out princess sticker books, a box of crayons, a couple of picture books, and magic markers, along with colored paper.

Monica's eyes filled with tears. "Such a sweet thing to do, Juanita."

Juanita smiled at Willow. "I know how busy I had to keep Willow when she was that age."

"Thank heavens, I'm on my own now," teased Willow.

Lily joined in the laughter and then stood to help with the drinks.

While Izzy played on the floor with her gifts, the women huddled around the table and listened as Lily told them of her plans.

"Good to get rid of the phone and hide your car," commented Rose.

"And meeting with lawyers is smart," Willow added. She turned to Monica. "Had you filed any complaint against Jeremy in New York?"

Monica hung her head and shook it. "Was too scared to do it."

Lily exchanged worried glances with the other Flowers and Juanita. "After we go shopping today, we're going to stay pretty close to Brian's condo until we get things sorted out."

"I'm happy to pick up any items you need," said Willow. "Just give me one of your lists."

Lily grinned. "You know me so well." She reached inside her pocketbook and handed a list to Monica. "Please add whatever you want to the list. I know some of the things you and Izzy like, but not all."

While Monica went to work on it, Alec surprised them by walking slowly into the room.

Lily and the others stood. "Alec! Nice to see you!"

"I understand we have guests." He smiled down at Izzy.

Izzy gazed up at him, her mouth open.

Lily held her breath, wondering what she would say.

Izzy got to her feet and stood before him, gazing up at him with wide eyes. "Are you my grandpa?"

Alec chuckled and reached down to pat her head. "No, but I'm old like one."

Amid the soft laughter of the group, Izzy nodded emphatically. "Grandpa."

Monica stood and went over to Alec. "We've been reading a book about a little girl's grandpa."

"Well, if I could, I'd gladly be her grandpa," said Alec, his eyes swimming with tears. "You must be Lily's sister, Monica."

"Yes. Thank you for sending the car to pick us up."

"My pleasure." Alec's smile, a little eerie spread across his thin face, was sincere.

Lily was touched by this sweet moment, but worry soon returned.

CHAPTER THIRTY-THREE

WILLOW

Willow was as touched as the other women by Izzy's thinking Alec was her grandpa. That, and the way her mother was so excited about Izzy's presence made her wish there was a special man in her life. But she also knew she needed to make her way in the hospitality industry in Palm Desert. She wasn't looking for just any job but one in top management. Since coming home to help Alec, she realized she was well suited to it.

Rose elbowed her. "What's up? You're a million miles away."

"Just thinking about the future." She glanced at Monica and said quietly, "Such a shame that her life has been ruined because of a guy like Jeremy."

"True," Rose said and turned to Izzy, who was showing her a sticker she'd placed on her arm. "Pretty."

"See?" Izzy said, holding up her arm for Willow to see.

"Yes, a pretty princess." She recalled the hours she'd spent with her dolls and later, watching Princess movies. Moana was her current favorite.

Lily stood. "Guess Monica and I better get ready to leave. We have a lot to do."

Willow got to her feet. "If you're going to park your car here, I'll take you to a car rental place, like you mentioned."

"That would be great," said Lily. "Here's the list of additional groceries and one of my credit cards to pay for them."

Willow started to protest, but when she saw the look of determination on Lily's face, she stopped.

Lily turned to Monica. "While you say goodbye to Izzy, I'll take care of the car. Okay?"

Willow watched Lily hug Izzy and felt another tug of regret, her emotions battling between having a family and having the freedom to pursue work in the demanding hospitality business. Sarah Jensen had proved she could work at the hotel only as a part-time staff member.

Later, after dropping Lily and Monica off at the car rental place in northeast Palm Desert, Willow headed to Albertson's to shop, glad for a day away from Brent and Trace Armstrong.

CHAPTER THIRTY-FOUR

LILY

The rest of the day turned into a whirlwind of activity. Lily and Monica got a car seat for Izzy, clothes, shoes, and personal items for both Monica and Izzy. Monica wanted to hold off on getting a burner phone until she had a chance to gather some of the personal information on her cell.

Every time Monica protested that Lily was spending too much money, Lily reminded her of the funds she had from selling her condo and the fact that she didn't want Monica using any of her credit cards, leading Jeremy to her new location.

On their way to the law firm where Lily worked., they talked about the need for Monica to change all her passwords on her various computer programs and apps.

As they entered the office, Bennett Williams walked into the reception area. He smiled at Lily and silently observed the bruises on Monica's face and the cast on her arm.

Lily made the introductions and then she and Monica followed him into his office. "Have a seat," he said, as he went behind his desk and sat down. He studied them solemnly, clasping his broad hands together.

"Monica, I'm sorry this has happened to you. Do you want to tell me exactly what occurred?"

Monica told how Jeremy had started out being sweet and charming, but gradually had blocked her from friends and eventually from going to work. "He'd hit me and tell me he loved me and he was sorry but that I was the one who'd made him angry. When I told him it wasn't working out, he threatened to take Izzy away from me, even though he'd terminated his rights before she was born."

Lily closed her eyes at the sight of tears rolling down Monica's face. "I should've guessed that things would get worse and worse."

"No, Lily," Monica said with more force than she'd previously shown. "I wanted to warn you, but I was too afraid he'd find out what I'd done and run with Izzy."

"Lily, fill me in on the present status of things," said Bennett. "We want to prevent this bastard from doing this ever again."

Lily explained what they were doing. "Brian says they can stay in the condo until his lease ends, which is in a couple more months."

Bennett nodded. "So, this Jeremy hasn't made further threats here in California?"

"No," scoffed Lily. "From New York, we believe, he's left vile messages on Monica's phone, but we're cancelling the contract on the phone so he can't reach her."

"It's important that we build a trail of threats or any other means of his trying to get to Monica. Note everything he says and does. If he should ever appear, you'll have substantial cause for a case. I would advise you to go to the police and talk to them so they're already aware of the situation for their records."

Feeling emotionally exhausted, Lily nodded. "Thank you for your time, Bennett."

"It's cases like these that make my blood boil." He rose. "Monica, you're lucky to have Lily for a sister. She loves you a lot."

"Yes, I know," Monica said, giving them both a tremulous smile.

They left the law office and returned to Alec's house to pick up Izzy.

When they arrived, Izzy was in the swimming pool with Rose, laughing as she kicked and splashed.

"I think we have a real swimmer on our hands," said Rose, smiling up at them. "She's fearless."

"Mommy! Auntie Lee! Look!" Izzy dunked her face in the water and came up smiling.

"Great job!" Monica encouraged. Lily clapped with her, thrilled to see Izzy so happy. Time would tell what Izzy had seen or overheard back home with Jeremy. For now, she seemed at peace with all the changes.

Willow came out of the house carrying a tray of drinks. "How about some iced tea or lemonade?"

"Sounds lovely," said Lily. "Okay, if we rest here before unpacking everything at Brian's?"

Monica nodded. "That would be great. I'm exhausted."

Lily herself was almost giddy with fatigue.

When they got ready to leave, Pedro helped them install the car seat for Izzy in the rental.

Then, with Izzy secured safely, they returned to Brian's condo.

Showing Izzy her new clothes was like celebrating Christmas all over again. Izzy was a little girl who loved frills, pink, and glitter. Each new play outfit, each new pair of shoes brought a squeal of delight from her.

"Can you imagine what she's going to be like as a teenager?" said Monica, laughing and shaking her head.

"She makes it fun," said Lily. "Now, let me help you with your things, and then I'm going to meet Brian at the new house."

"Time to put Izzy down for a nap," said Monica. "I want to

keep to a strict routine. I think that will help her feel secure here."

"I agree."

Together, they got Izzy quieted down and on her bed with her favorite blanket, her Teddy Bear, and the new stuffed bunny Juanita had bought her.

As she nodded off, Lily and Monica tiptoed away. In Monica's room, Lily helped her hang up items or store them in the bureau. "Later this week, we'll go to the outlet mall for more things."

Monica plopped down on the bed, moved some packages away, and looked up at her with such a defeated look, Lily's heart clenched.

"I'm so sorry I'm being such a nuisance," Monica said. "Maybe I should take Izzy and go somewhere else to keep you out of my mess."

Lily sat beside her broken sister and hugged her. "You're here where I want you to be. In time, everything will get sorted out. I'll take care of some things for you, but for most of them, we'll have to work together." She straightened and gave Monica a steady look. "I love you, Monica. You're my family."

Monica clutched her hands in her lap. "Yes, but you already have another family—those women, Brian, the people at the law firm. All of them would do anything for you."

"And now you," Lily said, realizing that among the other things that needed to be done was for Monica to make an appointment with a counselor. She'd never seen Monica so low.

Lily entered the house which she would one day share with Brian, feeling as if she had rocks tied to her feet. Though exhaustion was taking hold of her, she managed a smile at the sight of Brian running a vacuum over the newly installed carpet in the master suite.

"Wow! They moved fast," said Lily, admiring the sand-colored carpet that went well with the cream-colored painted walls and white trim.

"I think you scared them when you told them it was an emergency," grinned Brian. "I've directed the crew to do the guest room next. Mom will stay there."

"That's right, your mother will soon be here," said Lily. She wondered if she could handle one more stressful thing then remembered the kind woman on FaceTime and pushed her worries away. "By the time she comes this weekend, all the painting and carpeting should be done. We might not have the rugs for the tile flooring in the living and dining areas, but it doesn't look too bad without them."

"A lot of the furniture we ordered is being delivered tomorrow," said Brian. "I've arranged a conference call from here, so I'll be able to cover the deliveries."

"The cable people have done their work here?" Lily said, surprised.

Brian nodded and grinned. "It's amazing what kind of help you can get when you use the same people as the hotel does. They were very anxious to help out."

Lily couldn't help laughing. When Brian was determined to see something done, he made sure to handle it with his usual diplomacy, getting results.

He finished vacuuming, moved the machine out of the room, returned, and lowered himself onto the carpet.

"Ah, nice and thick." He patted the space next to him. "Have a seat. The beds come tomorrow." He wiggled his eyebrows playfully. "Now, we have a whole big room as our playground."

Lily sat down beside him and leaned up against him. "Have all the fun you want. Just don't wake me."

He chuckled. “That bad, huh?”

“Lots to think about and get done.”

“You’ve got your lists, right?” he teased.

She elbowed him playfully. “Where would we be without them?”

He gently cupped her cheek with a broad hand. “I love that you’re earnest and caring.”

“What about the kitchen items for your mother’s visit?” Lily asked, unable to stop thinking of things that needed to be done. “We made a list of things to order on line. Tomorrow, we can finish up at our local stores.”

“Okay. I’m getting hungry. Want to go out to dinner?”

She shook her head. “Monica’s cooking. Afterward, I’m going to bed.”

“Mmmm. Early bedtime? May I join you, fair lady?”

She fluttered her eyelashes playfully. “What do you think, handsome gentleman?”

He leaned down and kissed her.

Responding to it, she realized she wasn’t as tired as she’d thought.

The next morning, Lily lay in the empty bed in Brian’s condo reviewing things in her mind. It was to be another busy day with Monica and Izzy and again at Brian’s new house. She made a mental list of phone calls she needed to make, patted the empty space beside her, and got out of bed, hoping for the day when things would calm down and she and Brian would be together.

She opened the sliding door in the master suite and stepped outside in the early morning air. It was forecast to be another hot day, but the temperature at this hour was pleasant. She observed the rosy fingers of the rising sun reaching across the sky, and hope spread inside her.

She'd gone from living a somewhat boring existence to coping with so many new things her mind spun. The one constant in her hectic days was her love for Brian. He was already her rock, the love of her life. The future held even more opportunities for their love to grow deeper with the arrival of Ollie and his dog, making them a family.

Lily went back inside, showered, and dressed for another busy day.

When Monica walked into the kitchen later, Lily had a list of numbers for her to call—the police, a counselor, a physician, and a preschool for Izzy. She'd already texted Sarah Jensen for the name of the babysitter she'd requested, thinking they'd use her for Izzy.

Monica studied the sheet of paper Lily handed her. "Wow, sis! You're really good at this. No wonder people at your old law firm were so sad to see you go."

Lily smiled. "One of the best decisions I've ever made."

Monica studied her and sighed. "I want to be able to move on as best I can. You're just starting a life together with Brian. I don't want to interfere with that. I'll make these calls and then I'm going to do some errands on my own. It's important to me."

Lily tried to hide her alarm. "I'd feel more comfortable if you stayed here as much as possible. We don't know yet what Jeremy is up to or where he is."

"I've checked my phone. He hasn't left any more messages or tried to call."

"More reason to stay close," warned Lily. "And get rid of that phone for a burner."

"I'll get one today," said Monica. "And I know I have to stay close, but I also need to know I can be on my own."

Rather than argue, Lily remained quiet as they both turned

to Izzy, looking like a rumpled angel in her new pink nightgown. She hurried over to them, and seeing her mother standing, scooted into Lily's lap.

Lily wrapped her arms around her and nuzzled her neck which still smelled of the bubble bath soap from last night. "Hey, princess, did you get a good sleep?"

Izzy nodded. "Yes. Now, I'm hungry."

Pleased that Izzy had so quickly assumed a normal routine, Lily rose.

"I'll get Izzy's breakfast," said Monica, waving her away.

Lily shrugged. "Okay, I'm going to go to Alec's house and gather more of my things."

She left them thinking about Monica's need for freedom. It was a healthy sign. She couldn't imagine being trapped inside an apartment with a man like Jeremy controlling her every move.

Lily was relieved to find Rose and Willow sitting outside sipping coffee when she arrived at Alec's. She'd ask what they thought about giving Monica more space. Pleased to see her friends, she went into the kitchen before joining them.

"Hi, Lily! Nice to see you," said Juanita, handing her a cup of coffee. "Where is that adorable little Izzy?"

"Back at Brian's' condo with her mother," Lily responded, feeling a sense of pride. Izzy was a real cutie. "Thanks again for all your gifts. She loves them."

"It was so much fun for me to do that. I don't think grandchildren are in my near future." Juanita checked the time on the microwave. "Time to see to Alec."

"How's he doing?" Lily said. "He looked a little better yesterday."

Juanita's eyes filled with sadness. She shook her head. "Even though some days are better than others, it's all about the same. But he's a fighter and determined to make sure all goes well with the sale of the hotel."

"Alec's such a wonderful man," Lily said. "I think he liked it when Izzy thought he was her grandpa."

Juanita chuckled. "He *loved* it." She hugged Lily. "I'm praying for your sister and Izzy."

Lily hugged her back and went to join her friends.

"There she is," said Willow, waving to her and smiling. "We were just talking about you."

"How are things going?" asked Rose.

"That's what I want to talk to you about." Lily took a seat at the table and told them about Monica's wishes to become more independent.

"Do you think I'm being overly protective about not wanting her to do things on her own?"

"After being forced to be with a man who watched her every move, she might need to be on her own in order to heal. She wasn't always a victim, was she?" said Rose.

"No," Lily admitted. "I've always done a lot for her, but she's a very capable person who was trapped in a bad situation. She's agreed to call a counselor."

"Well, then, maybe the need for more space is a part of healing," said Willow.

"Okay, then," said Lily, "I'm going to tell her this evening that tonight is the last one I'll spend with her, that I'll move back here unless she wants me to stay. It'll be her choice. Still, I'd prefer that she not be doing lots of errands around town by herself."

"A nice compromise," said Rose.

"Thanks for hearing me out," said Lily. "I just want to keep both of them safe, you know?"

"Understood," said Willow. "We all do." She leaned forward. "What's new with you and Brian? He's moving into his house now?"

"Yes, he even slept there last night. He's really excited about having a place for Ollie and the dog. It's very cute. He's gone from being on his own to a father with an instant family. It's nice for me, too, to be part of it. I've FaceTimed with his mother and we're going to set up FaceTime between Ollie and me so we're all better acquainted. Brian's mother is very nice."

"He's such a great guy, I'm sure she is," said Rose. She reached across the table and squeezed Lily's hand. "I'm so happy the two of you are together. An unexpected love story."

"Like you," Lily said, smiling at her.

They both turned to Willow.

Willow laughed and held up her hand. "Stop doing that! Don't look at me. I've got work to do."

"We love you, Willow," said Lily.

"Yeah, we do," Rose said.

"Well, that's all the love I can handle right now. I have to be tough to face my opponents at work. Besides, Dan is dating someone he met through Tiffany, so that never-was-opportunity is gone."

"For now," said Lily. "He's still not ready to settle down."

Willow nodded. "Yeah, that's what Tiffany says too. I don't need a man in my life right now." She lifted her coffee cup. "Here's to the Desert Flowers!"

Lily raised her cup and grinned. Being part of the Desert Flowers was important to all of them.

CHAPTER THIRTY-FIVE

ROSE

After Lily left, Rose turned to Willow. "Hard to believe so many things have happened to Lily. She's changed so much."

"She's a lot tougher than I thought when we first met," said Willow.

Rose nodded. "She's had a rough childhood, and now this. It makes me happy that she's with someone like Brian."

"She's almost as lucky as you, huh?" Willow teased.

Laughter rose up out of her. "Who'd have thought I'd meet a man like Hank. I can't wait to marry him and make it official. But we both think it's right to wait until after the sale of the hotel goes through. Besides we want to work around the arrival of Sam and Rob's new baby."

"Makes sense," said Willow rising. "I've got to get ready for work. See you later."

Sitting alone, Rose let her thoughts drift. Years ago, she'd been deeply in love with Alec, had hoped he'd ask her to marry him. With Hank it was different—very sudden, but right. Once they got past Hank's interest in someone new, his daughters had come through with love and support. Like Lily, she was marrying a family, not just a single man. As if he knew she'd been thinking of him, Alec appeared.

Rose stood up and hurried over to help him to a chair. "It's a beautiful morning, Alec. Come sit with me for a while."

"Thanks," he said, leaning on her arm. "Mornings like this are lovely." His lips curved. "Not as lovely as you, though."

She chuckled. "Still haven't lost that charm, Alec."

"No reason to. Not even now with me dying," he said.

Rose felt the sting of tears and gripped his hand. "I'd give anything to make you well."

"I know, my dear. That's one reason you're here. To help me through to the end. Each of you Flowers holds a special place in my heart. Any news of Lily and her sister?"

"As a matter of fact, Lily was just here, wondering about the need to give Monica a little more space. Starting tomorrow, Lily will be back in her room here."

"Ah, I see. I like looking out and seeing the three of you together."

"Yes. It's amazing how close we're becoming under such unusual circumstances." Rose smiled at him. "Only someone like you could pull this off."

He grinned. "It's working. I got a call from Mitchell Armstrong today asking for more information about the three of you. I think he's very impressed with all you've done."

"Interesting," said Rose. She and Hank hadn't made any definite decisions about where'd they live or what they'd do when this job was over. Rose could continue her blog anywhere, but she really loved the desert.

CHAPTER THIRTY-SIX

LILY

Lily was a little hurt by Monica's delight at knowing this would be her last night staying at Brian's condo. She told herself it was because Monica was already showing signs of wanting to regain her independence, but Lily wondered if she'd been too pushy, too demanding of her sister, not only now, but through the years.

When Brian called to say that his conference call was over and he had time to go shopping for kitchen items with her, Lily was happy to have that time with him.

"Pick you up in fifteen minutes," he said.

"I'll be ready," she replied, looking up as Monica entered the kitchen. She clicked off the call. "What's up?"

"I need to borrow the car. I've got an appointment with a counselor," said Monica. "He has an unexpected opening and can see me now. Afterwards, I'll get a burner phone."

"Oh, but I've just made arrangements to go shopping with Brian. His mother is coming to town next weekend, and we need to get some things for the house. Should I tell him to hold off so I can go with you?"

Monica placed her fists on her hips. "I thought we discussed this, Lily. If I'm going to break my old habits of kowtowing to you and everyone else, I need to be on my own."

Lily held up her hands. "Okay, okay. I just want to help."

Monica's face softened. "I know, Lily, and I really appreciate it. Sorry for snapping at you."

Lily went over to Monica and hugged her. "I'm sorry too if

I sound like an old nag."

Monica smiled. "You sound like a mother, the mother you've always been for me. I love you for it."

"Thanks. I love you, too," said Lily. "Don't worry. Go to your appointment. I'll take Izzy with me. We'll make it a nice outing for her. Wait to leave while I get Izzy's car seat."

When Lily came back, Monica plucked the car keys from Lily's hand and kissed her on the cheek. "See you later."

Izzy came running into the kitchen. "Where are you going, Mommy?"

"On an errand. I'll be back soon. You're going shopping with Auntie Lee and Brian. It should be fun."

Izzy smiled up at Lily. "Shopping?"

"Uh, huh. We'll have fun!"

They waved goodbye to Monica and then Lily said to Izzy, "We'd better hurry and get you ready."

Brian appeared as Lily was putting extra tissue and a few sheets of paper towels in her purse. She'd learned from previous outings with Izzy that these were helpful items for runny noses and sticky fingers.

"Ready?" Brian asked her.

"We are," said Lily, giving him an apologetic look. "Monica has an unexpected appointment with a counselor and needed to take off."

"On her own?" Brian said, raising his eyebrows.

"We had a talk earlier and she wasn't about to listen to my suggestion of accompanying her," Lily said calmly for Izzy's sake. Izzy was staring at them both with a worried look.

"I see," said Brian, but Lily knew he was as concerned as she.

Between stores like Bed, Bath and Beyond and Home Goods, Lily and Brian were able to gather considerable amounts of needed items for the new house.

They'd easily agreed on white towels for the master bedroom, a soft green for the guest room, and a deeper green for Ollie's bathroom and sheets to match. When it came to kitchen and dining décor, Brian let Lily take the lead, while he concentrated on pots and pans and cooking utensils.

Izzy, riding in the cart, was kept busy playing with a set of measuring spoons until she grew too restless. Needing a break, Lily took her outside the store while Brian got in line at the checkout lane.

Lily's cell rang. *Monica.*

"Hey! What's up?" Lily asked, watching as Izzy sat in one of the chairs in the display area outside the store.

"Jeremy called," Monica said, her voice trembling. "He's here and I'm going to meet him and tell him to fuck off! I'm done with his stupid game."

"Whoa! Wait! I thought you were getting a burner phone and cutting off your cell."

"I was on my way to get the burner when he called. I know you're probably mad, but I have to take care of this myself. I don't want to live like this anymore."

"No, Monica! Please, don't ..."

"Here he is now," Monica said.

It took Lily a second to realize Monica had hung up. In a panic, she tried to call the number back, but there was no answer. Lily picked up Izzy and ran inside to find Brian. He'd paid for their things and was moving to the door. She hurried over to him. "Monica's meeting Jeremy. Call 911! Please! We have to go help her!"

"Hold on!" Brian said. "Monica's meeting him? When? Where?"

"I don't know. She didn't tell me. We have to look for the car. She said she was on her way to get a burner phone. That means we can check store parking lots." A sob escaped Lily as they hurried to his car and began to throw their purchases into the back.

Izzy began to cry as Lily buckled her into her car seat. Brian finished loading their things and slid behind the wheel.

Hardly able to hear above Izzy's wails, Lily tried to give Brian the details of the call and soon realized they had no way of knowing where Monica might be.

"We'll look for the car," said Brian. "It's a white Corolla. Right?"

"Yes, a newer one," said Lily, barely able to get the words out because of the lump in her throat and the nausea behind it.

Brian drove the short distance to the mall and began circling it, looking for the car.

"There!" said Lily. "Over there." She pointed to a white Corolla.

Brian pulled up next to it.

Lily jumped out of Brian's car and peered into the window of the rental. There were no signs of Monica.

"Stay with Izzy and the car," said Lily. "I'll run inside to see if I can find Monica or Jeremy."

"If you see Jeremy, keep your distance," warned Brian. "I'll call the mall security here and tell them what's happening."

Inside the mall, Lily kept a steady pace running along the concourse outside the stores, trying to catch a glimpse of either Monica or Jeremy. As she circled back, she glanced at people inside stores, pausing a moment and then moving on, become more and more frightened.

She returned to Brian's car. "Any sign of them?"

Brian shook his head.

"What are we going to do?" Lily's cry shattered the air.

"I don't know. We have no idea where they are or what kind

of car Jeremy might be driving." He placed a hand on her shoulder. "I'll go in and talk to security. Their cameras might have picked up something."

He left the car and hurried inside.

Lily did her best to stop shivering. Her mind was full of horrible pictures of Monica and Jeremy in a physical struggle that she knew Monica couldn't win.

When at last Brian returned to her, he shook his head. "Nothing shows on their cameras. We've placed a call to the police about a possible abduction, but they, like we, have no concrete facts. The only thing we can do is wait and pray Monica gets in touch with you again."

Lily lowered her head in her hands. Cries from deep within rose, filling the air around them with sounds of despair.

"I'm sorry, honey," Brian said, wrapping her in his arms.

From inside Brian's car, Izzy's wails were ear-piercing.

"Let's take Izzy back to my house," said Brian. "She's pretty upset. We need to keep her and ourselves as calm as we can."

Tears blurred her vision, but Lily nodded. "You're right. We need to protect her." They climbed into Brian's car.

"Where's Mommy?" Izzy asked. "I want Mommy!"

"We'll find her," said Lily forcing a calm to her voice she didn't feel. "In the meantime, Auntie Lee is here. And so is Brian." Lily couldn't hide the tears that rolled down her cheeks. A shiver crept along Lily's spine. Dear God! What would she do if something happened to Monica?

Back at Brian's house, Lily set Izzy in one of the new kitchen chairs at the table with juice and cookies and gave her a pen and paper to draw on. But neither she nor Izzy were content to sit still.

Brian carried in their purchases.

Trying to distract herself, Lily spent time removing tags,

placing towels and sheets in the washing machine, and hand washing silverware, dishes, and pots and pans. But her thoughts remained on Monica. "Please, God, please keep her safe," she murmured over and over again.

When she went to look for Izzy, Lily found her asleep on the master bedroom carpet next to the newly assembled bed. Lying down next to her, Lily wrapped an arm around her, wanting to protect Izzy from the awful feeling inside her that wouldn't go away.

Brian walked in, saw them, and lowered himself beside her. "I wish I could do something to make them both safe, but the only thing we can do is stay together while we wait for news."

"I know," said Lily, feeling helpless. "When Izzy wakes up, we should take her to the condo. If Monica can escape Jeremy, she might go there."

He stroked her hair. "I know how hard it is to feel so helpless."

"I wish she'd listened to me," Lily said. "I asked her not to go to places by herself until we knew more about Jeremy's whereabouts. And for her to arrange to meet him? It doesn't seem right. Did he still have that much influence on her? She was going to tell him off, but I wonder if it was more than that. I should've gone out with her."

"You can't blame yourself, Lily." He patted her back. "That would be unfair."

She sat up and kissed him. "Do you know how much I need you?"

He gave her a steady look. "I'm here, Lily. I'm here."

She snuggled up against him and cried softly, so as not to wake Izzy, afraid of the questions she might ask about her missing mommy.

CHAPTER THIRTY-SEVEN

LILY

At Brian's condo, Lily tried to tell herself that no news was good news, but she couldn't shake the feeling that Jeremy would somehow get his revenge.

Worried sick about Monica, Lily sat with Izzy, reading one of her new books to her. In the background, the muted television showed pictures on the screen. Though Lily kept glancing at it, there were no announcements of any new crimes.

"Why don't I drive over there and check the car once more?" said Brian. "I'll talk to the security people to see if anything has been reported."

Tears stung her eyes as she nodded. "That would be great. I don't know what else we can do until we hear from the police."

Brian shook his head. "Neither do I."

Izzy patted Lily's cheek for attention. "Where's Mommy?"

Lily's heart contracted. What was she supposed to say?

"She's out," Lily said. "But don't worry. We'll find her." Izzy deserved the truth because she had an awful feeling it was going to get worse.

"Now, let's go back to our story." The cute story about a bunny named Bob was as much for her diversion as it was for Izzy. When Lily could no longer sit still, she rose and began making supper. Monica had wanted to keep her on a strict schedule and the growing dark indicated it was time for Izzy's meal.

Rummaging in the refrigerator, Lily retrieved bread, eggs and milk. Toast and scrambled eggs were some of her niece's favorite things.

She'd just placed a plate of food in front of Izzy when Brian arrived back at the condo. Lily froze. "Any news?"

He shook his head and motioned for her to follow him out of the room. "We got the local news stations to agree to post a picture of Monica with a phone number to call if anyone has seen her."

"Oh, great idea. Thanks."

"They are the ones to thank." Brian sighed and rubbed a hand through his hair. "I don't know what to think, but it can't be good."

Lily gripped her hands together. "I have to remind myself that Monica is stronger than she looks."

"With a broken arm?" Brian asked her gently.

She let out a shaky sigh. "I wish she'd listened to me."

"I think we should print off photos of her and Jeremy from her Facebook page and give them to the police. That way, if they find him, they know who they're dealing with."

"Smart idea. I've got my computer set up in the kitchen. It's already hooked up to your printer. Give me a moment." Lily hurried back to the small office space she'd set up in the kitchen, went to Monica's Facebook page, and printed off some photographs for the police.

"Here." She handed Brian a sheaf of papers.

"Thanks. I'll take these to the police department and be right back."

Lily nodded, wishing she would stop feeling as if she might throw up. She glanced at Izzy and forced a smile at the questioning look she gave her.

###

With Izzy tucked into bed for the night, all the fears Lily

had kept at bay now wrapped around her like a python squeezing the air out of her. Brian offered to cook something, but Lily shook her head. "I can't eat anything right now."

He handed her a glass of water. "At least drink this."

Lily took the glass and lifted it to her mouth, thinking of how she'd fed Monica as a child. Sometimes that's all they'd had for a meal—water, peanut butter, and bread.

She took the glass of water out to the patio. The warm air caressed her, easing her nerves for only a moment before cold fear swept over her. No news might be good news, as she'd earlier thought, but she had an awful feeling she'd have heard from Monica by now if she was all right.

At the sound of the doorbell, she dropped the plastic glass, and hurried into the house.

Brian opened the door and stepped back, motioning a policeman inside.

Lily ran to Brian's side and grabbed hold of his arm. "Any news of my sister?"

The policeman bobbed his head. "I'm afraid so. There's been an accident on the I-10 involving Monica Weaver and a man named Jeremy O'Neill."

"Oh, my God! Is she all right?" Lily stared at the policeman and knew the answer from the look on his face.

"I'm sorry, ma'am. But there were no survivors."

Lily felt herself falling and then it all turned black.

Lily felt as if she were swimming in a dark pool as she struggled to open her eyes. She was lying on the couch in Brian's condo, she realized, and looked up into his concerned face.

"Hi, Lily. Do you know where you are?" Brian asked.

She frowned at him. "Yes. Here in the condo. What happened?"

"You fainted," said Brian. He handed her a cold compress. "Here. Hold this while I help you sit up."

She took the cloth and held it to her forehead as she got to her feet. At the sight of a policeman still standing by the door, the memory of his news rushed back. She straightened and moved forward, needing to know the details.

"Tell me everything," she said to the policeman.

Soon it all became clear. Jeremy was found behind the wheel, still buckled in. Monica was in the backseat, her hands tied behind her back. They suspected that on the way toward L.A., a struggle of some kind or another reason had caused Jeremy to lose control. The car went off the road, rolling over, until it ended up on the other side of the road.

"We were able to retrieve her purse from the car," the policeman said, handing her a paper bag holding the purse.

"Thanks," said Lily, hearing her voice ringing in her ears as if it was a recording gone bad.

"Thank you, sir," said Brian. "Where are they now?"

"At the morgue."

Brian put a comforting arm around her. "Thank you for your help."

The policeman nodded. "Sorry to bring you such bad news. Let us know if there's anything we can do for you."

Brian showed the policeman out the door and turned back to Lily. "Well, we have our answer. I'm very, very sorry about Monica."

Lily clasped a hand to her chest, feeling as if her heart was about to explode. The reality of losing her sister hurt like a physical pain. Monica was gone. She'd never be with them again.

She heard Izzy cry out in her sleep and turned to Brian as realization struck her like a blow to her belly. "Oh, my God! I'll have to tell Izzy! She's mine now."

CHAPTER THIRTY-EIGHT

ROSE

Rose stirred in her sleep then realized her cell was chirping. Half-asleep she reached for it, clicked on the call, and said, "Hello?"

The sound of sobbing filled her ears. All traces of sleep fled. She sat up. "Hello?"

"Rose, it's me, Lily. They found Monica. She's dead."

"Oh, Lily, I'm so sorry. What happened?"

"She and Jeremy died in a car accident."

Rose heard more sobbing. "Tell me what you need."

"I need you to help me with Izzy tomorrow. I have so much to do. So much I can barely think."

Rose heard the wobble in Lily's voice and tears gathered in her eyes. She was an only child but she knew how much Lily loved her sister. "Take a breath. Talk to me."

Lily told her about Monica's call from the mall and the long wait they'd had before hearing of the accident. "Izzy is now mine. Before I came to California, Monica had legal papers drawn up assigning me the custody of Izzy should anything happen to her." Lily sobbed. "It's almost as if she knew."

"Aw, honey. I'm very sorry. Of course, I'll help. Do you want me to pick up Izzy?"

"No. I want to drop her off, just like I did before. She'll think it's another adventure. I need her to get comfortable staying there, because I need to go to New York to take care of Monica's apartment and car, and to file legal papers. I'll speak to Alec and Juanita about Izzy staying there when I come."

"Okay, hon. We'll be here. If you don't mind, I'll give Juanita a heads-up so she knows what's going on. We'll try to make it as comfortable for Izzy as possible."

"Thank you," said Lily. "I don't know what I'd do without you. Brian has postponed his mother's visit and is going to meet her in Austin. It's what we thought would be best for everyone. So, I really need help from you, Willow, and Juanita to make it all work."

Rose's throat clogged with tears but she managed to say, "We're here to help you, Lily. Always."

CHAPTER THIRTY-NINE

LILY

Lily was lying in bed when she felt a hand touch her cheek. Startled, she opened her eyes and stared into Izzy's face. She turned and found Brian gone.

"Where's Mommy?" Izzy said, crawling up into bed next to her.

Lily tensed and quickly reviewed in her mind what she'd read online about telling young children about the death of someone dear. Straightforward talk was necessary.

"Come here, sweetie," Lily said, wrapping an arm around Izzy and drawing her close. "There's something I need to tell you. Mommy died in a bad accident. She's not coming back."

Izzy flipped over on her side and faced Lily. She patted Lily's wet cheek. "I want Mommy to come back."

"Me, too," said Lily, doing her best to be strong for her niece. "But that isn't going to happen. It makes me very sad but I can't do anything to change that."

Izzy's eyes widened. "She's not coming back? Never?"

She hugged Izzy to her and rubbed her back. "No, she's not. We'll do lots of things together to help remember her. I'm here to help you, along with Brian and my friends at Alec's house. It's okay to cry. It's okay to feel sad. I feel very, very sad too, because I loved your mommy very much."

Izzy drew a shaking breath and put her thumb in her mouth, settling a wide-eyed gaze on Lily.

Feeling ancient, Lily climbed out of bed and turned to her. "Do you want to stay there for a while?"

Izzy nodded, and Lily headed into the bathroom for a shower. The day wasn't about to get better.

The minute Lily walked into the kitchen at Alec's house and saw Rose, Willow, and Juanita, the tears she'd been able to hold inside all morning as she'd dressed and fed Izzy tumbled down her cheeks.

Each of the women came up and silently hugged her before turning to Izzy with bright smiles.

"Hooray! My little swimmer is here," said Rose.

"We're going to do sticker paper dolls, right, Izzy?" Willow said, holding up a colorful booklet.

Izzy glanced at Lily.

"Yes," Lily said, "you can swim and do stickers while I go on errands today."

"Will you come back?" Izzy asked in a small voice.

"Oh, sweet girl, Auntie Lee will return this afternoon. Okay?"

"Okay." Izzy hugged her.

Juanita handed her a cup of coffee and wiped tears from her cheeks. "Come sit with us while Rose helps Izzy into her swimsuit."

"Thanks," said Lily. She gave Juanita a grateful smile. "I really need this."

Lily sat at the table, took a sip of the hot liquid, and let out a long sigh. "My worst fears came true. I was so hopeful that getting Monica out of New York would save her."

Juanita shook her head. "That man was evil. It shouldn't happen to anyone, but it does. I'm so sorry."

"Stalking and physical abuse are inexcusable. It's an insidious thing—how one person's need for dominance can ruin another," said Willow. "Monica's isn't the first death like this, nor will hers be the last. This kind of abuse is real and too often deadly. We must get the police to act more strongly to cries for help in situations like these."

"True, but Monica never reported him. That's the other issue. The police department here has been very helpful," said Lily. "It's how we found out so quickly about Monica. They were circulating photos of her and Jeremy that we'd given them."

"Rose said Izzy is now yours," said Juanita, giving her a look of concern. "How does Brian feel about that?"

Fresh tears filled Lily's eyes. "We talked about it this morning. He says as long as we're going to be a family, we might as well have one of each—a boy and a girl. It's going to be tough to get us all used to one another, but we're determined to make it work. I think both Brian and I have been hungry for a family for a long time, though neither of us has acknowledged it until now."

Juanita squeezed her hand affectionately. "Both Ollie and Izzy will be blessed to have you and Brian for parents. Out of bad situations comes some good."

"Thanks," said Lily, hoping she and Brian would be able to give Ollie and Izzy the love and comfort they needed. Two children who'd suffered such devastating losses would need a lot of tender, loving care to deal with the trauma of losing their mothers.

After seeing Izzy happily swimming with Rose, Lily headed to Alec's private quarters.

She knocked on the door and opened it a crack. "Alec?"

"Come on in," he called. She walked into his living area and found him sitting at a desk. He smiled at her. "Good morning. What brings you here?"

"I have a favor to ask," she said, taking a seat in the chair he indicated for her. Trying not to cry, she told him about

Monica's death.

"My God!" He shook his head sadly. "I'm so sorry, my dear. What can I do for you?"

"I need to ask if Izzy can stay here while I go to New York to clean out Monica's apartment and file some legal paperwork. Brian and I have agreed it would be best if she stayed with people that she knows. This way he can travel to Austin to be with Ollie."

"Of course. Juanita and I will be thrilled to have her here. It gives me another opportunity to be a grandpa for a while."

Lily smiled. "Rose and Willow have promised to help. I'll stay only as long as I need to."

"You take your time, my dear, though I certainly understand your desire to spend as little time in New York as possible."

Lily rose and gave him a kiss. "Thanks so much. You're such a wonderful man."

He looked up at her, his eyes filling. "Like I told Rose, I love each of my Desert Flowers. I'd do anything for you."

She hugged him, too emotional to talk.

After a grueling couple of days of taking care of details following Monica's death and getting Izzy used to the thought of staying at Alec's house while she went to New York, it was time to leave. Monica had been cremated, and she and Brian agreed to hold off on any private service until a later time.

Lily put on a cheerful act worthy of an award as she dropped Izzy off at Alec's house. Once again, Juanita, Rose, and Willow were there to welcome them. By now, Izzy was comfortable with them and loved the attention they gave her. Still, Lily's heart clutched at the thought of leaving her. She hugged Izzy to her, wishing she could stay.

"Are you sure you don't want one of us to go to New York

with you?" Willow asked.

Lily nodded. "Thanks. I appreciate it, but this is something I need to do alone, a cleansing of a sort."

"Call us if you change your mind," said Rose.

Lily smiled and gave them a wave as she left. They were such dear friends.

Back at Brian's condo, saying goodbye to him was as difficult. With his arms around her, Lily leaned against him taking a moment to soak in the comforting feel of him. He'd become such a reassuring presence in her life, reminding her how strong she was, telling her over and over again how much he loved her, how everything would work out.

As she left him to go to the airport, she put on a brave front—smiling and waving to him, but inside she was weeping. Brian would head to Austin later that day. Ollie was due to come to Palm Desert in another four weeks, and he needed more time with Brian. While Lily found the idea of this new family overwhelming from time to time, she told herself they all needed one another.

The flight to New York was full of memories of Monica through the years. It was a way for Lily, she supposed, to begin the process of grieving for her sister. Lily was glad she'd answered Monica's call for help by moving to New York to be with her through her pregnancy, the birth of Izzy, and beyond. The best that had come of it was the strong, loving relationship she already had with Izzy.

Still, she wondered if she could've done something to prevent Monica's death. Brian told her not to take on that burden, but a part of Lily would always wonder about it. She hadn't liked Jeremy when she'd first met him, but Monica had been totally infatuated, loving how he called her beautiful, discounting his lack of ambition, and the way he ordered he around.

But Lily understood why Monica had fallen for him. The prettier of the two of them, Monica had faced a lot of verbal slaps from her mother for her pretty looks while her mother's own beauty was rapidly fading.

Remembering that, Lily vowed to be a loving parent to both Izzy and Ollie. As she'd done before telling Izzy about her mother dying, she'd reach out for all the help she could get. It was especially important now.

Izzy had asked for her mother a few more times and then after cuddling and talking about why she wouldn't be coming back, Izzy had stared at Lily, her round eyes awash with tears. Lily was sure that the subject would continue to come up, but for now, Izzy was doing her best to deal with her mother's sudden death. How could a four-year-old handle something a grown woman couldn't make sense of?

Opening the door to Monica's apartment, a shiver crept down Lily's back, making it difficult to move forward. Even now, with both Jeremy and Monica gone, the air inside reeked of hopelessness. Monica's death was so tragic. She was much too young to die, killing an unborn baby and leaving a small child behind her. Anger filled Lily, replacing the cold inside her with a hot rage. How dare Jeremy do this to her sister? To Izzy? To the baby? To her?

Hands fisted on her hips, Lily stared at the mess around her. Jeremy must have made it. The place was totally tossed, as if he'd been looking through cupboards and drawers, searching for what, she could only guess. One thing Lily knew for sure is that she didn't want anything here except family photos and papers, and Izzy's things. The rest was to be given as a donation to a local women's shelter. Even the car, which had been located at Kennedy Airport and was being returned to the police station in Ellenton, would be donated. She'd pack up what she wanted and hire the rest to be done. And if another tortured woman could use Monica's things, all the better.

Holding in sobs, Lily headed to Monica's bedroom. After working so many years at a law firm, she'd made sure Monica had placed important family papers, such as birth certificates and life insurance policies, in a fire-proof metal box in the back of her closet.

Lily went to the closet, pushed the hanging clothes out of the way, and found the container where she and Monica had placed it. Relieved, she brought it out and put it by the front door where she would stack personal things she'd packed up.

She went out to her rental car and unloaded the boxes, packing paper, and packaging tape she'd picked up at the nearby Office Depot on her way to the apartment. Having just moved out of her condo, she knew what supplies she'd need.

Inside the apartment, Lily went to Monica's bedroom, carefully going through all the drawers, selecting a few pieces of better jewelry to save for Izzy, leaving the rest to be donated.

In Izzy's room, she packed up a box of toys, nestling them among clothing and shoes that would still fit Izzy. She glanced around the room and decided to pack all the pictures and decorative items that Izzy might find comforting.

Then, too tired to do more, Lily left the apartment and headed to a local hotel. On the way, she stopped at a favorite Chinese restaurant. Sitting by herself at a table, Lily felt so alone she almost got up and left. Before she'd gone to California, she, Monica, and Izzy had loved coming there. Now, that would never happen again.

The waitress approached, and instead of ordering food for the restaurant, she ordered it to go, anxious to get out of there.

Later, in her hotel room, Lily picked at her food and called Juanita to see how Izzy was doing.

"She's been a little quiet, but Rose and Willow have kept her busy," Juanita assured her. "They all get along so well. Poor baby is tired, but I'm sure she'd like to hear from you. Wait a sec. I'll put her on the phone."

When Lily heard Izzy's sweet little voice say, "Hi, Auntie Lee", she fought for control.

"Hi, Sweetheart! Did you have a fun day with Rose and Willow and Juanita?"

"Yes! I can swim!"

"Wonderful!" said Lily. "Guess what? I'm sending you a big box of your old toys. They'll come soon."

"Toby?"

"Yes, Toby, the fish, and other things. Auntie Lee loves you. Say goodbye and let me talk to Juanita."

"'Bye."

"I don't know what you said, but Izzy is happy about something," said Juanita. "She's such a doll. We all love her."

"Thank you so much for being there with her. It means the world to me. I'm working as fast as I can to get back home. Will keep in touch."

Drained, Lily hung up and climbed into bed, not caring that she was still in her clothes.

The next morning, Lily looked at her list, grateful she was so organized. She'd hardly slept a wink. After breakfast, she placed a call to the head of the women's shelter to tell them what she had in mind. The head of the shelter eagerly accepted Lily's offer and agreed to send a volunteer over to the apartment to oversee the packers.

On the way to Monica's place, Lily stopped at the women's shelter and handed over the keys she'd picked up from the police and the title to the car.

The director's eyes filled as she accepted the donation. "You can't possibly know what a help this is going to be for one of our families. The household items, too. Thank you so much."

"You're welcome. I just wish my sister had been able to come to you. I think she'd be very pleased to know she's helping others."

"Sadly, we hear too many stories like your sister's," said the director, sighing and shaking her head. "I'm sorry for your loss and understand how devastated you must be. We do, however, appreciate your thought of us, and your desire to help others who are trying to escape their abusers. We'll see that some good comes of your sister's death." She squeezed Lily's hand. "Again, I'm so sorry."

Numb with grief, Lily merely nodded.

That afternoon, Lily walked into her old law office feeling like a total stranger. It seemed so small, the people like strangers.

David Bakeley, her old boss approached her with a sad expression. "Lily, it's nice to see you, but I'm sorry for the circumstances. I know how close you were to your sister. Come back to my office and we can take care of any paperwork. The probate of wills in New York is a slow process, as you know. But from what you said, everything else is in order, including the supervision of her little girl.

Lily nodded. "Yes, Izzy is under my care now. My fiancé and I plan to officially adopt her."

David's eyebrows rose. "A lot has happened to you in a relatively short time."

"Yes. Both good and tragic."

As she sat in David's office, she thought how fortunate she

was to have escaped her old, monotonous routine. It had been a decent life, but couldn't compare to what she'd found in California.

CHAPTER FORTY

ROSE

At Alec's house, Rose lifted Izzy out of the swimming pool, wrapped a towel around her, and hugged her close. Such a sweet little girl. She couldn't wait for Leah and Izzy to meet. They'd be adorable together. They both were bright, active, and loving.

Willow joined them on the pool deck. "How's it going? Izzy, I saw you swim. You're a little fish."

"Like Toby," said Izzy.

Willow gave Rose a questioning look.

"I gather it's a toy that Lily is shipping here for her."

"How's Lily doing? I haven't had a chance to talk to her. Brent and Trace are keeping me busy, trying to outdo every idea I come up with."

Rose couldn't hold back a frustrated sigh. "When is that nonsense going to stop?"

"I'm not sure. Not until they assign someone to become the resident manager or an assistant to that position. There's a part of me that would give anything to beat them at their game, but it's their hotel so I don't think that's going to happen."

"Whoa!" said Rose. "You can't take that attitude. You're better than both of them."

Willow shook her head. "I'm just trying to be real, that's all." Rose studied her but said nothing. She'd have a little talk with Hank tonight. Maybe there was something they could do to help Willow.

###

A day later, Rose stood with Willow and Izzy at the baggage claim area of the Palm Springs airport, waiting for Lily to arrive. Izzy wasn't the only one excited to see her. Rose had been surprised by how much she'd missed her, but then, the Desert Flowers had become a close trio.

Willow lifted Izzy in her arms so she could see Lily approaching them in the group of deplaned passengers making their way down a hallway toward them.

"Auntie Lee!" cried Izzy, wiggling to get down.

Rose's eyes misted as she watched Izzy run to Lily. Monica's death had struck Rose hard. The thought of a young pregnant mother being killed because of her crazy, stalker ex-boyfriend was devastating.

Lily's face was streaked with tears as she walked toward them carrying Izzy.

Rose and Willow embraced her.

"Welcome home," said Willow.

"We're glad you're back," added Rose. "We've all missed you."

Lily gave them a wry smile. "Not as much as I've missed you. I hope never to see New York again."

"That bad?" said Rose.

Lily nodded. "But now it's over." She kissed Izzy's cheek. "And now I've got my little Izzy back."

Izzy patted Lily's cheek. "Izzy love you."

"We all do," said Rose, dabbing at her eyes.

CHAPTER FORTY-ONE

LILY

The next day, Pedro helped Lily move her boxes and the few pieces of furniture from her condo out of Alec's garage and over to Brian's new house. Though they were staying at Brian's condo, she and Brian agreed to get things set up as quickly as they could at the house prior to his mother's visit.

Eager to make an excellent impression on Brian's mother, Lily made a game of unpacking at the house and allowing Izzy to play in the big boxes.

After a few hours, she called Sarah Jensen to get the phone number of the babysitter she'd previously recommended. It would be another new person in Izzy's life, but Lily wanted to get back to work. Monica's death had shaken her to the core and she needed to focus on something besides the unsettling thoughts of her sister. It would be good to get caught up on what was happening with the sale of the hotel.

She knew Rose and Hank were still working on promotional materials, including new signage at all three hotels in the Corona Collection. Willow was working on coordination of management of the three hotels, bringing their styles together.

Brian and she had discussed the timeline, but a lot depended on moving the two Blaise properties in Phoenix into compliance with the Desert Sage Inn style.

###

Lily eagerly opened the front door to Brian's house to greet Anna Rivera, the babysitter she was hoping to hire. Smiling at her, Lily noticed Anna's dark hair streaked with gray and the laugh lines radiated from bright, dark eyes.

"Hello, Anna. I'm Lily, and this is Izzy."

They shook hands, and Anna glanced at Izzy.

"Ah, such a precious child," Anna murmured, as she stepped inside. "I love this age."

"Yes, she's at a great age," Lily replied with a sense of pride. "We'll soon have another child join us, a boy of eight, named Ollie."

Izzy went to Anna and looked up at her. "Are you my grandma?"

Anna bent down in front of Izzy. "I'm not your grandma, but a special friend. My name is Anna. Can you say that?"

"Anna!" said Izzy.

Anna laughed. "See? Now we're friends."

"Come on into the kitchen. I've made some iced tea," said Lily. "Would you care for some?"

"Yes, thank you. That would be nice," Anna replied.

As Lily led Anna to the kitchen, she noticed Izzy take Anna's hand, and smiled. Izzy had always been a social child, but being at Alec's house among Lily's friends, had helped her get used to having new people in her life.

In the kitchen, Lily poured iced tea into two glasses, juice in another, and placed a plate of cookies on the table. After handing out the drinks, she sat opposite Anna eager to get to know her better. They talked about Anna's family, some of the jobs she'd had, and her thoughts about handling children. The more Lily learned, the more excited she was to have found her to help out with the children. Anna had raised a family of her own, had taught at a pre-school, and was now working for individual families as a means of enjoying the children.

"I'm new at motherhood," Lily confessed, holding Izzy in her lap. "I'm sure there's a lot you can teach me."

"Don't worry. We all make mistakes raising kids, but it's obvious you love Izzy. That's what counts more than anything else."

Lily let out a sigh. "That's what I'm hoping." She explained about Ollie. "I haven't met him yet, but we're going to start doing FaceTime together."

"Just be yourself," said Anna. "Kids know when you're not."

Lily nodded thoughtfully and turned the conversation to the particulars of the job.

They quickly agreed that Anna would start working three days a week when Lily would go to the law office and she'd be available for weekend evenings, if necessary.

"To begin with, the four of us will be spending a lot of time together to get used to one another," said Lily.

"I'll help in any way I can," said Anna.

By the time Anna got up to leave, Lily didn't think it at all too soon to give her a hug.

"Thanks for everything. You've helped reassure me."

Anna chuckled. "Being a parent is the hardest job you'll ever have, but it's worth it."

Lily saw Anna out and returned to unpacking, thrilled to think she'd have some help in the crucial days ahead.

That night, Lily had just put Izzy to bed when Brian arrived at the condo from his trip to Austin.

She raced to meet him. "Brian! So glad you're home." She turned as Izzy approached in her nightgown.

"It's okay. Come say 'hi' to Brian," Lily said, waving her forward.

Izzy gave him a shy smile and grabbed hold of Lily's hand.

Brian put down his suitcase, bent over, and ruffled her hair. "Hi, Izzy! Have you been a good girl while I've been gone?"

Izzy nodded emphatically. "I can swim." She lifted her arms to Lily to be held.

"That's great! I like swimmers. Lily says you're like a fish!"

Izzy leaned her head against Lily's shoulder and sucked her thumb, her gaze never leaving Brian as he straightened.

Lily gave him a kiss, wanting Izzy to know how she felt about him. Though Izzy was very comfortable with Lily's female friends, she was still a little cautious around Brian. She wondered if this behavior was related to Jeremy or not.

"Time for bed," Lily told Izzy. "I'll help Izzy get situated and meet you in the living room. There's a lot to talk about."

"How about a glass of wine while we catch up?"

"Mmm, that would be delicious."

Lily tucked Izzy in once more and after reading a short story, she hurried to the living room, anxious to share news with Brian.

He walked into the room, carrying two glasses of red wine. He handed her one and sat beside her on the couch. "Ah, I've missed you. I stayed a little longer than I thought because we have a bit of a problem with Ollie. He says he doesn't want to come to California with me, and he doesn't want to FaceTime with you."

"Oh, no! I thought he understood this would be his new home." Lily's stomach whirled with dismay.

"His aunt thinks he's just testing to see if he can stay with them. Up until now, he's been compliant about moving to Palm Desert. Upset about his mom. Susannah is going to talk with him to make sure he's again comfortable with the idea. She respects Becky's wishes for Ollie to be with me. My mother offered to fly to Austin to bring him here with her when she comes this weekend, thinking a visit or two before the move might help. Then Ollie can see for himself what his life would be like here. I talked to Susannah, and we agreed it was a good idea. Is that okay with you?"

"Yes," said Lily, trying to hide her disappointment about Ollie's behavior.

"Don't worry," said Brian, giving her a kiss. "He's a great kid, and smart."

Lily nodded, but she wanted to cry. What if they couldn't work things out?

While Anna took care of Izzy, Lily and Brian worked together to get the house arranged so both Ollie and Reenie could stay with them at the new house. The last of their furniture arrived, fitting easily with what Lily had saved from her condo. The rugs for the living and dining areas still needed to be delivered, but Lily didn't care as long as the rest of the move was completed.

On the morning of the day Reenie and Ollie were to arrive, Lily rose early and sat alone on the pool deck, wishing her nerves away. She wasn't worried about getting along with Reenie, but the anticipation of facing a little boy who'd already decided he didn't like her sent frissons of anxiety through her.

"What'cha doing?" asked Brian, walking up to her and giving her a sweet kiss on the mouth.

"Trying to get my nerve up to meet Ollie," she admitted. 'I'm afraid I'll ruin my chances with him by saying or doing something stupid. I understand what he's going through, watching his mother's health fail and dealing with her death. And then he's had to get used to the idea of a father and a grandmother he hadn't known. I don't want to be another source of stress for him when he's already hurt and confused.

What will I do if he decides he doesn't want to be here because of me?"

Brian pulled a chair up next to hers and gave her a steady look. "Just be yourself, Lily. Everyone loves you. Ollie will too." He put an arm around her. "You've been amazing dealing with Monica's death, tying up legal matters, and taking care of her things, along with turning this house into a home and helping with Izzy. I wish I could take you away somewhere to rest, but all I can do is offer my support."

She turned to him and caressed his cheek. "You mean so much to me, Brian. Okay, let's do this. Turn us into a family."

He grinned at her. "That's my girl."

That afternoon, Lily stood with Brian, holding onto Izzy's hand, praying things would go well. She recognized Reenie walking toward her and lifted a hand to wave, but her attention focused on the little boy walking with her.

Smaller than she'd thought, his features were so like Brian's, her breath caught. Ollie looked up at her. Behind his round eyeglasses his hazel eyes studied her.

She smiled and waved, but he didn't respond.

"You're here!" cried Brian, rushing forward to greet them.

He put an arm around his mother, quickly kissed her, then turned to Ollie. "Hi, son!" He hugged him.

Lily relaxed when she saw Ollie wrap his arms around Brian's waist.

Brian lowered Ollie on his feet. "I want you to meet Lily. I've told you about her before. And this little girl is Izzy. Can you say, 'Hi?'"

Ollie shook his head.

"Hi, Ollie," Lily said. "I'm so happy you could come for a visit." She turned and smiled at Reenie. "Hello, I'm Lily."

"So happy to meet you in person," said Reenie extending a

tanned hand to her.

Lily shook it and felt a smile cross her face. Brian's mother was adorable. Short and curvy, she oozed personality as her blue eyes studied Lily and traveled to Izzy.

"Hi, Izzy," Reenie cooed. "Aren't you sweet!"

"Are you my grandma?" Izzy asked, giving her a hopeful look.

Reenie beamed at her. "Why, yes, I could say that. After all, I'm going to be your grandma sometime soon." She turned to Lily. "I hope you don't mind."

"Not at all," said Lily, pleased. She smiled at Ollie. "She's your grandma too, Ollie."

Ollie studied Reenie and nodded, but kept his gaze averted from Lily.

"Let's get home, shall we?" Brian said, cupping Ollie's head with his hand and gently encouraging him to move.

Ollie remained silent, but stayed beside Brian.

Izzy studied him, then took hold of Ollie's hand.

Lily held her breath, wondering if Ollie would shake it off, but he continued to let Izzy hold his hand as they all moved forward.

When they went to get into Brian's car after picking up luggage, Lily said, "Why don't I sit in the backseat with the kids, Reenie? That will give you room up front."

"No," said Ollie. "Grandma, sit with me."

Reenie gave her a helpless look. "No problem, I'm happy to do it."

"Okay," said Lily, trying not to show her hurt.

CHAPTER FORTY-TWO

LILY

At home, Lily proudly showed Reenie the guest room. She'd worked especially hard to make it feel welcoming by placing a pitcher of ice water on a coaster on top of the bureau and a glass and a vase of fresh flowers beside it. "This is lovely," Reenie declared setting her purse on the chair next to the bureau. She faced Lily with a smile. "I'm so pleased to be able to stay here for a few days to get to know you. I've never seen Brian so happy."

Lily felt the sting of tears. Reenie's acceptance meant so much to her. "He makes me happy too. While you get comfortable, I'm going to check on Ollie."

Reenie gave her an encouraging pat on her arm. "Don't worry. Ollie will come around. He's missing his mother."

"I know," said Lily. "Poor kid. I know none of this is easy for him. I understand what he's going through. I'd do anything to have my sister back."

"Yes, of course. So much has happened to you in such a short amount of time. I admire your strength."

Lily sighed. "Without Brian, I don't think I could have made it."

She left Reenie and went to Ollie's room. Brian, Izzy, and Ollie were standing looking at the empty 20-gallon aquarium tank Brian had placed on a table. She walked over to them.

"What do you think, Ollie? This is where your lizard will live. You're going to have to help me, though. I'm afraid of them."

Ollie looked up at her with surprise.

"It's true," she said. "They frighten me."

"They won't hurt you," Ollie said softly.

"Well, it's a good thing you're here to show me." Lily put a hand on his shoulder and quickly took it off, wondering if she was moving too fast with him.

"I want one," said Izzy, pointing to the aquarium.

"Maybe when you're a little older. Not now," said Lily. "Later, when you're Ollie's age, we can talk about it."

"How about a swim in the pool?" said Brian, diverting Izzy's attention.

"Okay. Ollie, we have new swim trunks for you." Lily handed them to him.

He accepted them without looking at her.

Lily held in a sigh. "C'mon, Izzy, let's go get you changed."

After unpacking Ollie's clothes and getting his room squared away, Lily changed into her bathing suit and joined the others outside at the pool.

"Auntie Lee! Look at me!" cried Izzy, hanging onto the side of the pool and kicking.

Next to her, Ollie clung to the side of the pool, looking uncomfortable.

"It takes a while to get used to a pool," said Lily, stepping into the water and standing by him. "Brian, why don't you hold onto Ollie's hands and tug him along the surface, like a motorboat."

To demonstrate, she took hold of Izzy's hands and swished her through the surface of the water.

"Look, Ollie! I'm a fish!" said Izzy.

Ollie glanced at her and then allowed Brian to hold one of his hands and help him glide through the water.

Lily watched the tension leaving Ollie's stiff body and then went over to the steps and sat down beside Reenie.

"I'm very happy Brian found this house," said Reenie. "It's a perfect place for kids. Dogs, too. I've met Ollie's dog, Jack. He'll love the space."

"I hope so. Brian bought the house with all that in mind."

"Tell me a little about yourself, Lily. I know your sister died recently, leaving Izzy with you. Any other family?"

"No." Lily realized there was no point in making her family seem better than they were. She described what it was like growing up with her mother and the care of Monica she'd undertaken from a young age.

"Alcoholism is a horrible disease," Reenie said. "I'm sorry you had to go through all that. But I see how strong it's made you."

Lily looked at her with surprise. "I don't think I'm strong at all."

Reenie squeezed her hand. "It takes a strong person to handle everything that's been thrown at you. I hope this next phase of your life will be a little easier with Brian by your side." She chuckled. "And if he doesn't do right by you, you let me know and I'll ... I'll kick his butt!"

They laughed together.

"What are you two up to?" Brian asked, making his way over to them.

"Nothing," said Reenie. "Just getting to know your lovely lady."

Brian smiled and kissed Lily. "I'm a lucky guy, and I know it."

"That you are," said Reenie, beaming at them both. "A good thing, too, because it's going to take the two of you working side by side to pull this family together."

Lily glanced at Izzy and Ollie kicking and splashing as they played nearby. Looking at them, no one would guess the sorrow they carried. Ollie might be acting out a bit, but that was an honest reaction to what he was feeling. Though Izzy seemed content, at some point, Lily knew they'd have to talk more about her mother.

Later, after a light lunch and while Reenie and Izzy napped, Lily accompanied Brian and Ollie to the pet store. Though Brian had already spoken to the people there about Ollie's wish for a lizard, they were just going to pick up books about lizards and talk to the owner. Brian had already done some research and decided, as recommended, a Leopard Gecko was the best way to begin owning lizards.

The owner of the store remembered Brian and greeted them with enthusiasm. He brought out a number of books showing photographs of various types of lizards. Looking at the pictures with them sent a silent shudder through Lily, but she wasn't about to interfere with what Brian and Ollie had planned. If it took a lizard to help bring them all together, she'd try her best.

She stood aside as Ollie proudly held a gecko. He glanced at her and then said softly, "Don't be afraid, Lee."

Lily nodded, too touched to respond. It was the first time he'd reached out to her.

Brian glanced at her, well aware of her emotions.

After being reassured that one of the leopard geckos would be set aside for Ollie when he returned for good, they left with books and supplies for setting up the tank. Though he struggled with the bag holding all the purchases, Ollie proudly carried it to the car.

"What do you say?" Brian prompted, smiling at Ollie.

"Thanks. These are the best gifts ever! Will you help me set up the tank ... Bri ... D-Dad?"

Lily watched Brian's look of surprise turn to joy. To give

Brian a few moments to collect himself, she held the car door open so Ollie could slide in.

When they got back to the house, Izzy was on the couch, cuddling her stuffed bunny, just waking up. She saw Lily and ran to her. "You're here."

Lily picked her up. "Yes, I'm here. Did you have a nice nap?"

"No. I want Toby."

"Toby should be here in a few days," said Lily.

"Who's Toby?" Ollie asked, glancing from Izzy to Lily.

"Toby is Izzy's stuffed dolphin," said Lily. "One of her favorite toys. Izzy's just moved here, and we're waiting for the rest of her things to arrive."

"Oh," said Ollie, studying them both before walking away.

Reenie approached. "Izzy? I brought you some puzzles and other things to play with. Shall we take a look?"

Izzy wiggled to get down from Lily's arms. "For me?"

"Yes," said Reenie. "For you. They're in my room. Come, let's go look at them."

Brian had gone back to the garage. Glad for the opportunity to have some time alone with Ollie, she knocked on his bedroom door. "May I come in?"

Though he was lying on his bed, Ollie managed to shrug in a noncommittal way.

She walked over to his bed. "Okay, if I sit down?"

He lifted a shoulder, let it drop, and turned his face into his pillow.

"I thought I should let you know what happened to Izzy."

He rolled over and looked up at her with a questioning expression.

"Izzy's mother died in an automobile accident recently. That's why she's come to live with us."

"Is she sad?" Ollie asked with a look of concern.

"Yes, but she's young and doesn't fully understand what's happening. You, on the other hand, know exactly what you've lost and should feel free to be unhappy or angry about your own mother. It's okay. We're all very sad about it. But Brian and I are happy to have you with us. We want a family—a family with you."

Ollie sat up, shook his head, and pounded the pillow with a fist. "No! I want my Mom! I don't want you!" His face crumbled, and he began to cry, deep sobs that shook his body.

Lily pulled him onto her lap, into her arms and held him. She rubbed his back as tremors rippled through his body. "I'm so sorry, Ollie. I wish I could bring her back for you, but nobody can. The best we can do is remember how much she loved you and how much you loved her in return, and all the wonderful times you had with her."

"It's not fair," he said, sniffing. Tears lingered on his sweet face.

"It's not," she said with sympathy. "And that makes it worse."

"I want things to be the way they were," he murmured settling his head against her chest.

"I know," said Lily, continuing to rub his back in comforting circles. "I wish Izzy's mother was still alive too, but we're doing our best to make sure she knows how much we love her. We want to make you comfortable and happy here with us too. But you're going to have to be patient with me."

He sat back and studied her. "Why?"

"Because I'm learning to be a mother. Can I trust you to help me?"

Ollie's gaze penetrated her while he considered it. He finally nodded. "Okay."

"All right then. For starters, I want you to know you can talk about anything you want. You can tell me anything."

He scrambled off her lap and stood facing her. “Okay. Can I have another cookie?”

Pressing her lips together to keep from laughing, she nodded. “Let’s go.”

They walked into the kitchen together.

Brian studied them with concern. “Everything okay?” he said quietly as Ollie walked out to the patio eating the cookie.

“For the moment,” Lily said.

Brian kissed her. “I’m not sure what just happened, but I love you for it.”

“Thanks.” She smiled. “We’ve had a nice talk, but it’s only the first step.”

CHAPTER FORTY-THREE

WILLOW

At Brian's house, Willow proudly carried the large potted plant she'd purchased for Lily's party. Sarah Jensen held a gaily-wrapped package in her hand and opened the front door for Willow to haul the plant inside.

Lily greeted them with a smile. "Hello! Welcome! Come in. I want you to meet Brian's mother, Reenie, and then I want to show you around the house."

Willow gazed around. "It's beautiful so far. Love the openness." She set down the plant in a sunny corner. "Thought you could use this in the new house."

Brian approached. "Hi, there! Glad you could make it. We're having this get-together so our friends can meet my mother and my son, Ollie." He turned as Izzy ran up to Willow for a hug. "Guess you know Izzy pretty well," he added with a smile.

Willow hugged Izzy to her. "We're old buddies, aren't we?"

"Yes," Izzy said with a satisfied nod.

Willow set her down and followed Brian to where his mother was standing and talking to Rose and Hank.

"Mom, this is Willow Sanchez, another of the Desert Flowers we told you about," said Brian.

Reenie's smile was genuine as she studied her. "It's so nice to meet you. I swear you Flowers are all as pretty as the real ones. Lily has already told me how you're fighting for Alec's vision for the Desert Sage Inn. It's clear how much you mean to her." She glanced over at Lily talking to Sarah. "I'm very happy Brian found Lily. Of course, I had no idea I'd end up with an entire family, but I'm loving it."

"How's it going?" asked Willow. "So much has happened in such a short time."

Reenie grew more serious. "With the recent trauma they've all had, I'd say it's going remarkably well. Once things are calmer, Lily and Brian can think of a wedding. The marriage situation is a little backwards, but as I told my friends back in Florida, I believe the whole thing was somehow meant to be."

Willow smiled. She had the very same feeling. She'd seen the connection between Lily and Brian from the beginning and felt something was bound to happen between them. Maybe not quite like this, but it was all good.

CHAPTER FORTY-FOUR

LILY

Too soon it was time for Reenie and Ollie to leave. Lily helped Ollie pack his suitcase, tucking his brand-new stuffed lizard inside it as he wanted. He'd loved everything about the visit to the Living Desert Zoo and Gardens and had chosen the lizard as the one gift he could select.

"We'll put your books in your backpack so you can read them on the plane," said Lily, helping him to fit them inside. "We'll leave a few others here for when you come back. It'll only be a few weeks. Okay?"

Ollie nodded. Since their emotional afternoon together, Ollie had been very attentive to her, had called her Lee, but hadn't wanted to hug. Lily was sure time would take care of that, but it still worried her.

On the way to the airport, Lily was as silent as the others. Even Izzy, usually full of chatter, remained quiet, sensing the sadness of the moment.

Lily stared out the window, thinking of the last few days. Reenie's presence would be sorely missed. She was a sunny ray of optimism, giving Lily additional confidence. She'd already announced she couldn't wait to come back. Ollie had opened up considerably, but she understood his need to take his time.

Brian pulled up to the departure entrance for their flight,

and Lily got out of the car to say goodbye.

Reenie embraced her. "I'm so glad you're part of the family. Can't wait until you two make it official, but I understand why you're waiting. Keep in touch. FaceTime whenever you want. I can't wait for my friends to meet you."

Lily laughed. "I'd love to meet them."

As Reenie went to her son, Lily squatted and faced Ollie. "I want you to know how happy I am that you came for a visit. I'm happy too that I got to know you a little. You're so much like your father—thoughtful and kind. I already love you, Ollie. And when you're ready, I hope you'll love me too."

Ollie nodded, started to walk away, then turned and ran back to her. Throwing his arms around her, he almost knocked her off her feet. She held him close, loving the feel of him. He was a darling boy and would become a wonderful man. She'd help him in any way she could.

Brian helped her to her feet and lifted Ollie over his shoulder. She blew a kiss to them and went back inside the car to give them privacy.

When she glanced back at Izzy in her car seat, she wasn't surprised to see Izzy's eyes filling with tears. Izzy loved having people around. The coming weeks until Ollie returned would be lonely for her, Lily realized. Izzy and Ollie had become friends.

Back at the house, Lily put Izzy down for her nap and decided to stretch out in a deck chair by the pool. After the activity of the past few days, the house seemed unnaturally quiet. Still, she needed time to regroup and think about the days ahead.

Brian came out to the patio and sat down in a chair beside her. "That visit went well."

Lily nodded. "I really like your mother. She's upbeat and

kind."

"Yeah, she's the best. She helped me get through my depression following my injury and return to civilian life. And she's wonderful with both Ollie and Izzy."

"I wish she'd move here, but I'd never ask her to leave her friends," said Lily.

"I saw the way Ollie hugged you at the airport. You've been great with him," said Brian. "I think everything's going to be fine."

"Me, too, but it's going to take time. It might be wise for all of us to speak to a family counselor about how to deal with our grief, but I think we're going in the right direction."

Brian frowned and studied her. "Are you all right about not being married? It's something we both want, but the timing is a little awkward."

"I don't know what choice we have."

He lifted an eyebrow. "You don't?"

"Oh," she said, sitting up and smiling. "You mean it?"

Two days later, Lily dropped Izzy off at Alec's house for a new adventure with her special friends—Rose, Willow, and Juanita. Lily was pleased by Izzy's excitement, but then, at Alec's, Izzy had the run of the house with three doting women. Also, Alec made a point to see Izzy while she was there. Izzy still called him grandpa, which he loved, making it nice for all of them.

Willow greeted her at the door. "Come in. Hi, Izzy!"

Izzy waved and headed to the kitchen, while Lily set down her suitcase.

"I'm glad you and Brian will get a chance to rest, even if it's for only a couple of days," said Willow.

"Thanks," said Lily, "and thanks for taking care of Izzy for us." If she and Brian had their way, it wouldn't be only rest they'd be enjoying. She handed Willow a sheet of paper with the name of the inn where they'd be staying on the coast. The owner was a friend of Brian's.

"I'd better say goodbye to Izzy," said Lily and walked into the kitchen.

"Look!" said Izzy. "Auntie Rose gave me this." She held up a lime-green bikini as Rose joined them.

"Oh, my! How pretty!" Lily smiled at Rose. "Darling."

"I couldn't resist," Rose said. "I got one for Leah, too."

"A special gift for a special girl," said Juanita, ruffling Izzy's hair.

"Me?" said Izzy.

Juanita chuckled and gave her a hug. "Yes, you."

"See you later, Izzy," said Lily, bending over to give her a hug. "Have a great time! See you all later."

Lily watched as Izzy pranced beside Rose as they left the kitchen so she could try on her new swimsuit.

"Guess she'll be just fine," said Lily, smiling. "Again, thank you for giving Brian and me this time away. We really appreciate it." She wished she could tell them all their plans, but she'd promised Brian she'd keep their secret.

She left Alec's with a light heart. She'd heard of the Beach Rose Inn on the coast outside of Santa Barbara and couldn't wait to see the lovely inn for herself. There, she and Brian would have two whole nights together alone.

At the house, Lily carefully laid her dresses wrapped in plastic on top of her suitcase. While away, she'd have a chance to wear some of the summer dresses she'd bought. She'd packed a sweater and a shawl for the cool evenings she expected, but daywear was casual.

After loading the car, Brian got behind the wheel and turned to her with a smile. "Ready to do this?"

She grinned. "Yes! I can't wait."

He leaned over and gave her a lingering kiss on the mouth. When he pulled away, he gazed at her with affection. "Being with you feels so right."

"For me, too. It's never been this way with anyone else," said Lily. "I felt a connection to you from the beginning even before you stepped away."

He winked. "Not stepping away exactly. More like giving you time to think about me. I knew from the moment on that first walk together when you asked about my prosthetic that any relationship with you was going to be honest. I started falling then and have never stopped. I just didn't want to scare you away."

"Until I met you, I didn't believe in love at first sight," said Lily. "Now, I do."

He let out a sigh of satisfaction. "Well, then, we're doing the right thing."

"Do you think your mother will mind? Or my friends? In different circumstances, they'd be included."

Brian shook his head. "No, they'll understand. Besides, after we get Ollie home with us and everyone is in a routine, we're going to have the biggest, best party ever to celebrate."

"Okay, then, let's get married!" Lily said, trembling with joy.

The Beach Rose Inn was a charming, white Victorian whose roof gables were dressed with lace, making Lily think of a wedding cake. She knew from what Brian had told her that his friend, Evan Cooke, and his partner, Lance Perkins, had owned and operated the inn for over ten years and that it was a destination venue for very small weddings.

Evan met them at the reception desk and embraced Brian in a man-hug. "Great to see you, old friend."

Brian smiled. "You, too. I want you to meet my fiancée,

Lily. Soon to be my bride."

Evan gave her a quick hug. "A pleasure to meet you. Lance is very excited about the wedding. He's been rehearsing his lines so it will be perfect. I hope you two have your vows ready."

Lily glanced at Brian with dismay. She, who was always so organized, hadn't given a thought to it.

He smiled at her. "We just need to speak from our hearts."

She relaxed. Brian was right. Speaking from her heart would be easy because of him.

"Let me show you to your room," said Evan. "As you requested, Brian, one of my favorite suites has been reserved for you." He led them to a downstairs space in the back.

When Lily stepped inside the suite Brian had reserved, she couldn't help the smile she felt crossing her face. The Rose Room was perfect. The walls, painted a deep, rich red were edged with white trim. A tall, four-poster bed dominated a wall opposite a gas fireplace and displayed a fluffy, white duvet, accented by rose and green pillows. Beyond it, a sitting area sat next to a sliding glass door that opened onto a private little patio. The bathroom contained a double-size Jacuzzi tub and an over-sized shower.

She glanced at them and at Brian.

His grin was almost a leer.

"How nice. Thank you so much," Lily said as Evan went to the door.

"I'll leave you two alone. Tomorrow is a busy day, but tonight, Lance and I hope you'll join us for dinner. Two other couples are staying here, but they will be having dinner elsewhere."

Brian glanced at her and nodded. "That would be very nice."

After Evan left, he pulled her into his arms. "Are you sure

this is what you want? A private wedding. Just you and me?"

Lily smiled up at him, "This might be the only alone time we get for years. Let's enjoy it."

Brian laughed. "You're right."

After a late afternoon romp in bed, Lily showered to get ready for dinner. She was eager to know more about how Brian and Evan knew one another. They seemed like old friends.

The minute Lily walked into the dining room and saw Lance wearing shorts, she realized how Evan and Brian might have met. Lance was wearing a prosthetic similar to Brian's on his right leg.

Lance greeted her with a kiss. "So, my old hospital buddy is getting married. I'm happy to meet you, Lily. You must be a good woman to make this happen."

Brian put an arm around her. "She's the best. It didn't take me long to figure that out."

"I'm honored that you chose to come here for the wedding and have me conduct the ceremony." He turned to Lily and explained, "I've been deputized by the county clerk to conduct your wedding. I do this for others, of course, but I'm especially pleased to do it for you. I like to think the couples who get married here are off to a very happy start."

"We try, anyway," said Evan. He handed each of them a tulip glass filled with a bubbly liquid. "Thought we'd start with a champagne toast." He lifted his glass. "Here's to both of you and a long life together."

After dealing with so much death, Lily couldn't stop her eyes from filling. She gazed up at Brian with a shaky smile and clicked her glass against his, before doing so with the others.

"Thanks," Brian said. "Here's to all of us."

"Lance and I have prepared a special meal for you." Evan

nodded at Brian. "You said there were no food allergies, so we decided on Dungeness crab cakes, baked asparagus with hollandaise, and a lemon-rice side dish. It's one of our favorite meals. We hope you'll enjoy it."

"It sounds heavenly," said Lily, unable to remember when she'd had a relaxing meal like this. The sea air was already loosening the tension from the past several weeks. The wine and excellent meal would do the rest.

During dinner, talk was easy. As she'd thought, Brian had met Evan and Lance at the VA Hospital in Houston where they received care, training. and physical therapy services for the loss of their limbs and the prosthetics they chose to replace them. Like Brian, Lance had been injured by a roadside bomb in Afghanistan.

"Bad times," said Lance, shaking his head. "If I hadn't met and fallen in love with Evan, I might not have made it through the black period that followed."

"I was a nurse before I became a part of the hospitality industry," explained Evan. With his bright blue eyes and sunny disposition, Lily thought he must've been a wonderful nurse. In addition, he was a marvelous host. Lance, though quieter, was very attentive to their needs.

"This is delicious," Lily said, taking a last bite of the crab cake filled with crabmeat and little else.

"Lance is a great cook." Evan patted his round stomach. "It shows, but I don't worry about it. We both keep busy running this inn."

"The inn is stunning," said Lily. "As beautiful in its own way as the Desert Sage Inn."

Evan leaned forward. "How's Alec? I hear the situation isn't good."

"It's not," Lily said sadly.

"That's how we met," said Brian. "Working on the

transition of the hotel to the Blaise Group. It's confidential information that I'm sure you won't share."

Lance let out a sound of disgust. "Duncan Armstrong is already bragging about it. I can't understand how two brothers could be so different."

"As they're my clients, there's nothing I can say except I have the utmost respect for Mitchell."

"Agreed," said Evan. "Now, let's enjoy a nice after-dinner drink on the porch. It's a lovely evening." He turned to Lily. "We supply blankets for our guests, because the temperature can get quite chilly."

"Thanks. I think I'm going to need one."

By the time she'd finished a taste of brandy, and rocked back and forth in a rocking chair, listening to the waves rolling onto shore and retreating in a regular pattern, Lily wondered if she had the strength to make it back to their room.

Brian looked as relaxed as she felt when she finally forced herself to her feet. "This has been a lovely evening, but I'm ready for bed."

"I'll be right along," said Brian. "I just want to find out a little more about the new project Evan was telling us about."

She kissed his cheek. "Stay as long as you wish." She liked that he didn't feel forced to accompany her. She wanted time alone to savor this place, the new friends she'd made, and to go over plans for tomorrow—a day she'd once thought would never happen to her.

CHAPTER FORTY-FIVE

LILY

Lily awoke to the smell of bacon cooking. Stirring, she reached over and touched Brian. He instantly came awake. She smiled at him. "Morning, sweetheart. Today is already looking perfect."

He squinted at her. "It's still dark with these blinds drawn. What do you mean?"

She chuckled and reached for him. "I mean you. With you beside me like this on our wedding day, it's already wonderful. And if we open the blinds, I think we're going to find it sunny. I see bright light through the cracks between some of the slats."

He rolled over and embraced her. "With you by my side as my wife, every day will be sunny." His lips met hers, and she felt as if she was the luckiest woman in the world.

Sometime later, as they were sitting on the patio, sipping coffee that Lance had brought to their room earlier, a knock at the door indicated their breakfast was ready. Lily rose and went to answer it.

A pretty young woman with flowing blond hair smiled at her. "Breakfast is ready. May I bring it in?"

"Yes," Lily said, noting the rose in the glass vase and the metal covers on two plates on the tray. "You may place the tray on a table outside. It's such a beautiful morning, we're going to eat out there."

In no time, breakfast was laid out for them. "Enjoy your day. I'll see you later."

"Thanks. I understand you're going to be a witness for us."

The girl, whose name badge said Jenn, smiled shyly. "I love that part of my job." She brushed at her jeans. "Don't worry. I'll dress for the occasion."

Lily grinned. "You'll be fine." She was impressed that Evan and Lance had thought of everything. Though they technically needed only one witness for the marriage certificate, Evan had suggested two—himself and another. Working in a law office for so many years, Lily thought it was smart.

After a breakfast of Mimosas, scrambled eggs and bacon, and homemade biscuits, both Brian and she were ready for the day. Instead of a late afternoon wedding, Lily had opted for one in the morning. As she'd told Brian, she wanted to enjoy as much time as possible being his wife.

Now, as she prepared for the ceremony, she turned to Brian. "Will you zip me up?"

He gave her a teasing smile. "Isn't it bad luck for the groom to see the bride in her dress before the ceremony?"

"Not for us. We're here to help one another, so it doesn't count." She'd become accustomed to assisting Brian with little things like holding his walker as he rose from bed, steadying him as he first put on his prosthesis, even helping him put his pants on properly as she'd just done. While he'd been doing these things for himself for years, he seemed to enjoy her loving attention.

He zipped up the back of her dress and kissed the nape of her neck. "My beautiful, beautiful bride."

Blushing with pleasure, Lily studied herself in the mirror. The white, sleeveless dress was an understated beauty she'd found at a discount store featuring designer clothes. The dress accented her bust nicely and had a soft A-line look that emphasized her small waist. A border of embroidered white flowers along the hem was complimented by similar embroidery around the V-neck. She wore a simple drop-pearl necklace and pearl earrings.

"You're missing one thing," said Brian. He went over to the bureau, opened the drawer, and pulled out a blue box tied with a white silk ribbon.

"What's this?" said Lily. The smile that crossed his face was as bright as a ray of sun.

"It's for you. Something to remember our wedding day."

Lily carefully peeled off the ribbon and lifted the lid of the box. Inside was a blue-velvet box. She took it out and opened it. Inside was a bracelet—a sparkling band of diamonds. "Oh, Brian, it's beautiful!" she gushed. "I've never seen anything so perfect!"

"I wanted you to have something to match your wedding band. Let's put it on." He beamed at her as he wound it around her wrist and clasped it. "There! Like you said, it's perfect."

Gazing into the mirror, she flicked her wrist, staring at the shimmering rainbows the light on the bracelet created. Feeling as if she was in a dream, she turned to him for a kiss. "Thank you, Brian. I've never owned anything so beautiful."

"You deserve anything I can give you." He kissed her cheek. "Now, let's get married."

She laughed and, together, they went outside to the area the staff had prepared for the wedding.

Lily took a moment to gaze at the gazebo. White silk roses and small twinkling lights woven around the top of the railings added a softness to the painted white wood. In the open areas below the roof in each side section, a hanging basket held fresh flowers and overflowed with ivy. At the very center of the ceiling, a crystal chandelier sparkled. The effect was simple but gorgeous. A white cloth-covered table displayed a vase of pale-pink roses flanked by two white pillar candles. Lance, dressed in a dark suit, stood in front of the table. Jenn, now dressed in a pale pink sundress, and Evan stood at either side as witnesses.

Jenn handed her a nosegay of fresh, wild flowers and stood back as Lily and Brian took their places in front of Lance.

"Welcome," said Lance, beaming at them. He nodded to the harpist sitting in a chair on the grass outside the gazebo. She started playing music that made Lily think of angels and her sister. Monica would be so happy for her.

Lance led them through the usual ceremony. When it came time for Lily to say her vows, she paused for a moment and smiled at Brian, full of wonder that he'd chosen her and spoke softly, just for him.

"You said we should speak from our hearts, Brian. Mine is prompting me to tell you that you're everything I've ever wanted in a man to share my life." Her eyes filled, but she continued, struggling to find the best words. "We'll be sharing our love not only with each other, but the children we now have. I welcome them into my heart as well. Thank you for seeing the best in me when I can't see it for myself. I hope to return the happiness you give to me because you deserve it and much, much more. Each day, by thought and deed, I vow to show you how much you mean to me. I love you, Brian," her voice grew shaky, "my dear, darling husband."

Brian took hold of her hands and gazed at her, not bothering to hide the tears that trailed down his cheeks. "I never thought I'd find someone as perfect as you, accepting me as I am. I promise to spend the rest of my life honoring you in word and deed, building a life together."

They gazed at one another, silent, letting their tears of joy speak for themselves.

Lance coughed discreetly. "I guess you don't need me to tell you, but you may now kiss the bride."

Brian swept her into his arms. "This is the part I've been waiting for," he joked.

She laughed, and then his kiss was telling her much more.

The rest of the stay at the Beach Rose Inn was a blur of happiness for Lily. As much as she'd loved Brian from the moment they'd first walked together one early morning, exchanging vows and being married to him filled her with a deeper love.

As they packed for their return trip to Palm Desert, Lily was grateful they'd chosen to marry in a quiet, private ceremony that was stress free. She hoped her friends and Reenie would understand that and wouldn't be hurt by having missed it.

On the drive home, Lily replayed some of their special moments in her mind. She giggled at the memory of how many hours they'd spent in bed making love and talking. The fact that it had rained one afternoon and they didn't even know it spoke volumes.

They'd used the Jacuzzi tub and shower. One morning, Brian had tried to get out of the tub, slipped and landed back in the tub with a splash. When he'd sputtered and swore, she threw off the towel she'd been using to dry herself off and climbed right back in the tub, covering his face with kisses until he laughed so hard his frustration fled.

She'd loved lying naked in bed next to him, nestling against his strong body, talking about everything from their childhoods to their dreams for the future. It amazed her that coming from such different backgrounds, their goals were so alike.

It was comforting, too, to talk about their disappointments. Brian told her a little about surviving the war with the loss of part of his leg and how he still dreamed he was whole.

She told him more about her mother, how angry she'd become, how often she'd told Lily she wished she'd never had children. He'd wiped the tears from her eyes and told her they'd raise their children with love and support.

Brought out of her reverie by the sound of the conversation Brian was having with Reenie through the bluetooth speaker in the car, Lily focused on their words.

"Lily and I hope you aren't upset about missing the ceremony," said Brian. "Under the circumstances, we thought it was best for Ollie and Izzy for us to be married right away. Especially because we're about to begin the adoption process for both of them."

"Of course, I'm disappointed, but I understand," Reenie responded. "I love Lily and I'm thrilled that you have not only a lovely wife but two adorable children." She paused. "I was going to wait to tell you because I'm not sure how you'll feel about it, but I've begun investigating a move to Palm Desert. I want to be able to spend more time with you and my grandchildren. The condos I've been looking at online seem possible."

"Reenie! How wonderful!" declared Lily, not waiting for Brian to answer. "That would be a dream come true for me and the kids. I wanted to ask you to consider moving to California. We love you!"

Reenie was quiet and then said, "Oh, dear! Forgive me for crying, but I'm so deeply touched. Congratulations and best wishes to you both. We'll talk about this another time. I'm going to go now and have a good cry." She clicked off the call.

Brian took hold of Lily's hand. "Thank you, darling. That was really nice."

"It's true, Brian. Having your mother in Palm Desert would make our family even better. Your mother is the kind of mother I've always wished I'd had."

"The kind you're going to be," said Brian, lifting her hand for a kiss.

CHAPTER FORTY-SIX

WILLOW

The minute Willow saw Brian and Lily pull up in front of Alec's house, she hurried to Rose. "They're here. Five dollars says I'm right."

Rose shook her head. "I know enough about your premonitions or whatever you want to call them to not bet with you. But if you're right, I'll be both disappointed and happy for her."

While Juanita went to check on Izzy's nap, the two of them stood together by the open front door watching Lily and Brian emerge from his car.

Wearing a broad smile, Lily saw them and waved.

"What's that she's wearing on her wrist?" said Rose as Lily hurried toward them.

"Rose! Willow!" Lily threw her arms around Willow and turned to Rose. "Guess what! Brian and I are married!"

Willow held out her hand. "I win."

Rose tapped Willow's hand playfully. "Yeah but I was too smart to bet."

Lily frowned at them. "What's going on?"

"Willow had a strong feeling your time away was really a wedding trip," said Rose.

Willow placed her hand on Lily's shoulder. "I was going to tease you about it before you left, but then I knew you'd be worried about not inviting us."

Brian joined them and put an arm around Lily. "We needed to do something quickly because of the kids."

Lily clasped her hands. “Brian and I are going to have a big celebration after Ollie comes to live with us.”

“I’m happy for you, Lily,” said Willow. “You too, Brian. You’re going to make wonderful parents for those kids.”

“Yes. Congratulations to both of you,” said Rose. “We’ll be happy to celebrate with you later, but for now, I wish you both all the best.”

“Come on inside. My mother is just waking up Izzy now.” Willow clasped Lily’s right hand. “What a stunning bracelet.”

Lily smiled at her. “A wedding present from Brian.”

“It’s just a symbol of ... you know ...” stammered Brian.

Because Brian was usually someone who didn’t get flustered. Willow gave him an impulsive hug. “Yes, we all know how much you love Lily. We do too.”

Lily sighed loudly. “Oh, Willow, thank you and Rose for understanding.”

“I’m not going to go so easy on you,” said Rose, giving her a wink. “And we’ll just have to wait a bit longer for Willow to decide what kind of wedding she wants. Right, Willow?”

Willow felt her cheeks grow hot. “Dan has finally asked me out again.”

Lily gave Willow a high five. “Can’t wait to see what happens.”

Even though Willow’s stomach spun with excitement, she remained silent. Sometimes, being a desert flower, was safer that way.

CHAPTER FORTY-SEVEN

LILY

A few weeks later, Lily walked hand in hand with Brian through the house she loved like no other. Having grown up in chaos, moving often, and dealing with an unstable mother, Lily relished the feeling of love and security that filled this space. She gazed at the man beside her. Brian was the most decent, kindest man she'd ever known. And the love between them was real ... and hot.

Together, they were forming a family. Ollie was a darling boy who needed the love and attention she was more than willing to give to him. And Izzy had always been the child of her heart.

Quietly, she opened the door to Ollie's room and crept closer for a better look. He was sleeping on his stomach, sprawled across the bed as if he'd taken a flying leap and landed there. A book about lizards was open nearby. She carefully lifted it and placed it on the bedside table.

Bending over, she kissed his freckled cheek. He stirred, and she whispered, "We love you, Ollie." His body relaxed and he continued sleeping.

Jake, the labradoodle, rose and came over to her, nudging her hand for attention.

Brian, standing at her side, studied his son with a look of wonder. He reached out, gave Ollie a loving pat on the back, and bent to kiss him. When he turned to her, tears shone in his eyes.

They left Ollie's bedroom, closing the door halfway, and

went into Izzy's room. She was curled up on top of the pink princess sheet snuggling Toby, her stuffed fish. Her butterscotch hair spread across the pillow like a halo around her head. Her hand was near her mouth as if she'd decided to leave her option open as to whether she needed to suck her thumb as she'd taken to doing from time to time. Lily knelt beside the bed and kissed her cheek, loving the feel of her soft skin on her lips. This child, so precious to her, was a gift she hadn't expected. As much as she loved being a mother to her, Lily promised herself to keep the memory of Monica alive.

Brian smiled down at Izzy, reached over and rubbed her back gently. "So beautiful," he murmured.

They walked out of Izzy's bedroom and went to their own. Jake had already left Ollie's room to join them and was lying on his bed in the corner of the room, looking up at them with expectation.

Brian sat on the edge of the bed and tugged Lily down beside him. "Who'd have thought this all would've happened?"

"Not me. Not in a million years." She still felt as if she were living in a fairy tale, the old-fashioned kind where the ending was both sad and happy. Loose ends still needed to be tied up, but with Brian by her side, Lily knew she could face anything. And for the first time in her life, she had devoted friends like Rose and Willow, her fellow Desert Flowers, to be there for them. Her work with Alec wasn't over, but she'd continue to be a help to him no matter how long he lived beyond the sale of his hotel. He was the person who'd given her the opportunity to find a new life. She'd always be grateful to him.

Brian put his arm around her and said softly, "Seeing Ollie and Izzy tucked in their beds made me realize how important family is. Would you ... could you be willing to try for another?"

Lily smiled up at him. "You know how you like that I'm always a step ahead of you?" She paused, waiting for him to catch on, unable to stop a smile from crossing her face.

Brian pulled away from her and stared at her with rounded eyes. "Really? Do you mean it?"

She laughed at his look of delight. "I was going to tell you earlier, but then with Ollie getting moved in, I put it off. But it was on my list."

Chuckling, Brian swept her into his arms. "You and your lists. Do you have any idea how much I love you?"

As he drew her closer, a sigh of contentment escaped her. His hands caressed her belly reverently and then his lips met hers. The last couple of months had been full of every emotion she could think of, but here, in this moment, she knew she was truly blessed.

# # #

Thank you for reading *The Desert Flowers – Lily*. If you enjoyed this book, please help other readers discover it by leaving a review on Amazon, Goodreads, BookBub, or your favorite site. It's such a nice thing to do.

And be sure to read the other books in The Desert Sage Inn Series: *The Desert Flowers – Rose, The Desert Flowers – Mistletoe and Holly*, and *The Desert Flowers – Willow*.

Enjoy an excerpt from my book, *The Desert Flowers – Willow*, Book 3 in The Desert Sage Inn Series:

CHAPTER ONE

WILLOW

Willow Sanchez had a lot to think about as she grabbed a bottle of water and tiptoed outside in the quiet, early-morning hours on this late April day; her life had completely changed. She'd been happy to upend her teaching career in Boston and return home to help Alec Thurston, a man who was like a father to her and who was dying of cancer. He wanted her and two other women to oversee the sale of his hotel, the Desert Sage Inn, to The Blaise Hotel Group.

Alec called her, Rose Macklin, and Lily Weaver, his Desert Flowers, similar to Charley's Angels on an old television series. They'd each played a special part in his life and had talents that could help him preserve the image and reputation of his hotel with the transition to new ownership.

Restless, Willow breathed in the cool, clean air of the desert well aware the day would be a hot one. She decided to take advantage of the coolness and hike up to Alec's cabin, which was really a casita in the foothills above the inn with no running water, just a bed, table and chairs, and a fantastic view to relieve anyone's stress.

As she walked along the path by the inn's golf course, she admired the desert flowers, various shrubs, and palm trees against the backdrop of the adjacent foothills that added dimension to the green carpet of the fairways and putting greens. She noticed a bird pecking at a branch of a cactus and heard the whirring of wings before a brightly colored hummingbird darted at her pink T-shirt, hovered, and then took off looking for something better.

"'Bye, little hummer," she said playfully, perked up as always by these tiny birds. She loved the desert, hadn't realized how much she missed it at Boston University, where she taught business accounting in the School of Hospitality Administration. She'd lived in Palm Desert since she was a child while her parents worked at the inn and then directly for Alec in his home. Alec was the person who'd taught her to love the hospitality business. As her mentor, he'd helped her get into the hotel school at Cornell University. She'd always hoped one day to work at the inn with him, but now, with his illness, that wasn't going to happen. But after returning to her hometown a few months ago, she'd decided to stay in Palm Desert and seek work at other hotels if she didn't get the job she wanted at the Desert Sage Inn.

Thinking of her uncertain status, Willow began climbing on a trail up the foothills at the edge of the inn's property. Maybe the clear view would help settle her thoughts. Work and living arrangements weren't her only concerns. Dan McMillan, the sexy guy in charge of the fitness program at the Inn, had asked her out again. He'd attracted her from the beginning when Alec had hired him to conduct a teambuilding program for the three women before they started their work for him. But now she sometimes felt as if Dan thought of her as a sister, someone to have fun with, more than a woman he wanted in a lasting relationship.

Before returning to the desert, she'd had her heart shattered. The man with whom she thought she had a future had introduced her to his parents who'd rudely rejected her because of her immigrant parents and her working-class background. Unlike her ex, Dan wasn't prejudiced, but he didn't seem that serious about the future—with her or anyone else.

"Why would I set myself up for disappointment?" she asked a king snake she saw sunning itself on a rock about five feet off the trail.

The snake slithered into the rocks and brush away from the path, leaving behind an answer she knew was right. She'd go out with Dan, but she'd be careful about getting too close too fast. Still, she longed to find a man who was ready to commit to something long-term—someone who'd not only love her as she was but also understand her need to grow her career as an homage to Alec and to respect her independence.

Willow reached the casita and sat down on a bench outside it, grateful for the rest. She gulped a long swallow of water and slowly recovered her breath. The climb wasn't an easy one. But when she looked out at the scene below to the resort and then lifted her gaze to study the snowcapped mountains in the distance, she was glad she'd made the effort. The textured, blue-gray mountains always gave her a sense of peace, often a sense of purpose. Willow sat for several minutes while she contemplated the view, enjoyed the fresh breeze and the warmth from the sun, and sorted her thoughts.

As she descended the trail, fresh resolve filled her.

She was competing with the two sons of the owners of the

Blaise Group to become manager of the Desert Sage Inn. While Brent Armstrong was a spoiled brat, his cousin, Trace Armstrong, appeared to be the opposite—kind, thoughtful, and smart. Still, both were determined to take over the management of the inn after the sale went through. Willow knew she was as capable as they but that her chances of getting the job were next to none because it was, after all, a family business. Still, she'd do her best to protect the inn's reputation as Alec wished. She knew more about running it than they'd ever know.

She thought of the women she was working with. They made an interesting trio. Rose was the eldest of the three at fifty-two, recently engaged to Hank Bowers with whom she'd been assigned to work, and was, more or less, the leader. Lily Weaver and Brian Walden, the head of the Blaise Group transition team, had quickly married following a personal crisis for each of them, including the unexpected care of two children. Lily recently announced she was pregnant, leaving Willow, at thirty-one, the only unattached woman of the group. Maybe, thought Willow, that was the reason she was feeling so unsettled.

When Willow arrived back at Alec's house, she walked through it and out to the patio and pool in the back. Rose had just climbed out of the pool and was drying herself off with a towel. Tall and thin, with red hair and green eyes, she was a striking woman.

"Hey, girl! You're up early!" said Rose. "Where've you been?"

Willow smiled. "I hiked up to Alec's cabin. I needed to get a fresh perspective on things."

Rose immediately gave her a look of concern. "Is everything all right?"

Willow shrugged and sat down in one of the poolside chairs. "I just needed to think about the future. The closing of the sale of the inn is approaching, and I'm going to need to find another job here in the valley. I don't want to leave."

"You've done a fabulous job of heading the assistant team for the transition, I shouldn't think you'd have any trouble finding a good job in management." Rose came over to her and gave her a quick hug. "I'm happy to give you as many references as you want."

"Thanks. I'm not sure whether I'm going to rent or buy a place here, but that's something I'll think about after I get another job."

"Hank and I are still pondering living choices here. We're thinking of buying a house and then getting something smaller in Atlanta where his daughters live."

"You're still waiting to get married until after Alec leaves us?" Willow knew how Rose, like Lily, had thought at one time that Alec would marry her. But she and others in the valley had heard the story of how Alec's young wife, her cousin Conchita, and unborn daughter had died in a house fire for which he blamed himself. He had, Rose confessed, told her he'd never marry again, that his conscience wouldn't allow him to do that. Twisted a bit, perhaps, but true, thought Willow.

"Yes, I wouldn't feel right about moving out while Alec is still alive. I've promised to stay with him until the end. You know?" Rose said, sitting in a chair next to her. "Poor Lily had no choice, but I'm content to wait." She winked at Willow. "That'll give you a chance to catch up."

Willow chuckled and shook her head. "It might be a long time. Dan has asked me out, but I'm not sure it's going anywhere."

They looked up and smiled as Lily joined them. "Good

morning, you two! What's up?"

Lily was small and blond, almost waif-like until you knew the strength behind her.

"Nice to see you," said Rose to her. "Willow is thinking about her future, wondering where she's going to work, and ..." Rose paused for effect "... how her date with Dan will go."

Willow elbowed Rose playfully. "It's much more than worry about a date. I'm really concerned about where I'm going to work after our job for Alec is done."

"But she's staying here in Palm Desert," said Rose. "I'm not going to let her leave."

"Me either," said Lily. "And, Willow, as far as dating, you don't need to rush into anything. You'll know when the right man comes along."

Willow smiled her appreciation. "Thanks."

"How's Alec today? Anyone know?" Lily asked with a frown.

"I haven't spoken to any of the new nurses yet." Rose sighed. "Even after all this time of knowing what's going to happen, I still can't bear the thought of him dying."

"It's not time yet, is it? The nurses arrived to help Juanita, not because it's the very end for him. Right?" Lily's voice trembled with emotion.

"Yes," said Willow. "When it's time, Hospice will be brought in. My mother said he's trying his best to hang on until the sale of the hotel goes through."

"The three of us originally wanted to stay here for the duration of our job and as long as he lived. My situation has changed because of Brian and the kids, but as much as possible I want to be here for Alec," said Lily.

"How are things going with Izzy and Ollie?" Willow asked. At three, Izzy, Lily's niece and now her child, was adorable. And Ollie was a darling eight-year-old boy who'd unexpectedly entered Brian Walden's life as the child Brian never knew he had. After the trauma of his mother introducing him to his father and then dying of cancer, Ollie was now settling in with them.

Lily smiled. "Each day is better. Ollie still has some bad days, but Izzy adores him, which helps them both."

"You and Brian are so admirable," said Rose. "I love Hank's granddaughter, Leah, but I imagine it would be difficult to go from single and childless to married with children."

Lily let out a breath and shook her head. "I often wake up and wonder who I am. It all happened so quickly. But even though my sister's death was horrific, I'm in a good place. I have a man who loves me, the family I've always wanted, two wonderful friends, and a fulfilling career."

Willow and Rose squeezed her hands.

"The emotional abuse Jeremy put my sister through was awful," said Lily, unable to hide her pain. "I still wonder if I could've done something to get Monica away from him sooner and, perhaps, prevent her death. Maybe if ..."

Rose held up her hand. "Unh, unh. We're not going to let you go there. Right, Willow?"

"Right," she said firmly. "It's not worth the trip. Now, who wants coffee?"

They moved into the kitchen, and like many mornings, continued their conversation over a cup of java.

Later, as Willow entered the hotel to attend her meeting, she took a moment to gaze around the lobby. The understated color scheme of desert-sand brown worked with pops of purple and turquoise accents, giving a sophisticated, pleasant feel to the area. The Desert Sage Inn was all about the quality of guests' surroundings and the excellent service they could expect. Like Alec himself, you knew what you were going to get—an honest representation of what he offered.

She waved to her friend Sarah Jensen, a part-time assistant manager. She was a pretty, vivacious, brown-haired young mother who'd returned to her parents' home with a two-year-old son while her husband was doing his last stint in the army in Afghanistan. They often sipped cups of coffee at work together and on some evenings, went out for a glass of wine.

Willow laughed when Sarah gave her a thumbs-up signal. She and everyone else knew how difficult working with Brent Armstrong could be.

In the past Willow had wondered why Brent was the way he was. He came from a privileged background, had every opportunity handed to him, and yet was nasty, bossy, and ready to lash out at anyone who disagreed with him. After she met his father, Duncan, the younger of the two brothers who owned The Blaise Hotel Group, Willow understood. With a smaller share of the company than his brother, Duncan was aggressive, constantly trying to outdo Mitchell. He pushed Brent into thinking he was better than anyone else and that he, not Trace, should end up with a larger portion of the company. Unrealistic, but a continual squabble nevertheless. The fact that Brent bought into it didn't help.

Before going to John Rodriguez's office, Willow grabbed a cup of coffee from the guest hospitality coffee service in the corner of the lobby. She'd need all the caffeine she could get to keep on her toes with Brent around. He'd once copied her notes on a presentation she'd put together and tried to pass them off as his own.

When she got to the office, Brent and Trace were already there with John. "Good morning!" she said cheerfully and sat in the empty chair in front of John's desk.

"You're late," said Brent.

"Good morning," John said, giving her a smile. "We were

just chatting about the weather and sales figures. Though we're not a big conference center, some of our business comes from small group sales, and when bad weather comes into play across the country, it definitely is a factor."

"I've been working on an idea about coordinating sales from one Corona property to another through cross-promotions. I'm not quite ready to present it, but it could be a lot of fun for our guests," said Willow.

"Fun? Is it profitable for the Blaise hotels?" Brent said, scowling.

Willow rolled her eyes.

"I'm sure Willow has all three of the hotels in mind when she's talking about the Corona Collection," said John in measured tones.

Trace glanced at her and shook his head, apparently as tired of Brent as the rest of the staff at the hotel.

The meeting proceeded at a brisk pace. Willow was busy typing notes, starring a few of them for further investigation, when John stood.

"I have another meeting. We have only a few weeks before the transition of the hotels to the Corona Collection is to take place. I suggest that each of you make a list of questions you have about the timing that day so we can discuss it. A smooth transition is what we've all been working toward. Let's make it happen."

After he left the room, Brent said, "Wonder why he's so uptight?"

"Maybe because every time he spoke, you had to add something," Willow replied.

"Yeah, Brent, just cool it," said Trace. "It's annoying."

Brent stood and shrugged. "It's my job." He turned to Trace. "Want to grab a cup of coffee before we head to the links?"

Trace shook his head. "No, go ahead. I'll meet up with you later."

"Why?" Brent looked at Willow and then turned to Trace. "You're going to ask her? Don't bother. If she won't go out with me, she won't go out with you."

Willow watched Trace's cheeks color and felt sorry for him. "What did you want to ask me?"

Trace glanced at Brent and let out a sigh of irritation before facing her. "I'd like to take you to dinner tonight," he said quietly. "Are you free?"

Willow shook her head. "Not tonight, but I am tomorrow." She almost laughed at the look of surprise on Brent's face, and smiled sweetly at Trace. *How dare Brent make such a decision for her!*

Trace smiled and nodded. "Okay, then, I'll be in touch. Thanks, Willow."

Brent was still frowning as the two of them left the room.

Willow left John's office to print off the notes she'd been working on, wondering if she'd done the right thing. Trace was nice, good-looking, and ambitious, but he was part of a situation that was unsettling. She'd already been treated badly by one set of wealthy parents, why would she put herself into another vulnerable position? But it was too late now. She wouldn't go back on her word.

In the meantime, she had a date with Dan.

# # #

About the Author

A ***USA Today* Best-Selling Author**, Judith Keim is a hybrid author who both has a publisher and self-publishes. Ms. Keim writes heart-warming novels about women who face unexpected challenges, meet them with strength, and find love and happiness along the way. Her best-selling books are based, in part, on many of the places she's lived or visited and on the interesting people she's met, creating believable characters and realistic settings her many loyal readers love. She loves to hear from her readers and appreciates their enthusiasm for her stories.

Ms. Keim enjoyed her childhood and young-adult years in Elmira, New York, and now makes her home in Boise, Idaho, with her husband and their lovable miniature Dachshund, Wally, and other members of her family.

"And please check out my other books: "

The Hartwell Women Series
The Beach House Hotel Series
The Fat Fridays Group
The Salty Key Inn Series
Seashell Cottage Books
The Chandler Hill Inn Series
The Desert Sage Inn Series
Soul Sisters at Cedar Mountain Lodge
The Sanderling Cove Inn Series
The Lilac Lake Inn Series

"ALL THE BOOKS ARE NOW AVAILABLE IN AUDIO on Audible, iTunes, Findaway, Kobo and Google Play! So fun to have these characters come alive!"

Ms. Keim can be reached at **www.judithkeim.com**

And here's a link to where you can sign up for her periodic newsletter! **http://bit.ly/2OQsb7s**

She is also on Twitter @judithkeim, LinkedIn, and Goodreads. Come say hello!

Acknowledgments

And, as always, I am eternally grateful to my team of editors, Peter Keim and Lynn Mapp, my book cover designer, Lou Harper, and my narrator for Audible and iTunes, Angela Dawe. They are the people who take what I've written and help turn it into the book I proudly present to you, my readers! I also wish to thank my coffee group of writers who listen and encourage me to keep on going. Thank you, Peggy, Lynn, Cate, Nikki Jean, Mel and Megan. And to you, my fabulous readers, I thank you for your continued support and encouragement. Without you, this book would not exist. You are the wind beneath my wings.

www.ingramcontent.com/pod-product-compliance
Lightning Source LLC
Chambersburg PA
CBHW061607190726
48288CB00007B/2212
9781962452250